Kansas City Public Theatre

Woodneath Press
8900 NE Flintlock Rd.
Kansas City, MO 64157

Copyright © 2023 Woodneath Press
All rights reserved.

This book, or part thereof, may not be reproduced in any form without the written permission from the publisher or author, except for the inclusion of brief passages in a review.

FIRST EDITION

Print ISBN: 978-1-942337-36-2

For information visit our website:
www.mymcpl.org/story-center/publishing/woodneath-press

Cover design by Nathan Bowman
Cover photo by Mason Kilpatrick
Book layout and typography by Sahara Scott
Set in Times New Roman

Printed in the United States of America

Note: All plays in this volume have been protected under the copyright laws of the United States of America. These plays are for the reading public only and all performance rights, including professional amateur, motion picture, recitation, public reading, radio and television broadcasting, podcast, and the rights of translation into a foreign language are strictly reserved. Inquiries concerning these rights should be addressed to the author or Kansas City Public Theatre.

KANSAS CITY PUBLIC THEATRE PRESENTS

Their Own Devices

A Collection of Kansas City Playwrights

ELIZABETH BETTENDORF BOWMAN
NATHAN BOWMAN

CONTENTS

Introduction	by Kansas City Public Theatre	v
Acknowledgements		vii

The Plays

The Avocado Tree	Foreword	1
Play	by Sofiana Olivera Abalán	2
w/ Spanish Edition		
Her Own Devices	Foreword	123
Play	by Lindsay Adams Kennedy	124
Black Parent Union	Foreword	183
Play	by Gary Enrique Bradley-Lopez	184
Mirrors	Foreword	244
Play	by Kaitlin Gould	245
Family Spouses	Foreword	289
Play	by Prisca Jebet Kendagor	290

INTRODUCTION

Their Own Devices is a celebration of the first five years of Kansas City Public Theatre (KCPublic), a professional theatre company founded in 2017 with a mission to bring accessible theatre and new work development to the Kansas City community. This anthology features plays written by Kansas City-area playwrights whose work has been developed in some way by KCPublic. It is a testament to our dedication to promoting local artists and providing a platform for diverse stories and perspectives. When we were approached with the idea of developing this anthology, we thought it was the perfect way to celebrate the five-year anniversary of KCPublic, with all its challenges and successes. And we've had a lot of reasons to celebrate. In five short years, KCPublic grew from being an idea to being a home for accessible theatre and new work development in Kansas City. By our fifth year, KCPublic's new works programming had grown to a point that we were able to launch an annual new works festival to much success. Perhaps most noteworthy is that KCPublic was awarded the recognition of 2022 Arts Organization of the Year by the Missouri Arts Council and the State of Missouri.

When we started KCPublic, we had no idea that new work development would become so central to our identity as a company. We simply needed a launching off point. Rather than blow all our very little money on a single production, we decided to ease into it. The necessity of starting small arose directly from the mission of the company. KCPublic was founded with the mission of breaking down the socio-economic barriers that prevent people from experiencing professional performing arts. This mission is exemplified by the fact that all our productions, workshops or fully produced, are free-of-charge to the public in a variety of easily accessible locations. "Radical Hospitality" is the phrase we adopted that became the foundation of our approach, hence our company slogan "Be Radical." From the outset, we expected to make zero money, because that is quite literally the mission of the company. It was due to this financial reality that we started small by producing a series of new play workshops in a monthly program that we would eventually come to call "Theatre Lab."

When we started the program, it took place on the first Monday of every month at a now-closed artists' hangout, the Uptown Arts Bar. We called the program "First Mondays" (for obvious reasons) and sought playwrights to help populate our programming for the next year. Each month, we would hire a new playwright to present their work in a staged reading format with KCPublic. We hired the directors and actors for each piece and facilitated talkbacks between the playwright and the audience after each reading. The program grew over time, and we continued to build upon this process. We employed dramaturgs and other associates to ensure the process was as conducive to the needs of the playwright as possible. We created a volunteer reading committee to help us sort through play submissions. We started a playwriting residency that allowed us the focus to fully produce the new work of one area playwright each year.

After our first few months of programming, several things became clear to us. The first is that no two playwrights are at the same point in their writing process. We received submissions of first drafts alongside award-winning scripts that have had several staged readings already. This discrepancy required a specifically tailored process for certain playwrights who would have benefitted very little from a stage reading. As such, we allotted one Theatre Lab slot each season to a full, albeit minimal, production of a new work. For instance, *Mirrors* by Kaitlin Gould (included in this volume) was presented as a full production with a two-night run. Some plays were first presented as readings but were developed with the playwright beyond that and eventually produced as a part of our "mainstage" season with full budgets and a two-week run. *Her Own Devices* by Lindsay Adams Kennedy was the first of our plays that we took from page-to-stage in this way.

The second and most important thing we came to realize was how the development of new plays by Kansas City-area playwrights exemplified our mission in profound ways. The conception of theatre that has informed our vision from the beginning is that by its nature theatre is radically local. A live performance happens at a specific time, in a specific place, and that performance will never occur the exact same way twice. We participate in the theatre not in the isolation of our homes, but within a community of people, and as such, there are few tools more potent than theatre for engaging with people on issues that concern their lives and worldviews. For this reason, KCPublic envisions theatre as an essential cultural good that should be fully accessible to all members of the community. That is, theatre should be of and for the public at large, and not confined to the privileged few who can afford the price of a ticket that for many is a week's grocery bill. Not only that, but with its capacity to engage critically with audiences, it follows that theatre, to some degree, should engage with the unique qualities and viewpoints of the audience to which it is directed. To this end, producing playwrights who reflect the community of Kansas City, in all its diversity and contradictions, became central to our mission to produce theatre that is oriented to the public.

We titled this collection *Their Own Devices* to reflect our belief that Kansas City playwrights are specifically suited to write plays for a Kansas City audience. Any good play engages with themes that are universal in nature, but the universal is made known to us through the window of the particular. Who better to address the particular, and often contradictory worldviews of a mid-sized Midwestern city than the people who have made their lives here? When given the opportunity to have their voices lifted, this is what Kansas City playwrights have to share. These are their devices. We are honored to share the work of these talented playwrights with you, and we hope you find as much joy and meaning in their pieces as we have.

Elizabeth Bettendorf Bowman, Executive Artistic Director of KCPublic
Nathan Bowman, PhD, Producing Artistic Director of KCPublic

ACKNOWLEDGMENTS

Kansas City Public Theatre would not be here today if not for the support of so many people, organizations, and dedicated sponsors in our community. Free theatre isn't free, as we always say, and it is due to the ongoing support we receive that we are able to fulfill our mission of increasing arts accessibility across Kansas City and facilitating the development of our city's playwrights.

First, we must give a sincere thank you to Charlotte Street Foundation, including Amy Kligman, Patrick Alexander, and Laura Blumenberg, whose institutional support was instrumental in providing KCPublic with a launching pad. Their backing continues to facilitate so much of our programming, and we are indebted to them for their constant support. We would also like to thank all of the current and former members of KCPublic's board of directors who have worked tirelessly to ensure the successful execution of our programs and events, including: Marvin Bias IV, Kathy Breeden, April Brewer, Sarah Bronson, Nicole Crawford, Mark Exline, Laura Hambrecht, David Holmgren, Kris Kirkwood, Katie Lee, Delano Mendoza-Holt, Justin Mohn, Gary Mosby, Emmy Panzica-Piontek, Xavier Robles, Margaret Shelby, Derek Trautwein, Nixon Wegulo, Eric Woods, Inas Younis. We would like to thank the following individuals for their encouragement of KCPublic and for providing inspiration to us in their own unique ways: Felicia Londré, Joseph Dillman, Kayla Koester, Eric Rosen, Jessie Salsbury, Marissa Wolf, and Peter Zazzali. We want to thank ArtsKC, Missouri Arts Council, PH Coffee, Fountain City Winery, Guadalupe Centers, Latinx Education Collaborative, and the former staff of the Uptown Arts Bar for their support of our organization and especially of our new work programming. We especially want to thank all the artists, audiences, and donors who continue to show up time and time again because they believe that theatre should be made accessible to all members of our community regardless of income or zip code. And finally, we want to thank all of the playwrights we have worked with, who trusted us with their work, and whose words contribute so much to the diversity and vibrancy of the Kansas City theatre community.

THE AVOCADO TREE FOREWORD

Lucia Medina, a brilliant young architect, lives in a Latin American country in social and political upheaval with her father, Professor Don Francisco, and her young daughter, Katia. She yearns for a better life. When the violence in her country escalates, Lucia makes the difficult decision to emigrate to the United States. As the years go by, Lucia and her friend Ruben must face the unforeseeable consequences of the choices forced on themselves and their families. Through Lucia's experiences, we are given a glimpse into the realities of immigration, the struggles that come with leaving one's homeland, and the challenges of starting over in a new country. With themes of family, love, and the pursuit of a better life, *The Avocado Tree* by Sofiana Olivera Abalán offers a thought-provoking and emotionally charged performance that will leave you thinking long after the curtains close.

KCPublic worked with Sofiana over the course of two seasons. The play was first workshopped virtually in October 2020 via a reading that was presented to the audience on a Facebook live stream. This virtual performance was presented in English. In 2022, KCPublic, in its effort to produce a bilingual play each season, commissioned Sofiana to write a Spanish language version of *The Avocado Tree*. All lines that the characters would be speaking in Spanish, were translated into Spanish, along with the stage directions. This bilingual version of the play was presented in a concert reading format at Guadalupe Centers in April 2022.

The Avocado Tree
El Árbol de Aguacate

A Play

By/Autora: Sofiana Olivera Abalán

ACT I

Scene I - Will We Make it?

Setting:

NIGHT. A bus stop under a street lamp, on a street corner of a large sized city in a Latin American country.

Time: 1985

At Rise:

Bus stop.

Projection: The year is 1985. A Latin American country in turmoil.

Two SOLDIERS, with black stripes painted on their cheeks, enter the stage in combat mode. Their guns are drawn, and they move as if they are hunting for somebody. The sounds of sirens and occasional gunshots can be heard.

SOLDIERS exit stage without turning their backs to the audience.

Four people rush on stage from different directions and converge at the bus stop.

There is a LABORER, a PROFESSIONAL and an OFFICE WORKER. LUCIA MEDINA is an architect in her early thirties. She is carrying a shoulder bag with rolls of architectural plans. Her hair is shoulder length or longer.

     LABORER
Man! We missed it! Missed the last bus!

    PROFESSIONAL
   (voices without sound)
Shit!

PRIMER ACTO

Escena I - ¿Lo Lograremos?

Ambientación:

NOCHE. Una parada de autobús bajo un farol, en una esquina de una ciudad grande en un país latinoamericano.

Fecha: 1985

Telón:

Parada de autobús.

Proyección: El año es 1985. Un país latinoamericano en crisis.

DOS SOLDADOS, con rayas negras pintadas en sus mejillas, entran en el escenario en modo de combate. Sus armas están desenfundadas y se mueven como si estuvieran buscando a alguien. Se pueden escuchar los sonidos de las sirenas y disparos ocasionales.

Los SOLDADOS salen del escenario sin dar la espalda a la audiencia.

Cuatro personas se apresuran al escenario Desde diferentes direcciones y convergen en la parada de autobús.

Hay un OBRERO, un PROFESIONAL y un OFICINISTA. LUCÍA MEDINA es arquitecta de unos treinta años. Lleva un bolso al hombro con rollos de planos arquitectónicos. Su Cabello le llega a los hombros o más largo.

     OBRERO
¡Hombre! ¡Lo hemos perdido! ¡Perdimos el último autobús!

LUCIA
No. No,
(looking at her watch)
it's only ten past nine. We have almost an hour. There's time. There's one more coming.

OFFICE WORKER
Something is brewing. I saw the tanks roll out early on 8th Street.

PROFESSIONAL
It's something big.

OFFICE WORKER
Another coup?

          Questioning look from PROFESSIONAL.

LABORER
I bet the bus driver abandoned his route. Went home early.

PROFESSIONAL
We're screwed.

LABORER
Drivers are cautious.

OFFICE WORKER
Yeah, if they smell any trouble, they're the first to park their buses and hide.

LUCIA
There's nobody. The streets are empty.

      ALL are uncertain as to what to do.

PROFESSIONAL
Shit, now how am I going to get home now?

OFFICE WORKER
(evaluating while speaking)
I live some thirty blocks away. If I take side streets... get off the main streets...
(looking at his dress shoes)

PROFESIONAL
(mueve los labios sin hacer sonido)
¡Mierda!

LUCÍA
No. No,
(mirando su reloj)
son solo las diez para las nueve. Tenemos casi una hora. Hay tiempo. Hay uno más que va venir.

OFICINISTA
Algo se esta gestando. Vi los tanques salir temprano en la calle ocho.

PROFESIONAL
Es algo grande.

OFICINISTA
¿Otro golpe?

      Mirada cuestionadora de PROFESIONAL.

OBRERO
Apuesto que el chofer del ómnibus abandono su ruta temprano y se fue a casa.

PROFESIONAL
Estamos jodidos.

OBRERO
Los choferes son cautelosos.

OFICINISTA
Sí, si huelen algún problema son los primeros en parquear sus ómnibus y esconderse.

LUCÍA
Casi no hay nadie. Las calles están vacías.

      TODOS están inseguros a que hacer.

Not the best running shoes... Good night and good luck.

OFFICE WORKER exits running.

LUCIA
(yells behind OFFICE WORKER)
Get your handkerchief out!

LABORER
You're right. It's probably a good idea to get our handkerchiefs out early.

LUCIA and LABORER search their pockets, and each pull out white handkerchiefs.

PROFESSIONAL
Do you really believe that soldiers look for the white flag before they shoot?

LUCIA reacts. She unfolds her handkerchief slowly.

PROFESSIONAL (CONT'D)
(Scoffs)
Soldiers are trigger happy, Lady!

LABORER
I'll try anything that gives me a chance.

PROFESSIONAL
Just don't run like that dumb ass that just left. You'll pin a target on your heart.
(he zips up his jacket and pulls up his collar)

PROFESSIONAL exits walking hurriedly.

LABORER
Where'd you live?

LUCIA
North.

LABORER
I have a cousin close to Central Park. I'll stay there tonight.

PROFESIONAL
Mierda, ¿ahora cómo voy a llegar a casa?

OFICINISTA
(evaluando mientras habla)
Vivo a unas treinta cuadras de distancia. Si tomo calles laterales... evito las calles principales...
(mirando sus zapatos de vestir)

No son los mejores zapatos para correr... Buenas noches y buena suerte.

OFICINISTA sale corriendo.

LUCÍA
(grita detrás de OFICINISTA)
¡Saca tu pañuelo!

OBRERO
Tienes razón. Probablemente sea una buena idea sacar nuestros pañuelos temprano.

LUCÍA y OBRERO revisan sus bolsillos y cada uno saca su pañuelo blanco.

PROFESIONAL
¿Realmente crees que los soldados buscan la bandera blanca antes de disparar?

LUCÍA reacciona. Desdobla su pañuelo despacio

(burlón)
¡Señora, los solados tienen sus manos listas en el gatillo!

OBRERO
Yo intentaré cualquier cosa que me dé una oportunidad.

PROFESIONAL
Simplemente no corras como ese tonto que acaba de irse. Pondrías un blanco en tu corazón.

LUCIA
I'm just a few blocks past the Park.

LABORER
If we move fast we'll make it.

LUCIA
Wait!
(takes off her high heeled sandals)
I'll walk faster without them.

   LABORER and LUCIA exit waving their handkerchiefs up high.

(END OF SCENE)

   (se abrocha y levanta el cuello de su chaqueta.)

OBRERO
¿Dónde vives?

LUCÍA
Norte.

OBRERO
Tengo un primo cerca del Parque Central. Me quedaré ahí esta noche.

LUCÍA
Estoy a sólo unas cuadras del parque.

OBRERO
Si nos movemos rápido lo lograremos.

LUCÍA
¡Espera!
(se quita las sandalias de tacón alto)
Puedo caminar más rápido sin estas.

   OBRERO Y LUCÍA salen agitando sus pañuelos.

(FIN DE ESCENA)

Scene II - Where Is She?

Setting:

NIGHT. The MEDINA kitchen/ living room in a small and modest house. The table is set for two. There is a pail of water on the kitchen counter and a window above the sink. A big wall clock hangs above the window. In the living room there is a bookshelf packed with books. Next to the bookshelf there is a medium sized avocado plant in a pot. A few old baby girl toys are scattered around. Next to the front door there are dirty overalls and a few mechanic's tools. Classical music is playing from an old radio.
FRANCISCO MEDINA is a retired University Professor in his late sixties. He is waiting for somebody.

          DON FRANCISCO
         (looking up at the ceiling)
Please protect my daughter... Bring her home safely.

         DON FRANCISCO sits on his favorite sofa chair, opens a book, pretends to read and then looks up at the clock that reads 9:50 p.m.

She's never been this late.

         DON FRANCISCO stands and looks out the kitchen window.

         (END OF SCENE)

Escena II – ¿Dónde Está?

Ambientación:

NOCHE. La cocina / sala de estar MEDINA en una casa pequeña y modesta. La mesa esta puesta para dos. Hay un balde de agua en el mostrador de la cocina y una ventana sobre el fregadero. Un gran reloj de pared cuelga arriba de la Ventana. En la sala de estar hay una estanterestantería llena de libros. Junto a la estantería hay una planta mediana de aguacate en una maceta. Algunos juguetes viejos están dispersos alrededor. Junto a la puerta principal hay ropa sucia y algunas herramientas mecánicas. Música clásica suena desde un viejo radio.
FRANCISCO MEDINA es un profesor universitario, jubilado, de unos sesenta años. Está esperando a alguien.

         DON FRANCISCO
        (mirando hacia el techo)
Por favor, protege a mi hija… Tráela a casa a salvo.

         DON FRANCISCO se sienta en su sillón favorito, abre un libro, finge leer y luego mira hacia el reloj que lee 9:50 p.m.

Nunca ha llegado tan tarde.

         DON FRANCISCO se para y mira por la ventana de la cocina.

         (FIN DE ESCENA)

Scene III - I Got It!

Setting:

NIGHT. A stoop in front of the MEDINA home.

LUCIA enters still holding her sandals in her hand. She stops on the stoop and tucks away her handkerchief.

DIEGO a man in his mid-thirties, wearing a hooded sweatshirt, enters. He appears nervous. He keeps looking behind his back to see if anybody is following him.

            DIEGO
Lucía!

            LUCIA
Diego! You scared me! What're you doing out? It's already curfew.

            DIEGO
I got it!
    (pulls out a red passport from his sweatshirt pouch and hands it to LUCIA)

Your visa! I got a visa stamped in your passport.

            LUCIA
¡Dios mío! Finally!

    (opens passport, examines it)

One month. A visa for one month.

            DIEGO
And here's your plane ticket. It's for Sunday.

    (hands LUCIA a plane ticket)

You'll begin a new life in three days. I'll pick you up in my taxi. Take you to the airport.

Escena III – ¡Lo Tengo!

Ambientación:

NOCHE. Entrada frente a la casa MEDINA.

LUCÍA entra todavía con sus sandalias en la mano. Se detiene en la grada y guarda su pañuelo.

DIEGO un hombre de unos treinta años, vestido con una sudadera con capucha entra mirando a sus espaldas para ver si alguien lo está siguiendo.

            DIEGO
¡Lucía!

            LUCÍA
¡Diego! ¡Me asustaste! ¿Qué estás haciendo afuera? Ya es hora de toque de queda.

            DIEGO
¡Lo tengo!
    (saca un pasaporte rojo del bolsillo de su sudadera y se lo entrega a Lucía)

¡Tu visado! Te conseguí una visa sellada en tu pasaporte.

            LUCÍA
¡Dios mío! ¡Finalmente!
    (abre el pasaporte y lo examina)

Un mes. Una visa por un mes.

            DIEGO
Y aquí esta tu boleto de avión. Es para el domingo.

    (entrega a Lucía un billete de avión)

Comenzarás una nueva vida en tres días. Te recogeré en mi taxi. Yo te llevo al aeropuerto.

LUCIA
God, I've been waiting years for this.
(kisses passport and tucks it away in her pouch)

I'd almost lost hope.

DIEGO
Does Don Francisco know yet?

LUCIA
No, not yet.

DIEGO
When are you going to tell him?

LUCIA
Tonight.

DIEGO
You know, your old man adores you. You're all he has left after your mother died.

LUCIA
I know. .... Gracias, Diego. I'll be ready Sunday.

DIEGO exits. LUCIA puts on her sandals and freezes in place as she grabs the front doorknob of the MEDINA house.

(BLACKOUT)

(END OF SCENE)

LUCÍA
Dios, he estado esperando años por esto.
(besa el pasaporte y lo guarda en su bolsa)

Casi había perdido la Esperanza.

DIEGO
¿Ya lo sabe Don Francisco?

LUCÍA
No, todavía no.

DIEGO
¿Cuándo se lo vas a decir?

LUCÍA
Esta noche.

DIEGO
Sabes, tu viejo te adora. Tu eres todo lo que tiene después de la muerte de tu mama.

LUCÍA
Lo sé. …. Gracias, Diego. Estaré lista el domingo.

DIEGO sale. LUCÍA se calza las sandalias y se congela en lugar cuando agarra la perilla de la puerta de la casa MEDINA.

(TELÓN)

(FIN DE ESCENA)

Scene IV - Take a Number

Setting:

MORNING. U.S.A. Consulate office in a foreign country. The American flag and a framed picture of President Carter are prominently displayed. There is a counter with thick, bulletproof glass in front. The small waiting area in front of the counter has two rows of chairs.

Time: 1980

At Rise:

Lights up on people sitting, waiting. They are all holding big call ticket numbers and manila envelopes.

Projection: The year is 1980. The U. S. Consulate office in a Latin American country. A young CONSULAR CLERK sits on a high chair behind the glass and speaks through a microphone. There is a U.S. MARINE standing close to the CLERK's window. A person is standing at the counter being interviewed by the CLERK.

In the front row PERSON holding #96 sits next to PERSON holding #35. PERSON #96 is a heavy-set older woman. A younger LUCIA is holding #55 and is sitting next to RUBEN. RUBEN is a young Hispanic man in his thirties. He holds #54.

                PERSON #96
Three hours standing in line.
                (rubbing her legs)

My legs are killing me.

                PERSON #35
It's all good. Today's our lucky day. We're inside the building.

Escena IV – Toma un Número

Ambientación:

MAÑANA. Oficina de un Consulado Americano en un país extranjero. La bandera estadounidense y una foto enmarcada del presidente Carter figuran prominentemente. Hay un mostrador con un vidrio grueso a prueba de balas en el frente. La pequeña sala de espera frente al mostrador tiene dos filas de sillas.

Fecha: 1980

Telón:

Las luces prenden sobre gente sentada esperando. Todos tienen tickets grandes y sobres de manila.

Proyección: El año es 1980. Oficina del Consulado Americano en un país latinoamericano.
Un joven EMPLEADO CONSULAR se sienta en una silla alta detrás del vidrio y habla a través un micrófono. Hay un MARINE AMERICANO de pie cerca de la ventana donde atiende el EMPLEADO CONSULAR. Una persona está parada cerca al mostrador siendo entrevistada por el EMPLEADO CONSULAR.

En la primera fila de asientos la PERSONA que sostiene el # 96 se sienta al lado de la persona que sostiene el # 35. PERSONA #96 es una mujer mayor, subida de peso. LUCÍA más joven está sosteniendo el # 55 y está sentada junto a RUBÉN.

RUBÉN es un joven hispano de unos treinta años. Tiene el número

                PERSONA #96
Tres horas haciendo cola.
                (frotándose las piernas)

PERSON #96
I got here at six. As soon as curfew lifted, I rushed out my door. Got one of the last tickets.

PERSON# 35
This is my third try. I live South, over an hour away. Last night I stayed at my cousin's place, he's closer.

PERSON #96
I pray it's our lucky day. My son sent me a plane ticket. It's been fifteen years since I've seen him.

PERSON #35 makes the sign of the cross.

RUBEN
I was surprised to see you here this morning.

LUCIA
Yeah, well, like everybody else, I'm trying.

RUBEN
(looking around)
Where's Carlos? Is he applying separately?

LUCIA
I don't know.

Ruben looks at LUCIA confused.

We're not together anymore.

RUBEN
Oh, I didn't know.... You two been together since... junior high?

LUCIA
Too long.

AUDIO (V.O.)
Number 35! Number 35!

Person at the counter exits and PERSON # 35 goes to the window.

Mis piernas me están matando.

PERSONA #35
Todo está bien. Hoy es nuestro día de suerte. Estamos dentro del edificio.

PERONA #96
Llegué aquí a las seis. Apenas se levantó el toque de queda salí corriendo por mi puerta. Alcancé uno de los últimos tickets.

PERONA #35
Este es mi tercer intento. Vivo en el sur, a más de una hora de distancia. Anoche me quedé en casa de mi primo, él está más cerca.

PERONA #96
Rezo para que este sea nuestro día de suerte. Mi hijo me ha enviado un boleto de avión. Han pasado quince años desde que lo he visto.

PERSONA # 35 hace la señal de la cruz.

RUBÉN
Me sorprendió verte aquí esta mañana.

LUCÍA
Si, bueno, como todo el mundo, estoy tratando.

RUBÉN
(mirando a su alrededor)
¿Dónde esta Carlos? ¿Está solicitando por separado?

LUCÍA
No lo sé.

RUBÉN mira a LUCÍA confundido.

Ya no estamos juntos.

RUBÉN
Oh, no lo sabía... Ustedes dos han estado juntos, ¿desde la secundaria?

LUCIA
What about you? I'm surprised to see you here too.

RUBEN
After what happened to Ricky, I have to leave.

LUCIA
I understand.

RUBEN
I miss him.... Everyday. ... He was in his last year of residency. Looking forward to opening a practice.

LUCIA
It was a senseless killing. I am sorry.

> PERSON # 35 leaves the counter, and she appears to be crying on her way out. ALL look at her as she exits.

RUBEN
This is going to sound really weird, but you look good, prettier than ever. Being on your own has given you a... a kind of glow, a radiance.

LUCIA
(smiles)
It's probably my mommy hormones. I'm expecting.

RUBEN
Oh, congratulations!

LUCIA
Thanks.

RUBEN
Do you know? Boy or girl?

LUCÍA
Demasiado tiempo.

AUDIO (V.O.)
¡Número 35! ¡Número 35!

> La persona en el mostrador sale y la PERSONA # 35 se acerca a la Ventana.

LUCÍA
¿Y tú? Me sorprende verte aquí también.

RUBÉN
Después de lo que le pasó a Ricky, tengo que irme.

LUCÍA
Entiendo.

RUBÉN
Lo extraño... Todos los días… Estaba en su último año de residencia. Ilusionado con abrir un consultorio.

LUCÍA
Fue un asesinato sin sentido. Lo siento.

> PERSONA # 35 se retira del mostrador y parece estar llorando al salir. TODOS la siguen con la mirada cuando sale.

RUBÉN
Esto va a sonar muy raro, pero te ves muy bien, más bonita que nunca. El estar sola te ha dado una especie de resplandor, de radiancia.

LUCÍA
(sonríe)
Probablemente sean mis hormonas de mamá. Estoy esperando.

RUBÉN
¡Oh! ¡Felicitaciones!

LUCIA
No. But I'm hoping for a girl. I'm going to name her Katia, after my mother.

RUBEN
You know, you look so much more like your mother with your hair short.

LUCIA
Thanks. My poor Mom wanted so much to live long enough to meet her first grandchild. God did not grant her wish.

RUBEN
Everybody in the neighborhood loved Doña Katia. *(a pause)* Does Don Francisco know you're here?

LUCIA
No, these things take some time. Right now, he's devastated with my mother's passing. I figured I'd let him know when I actually get a visa.

AUDIO (V.O.)
Number 54! Number 54!

RUBEN
That's me!

LUCIA
Good luck!

RUBEN heads to the window.

RUBEN
Good morning!

CONSULAR CLERK
Ticket, please.

RUBEN passes his ticket under the glass window.

CONSULAR CLERK
(does not look at RUBEN)
Name?

LUCÍA
Gracias.

RUBÉN
¿Sabes? ¿Niño o niña?

LUCÍA
No. Pero desearía una niña. La voy a llamar Katia, en honor a mi madre.

RUBÉN
Sabes, te pareces mucho más a tu madre con tu cabello corto.

LUCÍA
Gracias. Mi mamá deseaba tanto mantenerse viva hasta conocer a su nieto. Dios no le concedió su deseo.

RUBÉN
Todos en el vecindario amaban a Doña Katia. *(una pausa)* ¿Sabe Don Francisco que estas aquí?

LUCÍA
No, estas cosas toman tiempo. Ahora esta devastado con la muerte de mi madre. Pensé que se lo haría saber cuándo consiga la visa.

AUDIO (V.O.)
¡Número 54! ¡Número 54!

RUBÉN
¡Ese soy yo!

LUCÍA
¡Buena suerte!

RUBÉN se dirige a la ventanilla.

RUBÉN
¡Buenos días!

SECRETARIO CONSULAR
Ticket, por favor.

RUBEN
Rubén García Martinez.

CONSULAR CLERK
Address?

RUBEN
San Pedro 590, Barrios Altos.

CONSULAR CLERK
Age?

RUBEN
Thirty-one.

CONSULAR CLERK
Civil status?

RUBEN
Single.

CONSULAR CLERK
Children?

RUBEN
No children.

CONSULAR CLERK
Application form and passport.

RUBEN passes his passport and an application form under the glass.

CONSULAR CLERK
(inspects documents carefully)
Your passport has your first name spelled with an "i" and your application has it spelled with an "e". What is the correct spelling of your name?

RUBEN
It's an "E".... R-U-B-E-N

RUBÉN se dirige a la ventanilla.

RUBÉN pasa su ticket por debajo de la ventana de vidrio.

SECRETARIO CONSULAR
(sin mirar a RUBÉN)
¿Nombre?

RUBÉN
Rubén García Martínez.

SECRETARIO CONSULAR
¿Dirección?

RUBÉN
San Pedro 590, Barrios Altos.

SECRETARIO CONSULAR
¿Edad?

RUBÉN
Treinta y uno.

SECRETARIO CONSULAR
¿Estado civil?

RUBÉN
Soltero.

SECRETARIO CONSULAR
¿Hijos?

RUBÉN
No tengo hijos.

SECRETARIO CONSULAR
Formulario de solicitud y pasaporte.

RUBÉN pasa su pasaporte y la solicitud por debajo de la ventanilla.

SECRETARIO CONSULAR
(inspecciona los documentos cuidadosamente)

CONSULAR CLERK
I must file your application with the spelling in your passport. If that is a misspelling, you must bring a passport with the correct spelling.

RUBEN
A new passport?

CONSULAR CLERK
Yes.

RUBEN
(uncertain)
Okay.

CONSULAR CLERK takes time to review the application.

CONSULAR CLERK
(with disbelief in his voice)
Mr. García Martinez, you're applying for an immigrant visa to the United States and you're not declaring a preferential status?

RUBEN
Yes,... I think so. ... What's a preferential status?

CONSULAR CLERK
Preferential status is given to spouses, children, and siblings of United States citizens. Applicants with this status are moved to the front of the waiting list. Do you have any immediate family member that is a citizen of the United States?

RUBEN
No. I have friends. Does that count?

CONSULAR CLERK
The relationship has to be by blood or marriage.

SECRETARIO CONSULAR
(inspecciona los documentos cuidadosamente)
Su pasaporte tiene su nombre escrito con una "i" y su solicitud lo tiene escrito con una "e." ¿Cuál es la ortografía correcta de su nombre?

RUBÉN
Es una "E." R-U-B-E-N

SECRETARIO CONSULAR
Debo presentar su solicitud con la ortografía que figura en su pasaporte. Si esa ortografía es un error, debe traer un pasaporte con la ortografía correcta.

RUBÉN
¿Un nuevo pasaporte?

SECRETARIO CONSULAR
Sí.

RUBÉN
(inseguro)
Bien.

El SECRETARIO CONSULAR se toma tiempo para revisar la solicitud.

SECRETARIO CONSULAR
(con incredulidad en su voz)
Señor García Martínez, ¿está solicitando una visa de inmigrante a los Estados Unidos y no declara un estado preferencial?

RUBÉN
Sí... Creo que sí. ¿Qué es un estado preferencial?

RUBEN
No, I have nobody.

CONSULAR CLERK
(flips through paperwork as if looking for something)
Some professions also receive preferential status. What's your profession Mr. García Martinez?

RUBEN
I'm a schoolteacher. I teach music.

CONSULAR CLERK
(in matter-of-fact tone)
Currently, there is no preference for schoolteachers. The United States does not need school music teachers.

RUBEN
Okay.

CONSULAR CLERK
You will be placed at the end of the waiting list.

RUBEN
Okay.

CONSULAR CLERK
(stamps multiple papers)
I'm going to assign you case number 343455. When you want to inquire about your status on the waiting list you must refer to this number. Do you understand?

RUBEN
Yes.

CONSULAR CLERK
Twenty-four months before you are granted a visa you will receive a letter giving you the time and date for an interview here at the Consulate.

SECRETARIO CONSULAR
El estado preferencial se otorga a las parejas, hijos y hermanos de ciudadanos de los Estados Unidos. Los solicitantes con este estatus son puestos al comienzo de la lista de espera. ¿Tiene algún familiar inmediato que sea ciudadano de los Estados Unidos?

RUBÉN
No. Tengo amigos. ¿Eso cuenta?

SECRETARIO CONSULAR
La relación tiene que ser por sangre o matrimonio.

RUBÉN
No, no tengo a nadie.

SECRETARIO CONSULAR
(hojea el papeleo como si estuviera buscando algo)
Algunas profesiones también reciben un estatus preferencial.

SECRETARIO CONSULAR (continuación)
¿Cuál es su profesión Señor García Martínez?

RUBÉN
Soy maestro de escuela. Enseño música.

SECRETARIO CONSULAR
(en tono práctico)
Actualmente no hay preferencia para maestros de escuela. Los Estados Unidos no necesita maestros de música de escuela.

RUBÉN
Okay.

SECRETARIO CONSULAR
Se le colocará al final de la lista de espera.

RUBÉN
Sí.

CONSULAR CLERK
While you are waiting for your interview if you move from the address you have given me today you must come and amend your application. Do you understand? This is very important.

RUBEN
Yes.

CONSULAR CLERK
Also, at all times, while you are waiting you must keep a valid passport. You must never allow your passport to expire. Do you understand?

RUBEN
My passport is new. It's valid for ten years.

CONSULAR CLERK
Thank you, Mr. García Martinez for applying to emigrate to the United States of America.

(BLACKOUT)

(END OF SCENE)

SECRETARIO CONSULAR
(sella múltiples documentos)
Le voy a asignar a su caso el número 343455. Cuando quiera preguntar sobre su estatus en la lista de espera debe referirse a este número. ¿Usted me entiende?

RUBÉN
Sí

SECRETARIO CONSULAR
Veinticuatro meses antes de que se le otorgue una visa, recibirá una carta que le dará la hora y la fecha para una entrevista aquí en el Consulado. Mientras espera su entrevista si se muda de la dirección que esta hoy en su solicitud, debe venir a informarnos del cambio. ¿Usted me entiende? Esto es muy importante.

RUBÉN
Sí.

SECRETARIO CONSULAR
Además, en todo momento, mientras que está esperando usted debe mantener un pasaporte válido. No debe permitir que su pasaporte se expire. ¿Usted me entiende?

RUBÉN
Mi pasaporte es nuevo. Tiene una validez de diez años.

SECRETARIO CONSULAR
Gracias Señor García Martínez por solicitar emigrar a los Estados Unidos de América.

(TELÓN)

(FIN DE ESCENA)

Scene V - Find a Way

Setting:

DAY. MEDINA living room. Set is similar to Scene II. The avocado plant and the clothes close to the door are not there. The bookshelf is less crowded.

Time: Four months later. 1980

At Rise:

A very pregnant LUCIA is sitting on the sofa with her feet up.

The doorbell rings.

              LUCIA
Come in! Door's open!

    RUBEN walks in carrying a grocery bag.

             RUBEN
Hi, Lucía! I was in the neighborhood and thought I'd stop to see how you're doing.
    (kisses LUCIA on the cheek and rubs her belly)

How's my little girl today?

              LUCIA
Any day now. The doctor has me scheduled for Tuesday, but she said contractions could start any day.

             RUBEN
I brought you some milk and fruit...
    (sets milk and fruit on the counter)
... and my mother knitted a blanket for baby Katia.
    (hands LUCIA a baby blanket)

              LUCIA
Oh, this is so beautiful. So soft. Thank you, Rubén, and please thank your mom for me.

Escena V – Encuentra una Manera

Ambientación:

DÍA. Sala de estar MEDINA. Escenario es similar al de la Escena II. La planta de aguacate y la ropa cerca de la puerta no están allí. La estantería tiene menos libros.

Fecha: Cuatro meses después. Año 1980

Telón:

Una LUCÍA bastante avanzada en su embarazo está sentada en el sofá con los pies en alto.

Suena el timbre.

              LUCÍA
¡Entre! ¡La puerta está abierta!

    RUBÉN entra con una bolsa de mercado.

             RUBÉN
¡Hola, Lucía! Estaba en el vecindario y pensé que pasaría a ver como estás.
    (besa a LUCÍA en la mejilla y le frota el vientre)

¿Cómo está mi niña hoy?

              LUCÍA
Ahora es cualquier día. El médico me tiene programada para el martes, pero me dijo que las contracciones pueden comenzar cualquier día.

             RUBÉN
Te traje un poco de leche y fruta...
    (pone leche y fruta en el mostrador)

Y mi madre tejió una manta para la bebe Katia.
    (le entrega a LUCÍA una manta de bebe)

RUBEN
You know you're like family. Let's see, we've been friends some ... twenty-five years?

LUCIA
Since Ms. Ramos sat us next to each other and had us hold hands. You could call it, love at first sight.

RUBEN
(laughing)
At five?

LUCIA
(flirtatious)
Yes! I make up my mind fast.

RUBEN
(shaking his head)
Lucía, Lucía ...

LUCIA
I know, I know.

RUBEN
Ah, you're the sister I never had.

LUCIA reacts with mocking disgust.

I remember when we used to run together. In high school. You were a really good runner. I always thought you would end up representing our country in the Pan American Games.

LUCIA
You were not bad yourself.

RUBEN
Nah! I just trailed you. Your Mom bribed me to always go with you, to protect you. She was afraid for you, running alone on the streets. She was afraid of your safety and since Carlos was not a runner she couldn't ask him. So, we made a deal.

LUCÍA
¡Oh! Esto es tan hermoso. Tan suave. Gracias Rubén, y por favor agradécele a tu mama por mí.

RUBÉN
Sabes que eres como mi familia. A ver, hemos sido amigos unos... ¿veinticinco años?

LUCÍA
Desde que la Señora Ramos nos sentó uno al lado del otro y nos hizo tomarnos de la mano. Podría llamarlo amor a primera vista.

RUBÉN
(riéndose)
¿A los cinco años?

LUCÍA
(coqueta)
¡Sí! Me decido rápido!

RUBÉN
(sacudiendo la cabeza)
Lucía, Lucía ,,,

LUCÍA
Ya sé. Ya sé.

RUBÉN
Eres la hermana que nunca tuve.

LUCÍA reacciona con disgusto burlón.

RUBÉN (continuación)
Recuerdo cuando corríamos juntos. En el colegio. Eras una buena corredora. Siempre pensé que terminarías representando nuestro país en los Panamericanos.

LUCÍA
Tú no eras nada mal, tampoco.

LUCÍA
(incredulous)

She bribed you?

RUBEN
Yup! She gave me money for ice cream after each run.

LUCIA
And here I always thought you came with me because you liked me.

RUBEN
Oh, I've always liked you Lucia, you know that...But, ice cream three times a week, that's a real motivator.

LUCIA
(laughing)
I can't believe my mom. And I can't believe you guys hid your little plot from me for so long.

RUBEN
So, what happened with Carlos? You were head over heels with him. I thought you guys were going to tie the knot.

LUCIA
I caught him in bed with Carmen a week after we found out I was pregnant.

RUBEN
Hummm... He's cheated before. What changed?

LUCIA
What changed? I'm expecting a child now. It's different.

RUBEN
It's hard to raise a child alone.

LUCIA
It's over Rubén. I'm not taking him back again. This time, it's really over.

RUBÉN
¡No! Yo solo te seguía. Tu mamá me sobornaba para siempre ir contigo, para protegerte. Tenía miedo de que corras sola por las calles. Tenía miedo por tu seguridad, y como Carlos no era corredor, no le podía pedir a él. Entonces hicimos un trato.

LUCÍA
(incrédula)
¿Te sobornó?

RUBÉN
¡Si! Me daba dinero para un helado después de cada Carrera.

LUCÍA
Y yo pensaba que siempre venias conmigo porque te gustaba.

RUBÉN
Oh, siempre me has gustado Lucía, tu sabes eso ... Pero, helado tres veces a la semana ese si era un verdadero motivador.

LUCÍA
(riéndose)
No puedo creer a mi mamá. Y no puedo creer que ustedes lo escondieron de mí su arreglo por tanto tiempo.

RUBÉN
Entonces, ¿qué paso con Carlos? Tu estabas loca por él. Yo pensé que ustedes iban a casarse.

LUCÍA
Lo encontré en la cama con Carmen una semana después de que nos enteramos que estaba embarazada.

RUBÉN
Hummm... Te ha engañado antes. ¿Qué cambio?

RUBEN
You're gonna need help.

LUCIA
It's over.

> A beat.

RUBEN
You know.... I've been thinking, I could help you with Katia.... be a father for her.
LUCIA is surprised.
Wait, ... hear me out. I know, we've talked about this before. But things are different now. We're older. Neither of us have partners. We get along great.

LUCIA
(biting her lip)
You'd be a great father. I have no doubt. ... But, I want more than a brother.

> RUBEN moves away from LUCIA.

Just promise me you'll be careful.

> A beat.

RUBEN
Did you hear that Sylvia is in the United States?

LUCIA
Yes. The quietest student found a way out.

RUBEN
Her sister told me that she's doing really well. She's helping them with some money every month.

LUCIA
I wonder how she did it.

RUBEN
Have you heard anything from the Consulate?

LUCIA
No, and I don't expect to hear from them any time soon. I was going to tell you. I've been asking around and found out that it takes a real long time to get a visa.

LUCÍA
¿Qué cambio? Estoy esperando un hijo ahora. Es diferente.

RUBÉN
Es difícil criar a un niño sola.

LUCÍA
Se acabó Rubén. No lo voy a aceptar de vuelta. Esta vez, de a verdad se acabó.

RUBÉN
Vas a necesitar ayuda.

LUCÍA
Se acabó.

> Una pausa.

RUBÉN
Sabes,... He estado pensando, podría ayudarte con Katia... ser un padre para ella.
(LUCÍA se sorprende)

Espera, escúchame. Lo sé, hemos hablado de esto antes. Pero las cosas son diferentes ahora. Somos mayores. Ninguno de los dos tiene una pareja. Nos llevamos muy bien.

LUCÍA
(mordiéndose el labio)
Serías un gran padre. No tengo ninguna duda … Pero, quiero más que un hermano.

> RUBÉN se aleja de LUCÍA.

LUCÍA *(continuación)*
Solo prométeme que tendrás cuidado.

> Una pausa.

RUBÉN
¿Escuchaste que Sylvia está en los Estados Unidos?

LUCÍA
Si. La estudiante más calladita encontró una salida.

RUBEN
I assumed it wasn't going to be fast. Like you said before, these things take time.

LUCIA
I heard decades. Twenty, thirty, forty years to get a visa to the United States.

RUBEN
I don't believe that.

LUCIA
They say that if you don't already have family there, you'll wait a lifetime.

RUBEN
C'mon, why would the Consulate even accept applications if they're going to take that long?

LUCIA
(visible reaction)
They couldn't quite advertise they take that long. That would be...embarrassing. Politically embarrassing.

RUBEN
That doesn't make any sense.

LUCIA
I'm not making it up. People know these things.

RUBEN
Then, I guess we'll just have to wait a little longer than I thought.

LUCIA
A little longer?

RUBEN
Eventually, our turn will come up.

LUCIA
Are you serious? .... I'm not waiting.

RUBEN
What? What're you gonna do?

LUCIA
I've been talking to Diego, Doña Ramona's oldest son. Remember him? He was one year ahead of us in school.

RUBÉN
Su hermana me dijo que le está yendo muy bien. Que les está ayudando con algo de dinero cada mes.

LUCÍA
Me pregunto como lo hizo.

RUBÉN
¿Has escuchado algo del Consulado?

LUCÍA
No, y no espero escuchar nada de ellos en el corto plazo. Te lo iba a contar, he estado preguntando por ahí y descubrí que se toma muchísimo tiempo obtener una visa.

RUBÉN
Asumí que no iba a ser rápido. Como dijiste antes, estas cosas toman tiempo.

LUCÍA
Escuché décadas. Veinte, treinta, cuarenta años para obtener una visa a los Estados Unidos.

RUBÉN
No creo eso.

LUCÍA
Dicen que si no tienes familia allá, vas a esperar toda una vida.

RUBÉN
Vamos, ¿por qué aceptaría el Consulado solicitudes si se va a tomar tanto tiempo?

LUCÍA
(reacción visible)
No podrían anunciar que tardan tanto. Eso sería vergonzoso. Políticamente vergonzoso.

RUBÉN
Eso no tiene ningún sentido.

LUCÍA
No lo estoy inventando. La gente sabe de estas cosas.

RUBEN
Yes, the taxi driver?

LUCIA
Yes, him. Last week he told me he could introduce me to a friend that sells visas.

RUBEN
Sells visas?

LUCIA
Yes, I'm going to meet with him after Katia is born.

RUBEN
Sounds shady, dangerous.

LUCIA
You wanna come? We could go together?

RUBEN
I don't trust Diego. Are you sure you want to do that?

LUCIA
Are you going to wait thirty, forty years?

LUCIA & RUBEN hold their gaze for a beat.

RUBEN
But... to travel with a bought visa? Illegally?

LUCIA
(facial reaction)
Don't you get it? This... this crazy world we live in is never going to change. Not in our lifetimes. There's ab-so-lu-te-ly nothing you or I can do to change that.... We're insignificant grains of sand in a huge sandstorm.

RUBEN
I can't. I have to have certainty.

RUBÉN
Entonces, supongo que tendremos que esperar un poquito más de lo que pensaba.

LUCÍA
¿Un poquito más?

RUBÉN
Eventualmente llegará nuestro turno.

LUCÍA
¿Hablas en serio? …. Yo no voy a esperar.

RUBÉN
¿Qué? ¿Qué vas a hacer?

LUCÍA
He estado hablando con Diego, el hijo mayor de Doña Ramona. ¿Te acuerdas de él? Estaba un año delante de nosotros en el colegio.

RUBÉN
Si, el taxista.

LUCÍA
Sí, él. La semana pasada me dijo que me podía presentar a un amigo que vende visas.

RUBÉN
¿Vende visas?

LUCÍA
Sí, me voy a reunir con él después de que nazca Katia.

RUBÉN
Suena oscuro, peligroso.

LUCÍA
¿Quieres venir? ¿Podríamos ir juntos?

RUBÉN
No confío en Diego. ¿Estas seguras que quieres hacer eso?

LUCIA
(touching her belly)
I want a better life for us.

A younger DON FRANCISCO enters carrying a box of books with a brown paper bag on top.

DON FRANCISCO
Hello, *mi'ja!* Hello, Rubén! So nice of you to come visit.

RUBEN
Good afternoon, Don Francisco! Lemme help you with that box.

RUBEN takes the box from DON FRANCISCO and sets it on the kitchen table.

LUCIA
Hello, Father! How was the University today? Are you bringing home more books?

DON FRANCISCO
Yes, another box.

RUBEN
Don Francisco, I was surprised to hear that you're retiring, you're still young.

DON FRANCISCO
(smiling)
Oh, it wasn't my choice, Rubén. A young Professor, a man with 'connections,' wanted my job.

RUBEN
That's just not right!

DON FRANCISCO starts stacking his books on the bookshelf.

DON FRANCISCO
Right? Right is subjective. Each person has their own personal definition, 'it's the way they see it.'
(observing the full bookshelf)

The Avocado Tree/ El Árbol de Aguacate 24

LUCÍA
¿Vas a esperar treinta, cuarenta años?

LUCÍA y RUBÉN mantienen la mirada por un momento.

RUBÉN
¿Pero … viajar con un visado comprado? ¿Ilegalmente?

LUCÍA
(reacción facial)
¿No lo entiendes? Este … este mundo loco en que vivimos nunca va a cambiar. No en nuestras vidas. No hay ab-so-lu-ta-men-te nada que tu o yo podamos hacer para cambiar eso. Somos apenas granos insignificantes de arena en una tormenta de arena.

RUBÉN
No puedo. Tengo que tener certeza.

LUCÍA
(tocándose el vientre)
Quiero una vida mejor para nosotras.

Un más joven DON FRANCISCO entra Cargando una caja de libros con una bolsa de papel sobre ellos.

DON FRANCISCO
¡Hola, mi 'ja! ¡Hola, Rubén! Es muy agradable que hayas venido a visitor.

RUBÉN
¡Buenas tardes, Don Francisco! Déjeme ayudarle con esa caja.

RUBÉN toma la caja de DON FRANCISCO y la coloca en la mesa de la cocina.

LUCÍA
¡Hola, papá! ¿Como estaba la Universidad hoy? ¿Estas trayendo a casa más libros?

DON FRANCISCO
Sí, otra caja.

RUBÉN
Don Francisco, me sorprendio saber que usted se jubila, aún es joven.

Looks like I'm going to have to build a new bookshelf.

RUBEN
The University will not be the same without you. You've helped so many students. I know, I would never have graduated if it wasn't for your constant support and encouragement.

LUCIA
Father, what's in the paper bag?

DON FRANCISCO
Oh! I have a surprise for you.

DON FRANCISCO pulls out of the paper bag a small avocado plant that is sprouting from a pit and proudly displays it.

Lunch three months ago!

RUBEN
(inspecting the plant)
An avocado.

DON FRANCISCO
The most delicious fruit from the Americas.
(inspects the small pot)

Looks like I'll need to re-pot soon. These roots are growing fast.

RUBEN
Avocados have big roots. They take up a lot of space.

LUCIA
(chuckling)
An avocado will never grow here.

DON FRANCISCO sets the small pot on the windowsill.

DON FRANCISCO
As long as it has sunlight, it'll grow.

DON FRANCISCO
(sonriendo)
Oh, no fue mi decisión, Rubén. Un joven Profesor, un hombre con "conexiones" quería mi trabajo.

RUBÉN
¡Eso no es correcto!

DON FRANCISCO comienza a poner sus libros en la estantería.

DON FRANCISCO
¿Correcto? Correcto es subjetivo. Cada persona tiene su propia definición personal, 'es la forma en que ellos lo ven.'
(observando la estantería de libros llena)

Parece que voy a tener que construir un nuevo estante.

RUBÉN
La universidad no va ser igual sin usted. Usted ha ayudado a tantos estudiantes. Yo se que nunca me hubiese graduado si no fuera por su constante apoyo y aliento.

LUCÍA
¿Papá, qué hay en la bolsa de papel?

DON FRANCISCO
¡Oh! Tengo una sorpresa para ti!

DON FRANCISCO saca de la bolsa de papel una pequeña planta de aguacate que esta brotando de una pepa, y la exhibe con orgullo.

¡Mi almuerzo hace tres meses!

RUBÉN
(inspeccionando la planta)
Un aguacate.

DON FRANCISCO
La fruta más deliciosa de las Américas.
(inspeccionando la pequeña maceta)

DON FRANCISCO *(continuación)*
Parece que pronto tendré que cambiar de maceta. Estas raíces están creciendo rápido.

RUBEN
Avocados take five, six years I think, to produce any fruit.

LUCIA
Six years! Father, you're crazy! You're going to wait that long?

DON FRANCISCO
Patience, Lucia. Patience is something your generation has lost. Today, everybody wants everything too fast. Anything worthwhile takes time. Time to grow... time to simmer... and time to create.

LUCIA
(reacts to a contraction)
I think it's time.

RUBEN
Don Francisco, it's time to meet your granddaughter!

DON FRANCISCO
Precious life! A new generation of Medinas.

(BLACKOUT)

(END OF SCENE)

RUBÉN
Los aguacates tienen raíces grandes. Ocupan bastante espacio.

LUCÍA
(riendo)
Un aguacate nunca crecerá aquí.

DON FRANCISCO coloca el pequeño macetero en el alfeizar de la Ventana.

DON FRANCISCO
Mientras tenga luz del sol, crecerá.

RUBÉN
Creo que los aguacates tardan cinco, seis años en producir fruta.

LUCÍA
¡Seis años! ¡Padre, estás loco! ¿Vas a esperar tanto tiempo?

DON FRANCISCO
Paciencia, Lucía. La paciencia es algo que tu generación ha perdido. Hoy en día todo el mundo quiere todo demasiado rápido. Cualquier cosa que valga la pena lleva tiempo. Tiempo para crecer,... tiempo para macerar ... y tiempo para crear.

LUCÍA
(reacciona a una contracción)
Creo que es hora.

RUBÉN
¡Don Francisco, es hora de conocer a su nieta!

DON FRANCISCO

¡Vida preciosa! Una nueva generación de Medinas.

(TELÓN)

(FIN DE ESCENA)

Scene VI - And You're Worth?

Setting:

An empty, seedy bar in a bad part of the city.

Time: Six months later. 1980.

At Rise:

DEALER, an older man with a two-day beard and an unkept look, is drinking alone.

DIEGO and LUCIA enter and approach the DEALER's table.

              DIEGO

Hey!

        DEALER acknowledges DIEGO with a head movement.

        DIEGO sits and indicates to LUCIA to do the same.

This is my friend I told you about. The one that needs a special favor.

              DEALER
    (assesses LUCIA slowly as he drinks his beer)

Waiter! My friends are thirsty!

        WAITER rushes in bringing filled mugs of beer.

        DEALER and DIEGO drink, but LUCIA does not pick up her mug.

              DEALER

What? You're going to offend me?

        DIEGO nudges LUCIA urging her to drink. LUCIA takes a sip.

The Avocado Tree/ El Árbol de Aguacate 27

Escena VI – ¿Y Tú Cuanto Vales?

Ambientación:

Un bar vacío y sórdido en una mala zona de la ciudad.

Fecha: Seis meses después. Año 1980.

Telón:

TRAFICANTE, un hombre mayor con una barba de dos días y una apariencia descuidada, esta bebiendo solo.

DIEGO y LUCÍA entran y se acercan a la mesa del TRAFICANTE.

              DIEGO

¡Hey!

        TRAFICANTE reconoce a DIEGO con un movimiento de la cabeza.

        DIEGO se sienta y le indica a LUCÍA que haga lo mismo.

Esta es mi amiga de la que te hable. La que necesita un favor especial.

            TRAFICANTE
    (evalúa a LUCIA lentamente mientras que bebe su cerveza)

¡Camarero! ¡Mis amigos tienen sed!

        CAMARERO se apresura a traer vasos de cerveza.

        TRAFICANTE y DIEGO beben pero LUCÍA no levanta su vaso.

            TRAFICANTE

¿Qué? ¿Me vas a offender?

        DIEGO le da un codazo suave a LUCÍA instándola a beber.

DEALER (CONT'D)
What's that? I want to see you drink with *gusto. Con ganas!*

> LUCIA picks up her mug and takes a long drag.

Better.
(sits back, lights a cigarette)

I'm starting to like your friend here.

DIEGO
That's what we wanted to talk to you about. My friend here needs help, and you are the only person that can help her. She needs a visa.

DEALER
(to LUCIA)
You want to leave? A nice girl like you? Where's your husband?

LUCIA
I'm not married.

DEALER
Pregnant?

LUCIA
No.

DEALER
Children?

LUCIA
No.

> DIEGO turns toward LUCIA and looks at her quizzically.

DEALER
A pretty thing like you, all alone?

> LUCIA gives a facial reaction.

Where? Where you wanna go?

> LUCÍA toma un pequeño sorbo.

¿Qué es eso? Quiero verte beber con gusto. ¡Con ganas!

> LUCÍA levanta su vaso y bebe la cerveza.

Mejor.
(se reclina en su asiento, y enciende un cigarillo)

Me está empezando a gustar tu amiga.

DIEGO
De eso es de lo que queríamos hablarte. Mi amiga aquí necesita ayuda y tú eres la única persona que la puede ayudar. Necesita una visa.

TRAFICANTE
(a LUCÍA)
¿Quieres irte? ¿Una chica tan agradable como tú? ¿Dónde está tu esposo?

LUCÍA
No estoy casada.

TRAFICANTE
¿Embarazada?

LUCÍA
No.

TRAFICANTE
¿Hijos?

LUCÍA
No.

> DIEGO se vuelve hacia LUCÍA y la mira con curiosidad.

Los Estados Unidos.

> TRAFICANTE comienza a reírse a carcajadas, mientras que DIEGO empieza a hablar.

LUCIA
The United States.

DEALER starts laughing loud as DIEGO begins to speak.

DIEGO
(turning toward LUCIA)
I thought...

DEALER
You couldn't afford a visa from here to there.

DIEGO
(toward DEALER)
You can buy visas to the United States, too?

DEALER
Of course. Everybody has a price. Uppity gringos included.

(toward LUCIA)

There's work in Spain. It's easier with the language. Everybody is going there now..... You speak English?

LUCIA
Un poquito.

DEALER
You're even more screwed.

DIEGO
English is hard. I've done the night classes for years, but it just doesn't stick. I can never get the words in the right order. It's all backwards.

DEALER
Even if I spoke English I wouldn't go North. It's better in Europe. It's more of a ... What do they say?... a 'melting pot.' I'd even choose freezing cold Canada over gringo-land.

DIEGO
A friend told me that in Canada you get a place to live when you get there.

DEALER
Yeah. It's true.

TRAFICANTE
¿Una cosa tan bonita como tú, solita?

LUCÍA da una reacción facial.

¿Dónde? ¿A dónde quieres ir?

LUCÍA
DIEGO
(volteando hacia LUCÍA)
Pensé...

TRAFICANTE
No podrías pagar una visa de aquí para allá.

DIEGO
(hacia el TRAFICANTE)
¿También se pueden comprar visas a los Estados Unidos?

TRAFICANTE
Por supuesto. Todo el mundo tiene su precio. Gringos sobrados incluidos.
(hacia LUCÍA)

Hay trabajo en España. Es más fácil con el idioma. Ahora todo el mundo está yendo allí... ¿Hablas inglés?

LUCÍA
Un poquito.

TRAFICANTE
Estas aún más jodida.

DIEGO
Inglés es difícil. He ido a las clases nocturnas por años, simplemente no se me pega. Nunca puedo poner las palabras en el orden correcto. Todo es al revés.

TRAFICANTE
Incluso si hablara inglés, no iría al norte. Es mejor en Europa. Es más, ... ¿Cómo es que dicen? ... 'un crisol.' Incluso elijaría el frígido Canadá en lugar de la tierra gringa.

DIEGO
Un amigo me dijo que en Canadá te dan un lugar para vivir cuando llegas ahí.

DIEGO
Can you imagine? A nice house to live, just for going to work there.
(he can see the image in his mind's eye)

LUCIA
Soooo, can you get me permission for Spain?

DEALER
As a favor to my friend here, it can be arranged. Diego and I go back a long time. A friend of his is my friend. *Salud!*

DIEGO
How does it work?

DEALER
(toward LUCIA)
I'll get you a visa for Mexico. I can get it tomorrow, if you want. Then, when you're there I'll arrange an entry visa for Spain, Germany, Canada. Wherever you want.

> A beat.

LUCIA
And to the United States?

DEALER
Persistent, eh... I like that.

DIEGO
(toward LUCIA)
Canada sounds better.

DEALER
If you're stuck on getting your American dream, you can walk there. I'll get you to Mexico. Then, you pay a *coyote* to take you across. You'll have no trouble finding those cabrones.

LUCIA
How much to Mexico?

> DEALER writes two numbers on a napkin and hands it to LUCIA. He points at the numbers as he speaks.

TRAFICANTE
Sí. Es cierto.

DIEGO
¿Te puedes imaginar? Una bonita casa para vivir, solo por ir a trabajar ahí.
(puede ver la imagen en el ojo de su mente)

LUCÍA
¿Entonces, me puede obtener permiso para España?

TRAFICANTE
Como favor a mi amigo aquí, puede ser arreglado. Diego y yo nos conocemos hace mucho tiempo. Una amiga de él, es mi amiga. ¡Salud!

DIEGO
¿Cómo funciona?

TRAFICANTE
(hacia LUCÍA)
Te conseguiré una visa para México. Puedo conseguirlo mañana, si quieres. Luego cuando estes allí, te arreglaré una visa de entrada a España, Alemania, Canadá. Donde quieras ir.

> Una pausa.

LUCÍA
¿Y a los Estados Unidos?

TRAFICANTE
Persistente, eh... Eso me gusta.

DIEGO
(hacia LUCÍA)
Canadá suena major.

TRAFICANTE
Si estas empeñada en conseguir tu sueño americano, puedes caminar hasta allí. Te llevaré a México. Luego le pagas a un *coyote* para que te ayude a cruzar. No tendrás ningún problema encontrando a esos cabrones.

LUCÍA
¿Cuánto a México?

DEALER
This, to Mexico and this, to Spain, Canada or Germany. All the same.

LUCIA
(looks at the numbers on the napkin)
Wow! That's a lot!

DEALER
(laughs)
What'd you expect?

LUCIA passes the napkin to DIEGO.

DIEGO
Maaan...!

LUCIA
It's more than a year's salary.

DIEGO
Is...is the air ticket included?

DEALER
Yes. Full service. Complete package deal. I only take American dollars.
(turning toward LUCIA)
Your stay in Mexico City for a few days is also included.

Awkward silence.
A beat.

DEALER (CONT'D)
(to LUCIA)
Stand up.

Uncertain, LUCIA stands up.

(gesturing with his hands)
Unbutton that big, ugly sweater you have there.

LUCIA obeys.

Take it off.

LUCIA takes her sweater off.

Turn around.

The Avocado Tree/ El Árbol de Aguacate 31

TRAFICANTE escribe dos números en una servilleta y se lo entrega a LUCÍA. Señala los números mientras habla.

TRAFICANTE
Esto, es a México, y esto a España, Canadá, o Alemania. Todo es igual.

LUCÍA
(mira los números en la servilleta)
¡Wow! ¡Eso es un montón!

TRAFICANTE
(riéndose)
¿Qué esperabas?

LUCÍA le pasa la servilleta a DIEGO.

DIEGO
¡Woo...!

LUCÍA
Es más que el salario de un año.

DIEGO
¿El... el billete de avión está incluido?

TRAFICANTE
Sí. Servicio completo. Paquete completo. Solo acepto dólares americanos.

(volteando hacia LUCÍA)

TRAFICANTE (continuación)
Tu estadía por unos días en la ciudad de México está incluida.

Silencio incómodo.
Una pausa.

(a LUCÍA)
Párate.

Incierta, LUCÍA se pone de pie.

(gesticulando con sus manos)
Desabotona ese suéter grande y feo que tienes puesto.

> DEALER slowly evaluates LUCIA's body. LUCIA remains still.

DEALER (CONT'D)
I like 'em with more meat on their bones. With something to grab.

But I could be persuaded...

> LUCIA quickly puts on her sweater and sits down.

LUCIA
I'll get the money. Make payments. It's just going to take me some time.

DEALER
(laughs)
Chiquita, you're not ready for this.
(shakes his head in disbelief)

Go home!

> LUCIA reacts with stubbornness.

DEALER (CONT'D)
As a friend, lemme give you some real good advice, the only thing a woman without papers has is her body. It'll be taken or it'll be sold many times in the path you want to take. .... Women that survive learn that quickly....
Go home!

(BLACKOUT)

(END OF SCENE)

> LUCÍA obedece.

TRAFICANTE (continuación)
Quítatelo.

> LUCÍA se quita el suéter.

Date la Vuelta.

> TRAFICANTE evalúa lentamente el cuerpo de LUCÍA. LUCÍA permanece quieta.

TRAFICANTE (continuación)
Me gustan con más carne en los huesos. Con algo para agarrar. Pero podría ser persuadido...

> LUCÍA rápidamente se pone su suéter y se sienta.

LUCÍA
Conseguiré el dinero. Haré pagos. Solo me va a llevar un tiempo.

TRAFICANTE
(riéndose)
Chiquita, no estas lista para esto.
(sacude la cabeza con incredulidad)

¡Vete a casa!

> LUCÍA reacciona con terquedad.

TRAFICANTE (continuación)
Como amigo déjame darte un buen consejo, lo único que una mujer sin papeles tiene es su cuerpo. Va ser tomado o va ser vendido muchas veces en el camino que quieres andar... Las mujeres que sobreviven aprenden eso rápido...
¡Vete a casa!

(TELÓN)

(FIN DE ESCENA)

Scene VII - Back to the End of the Line

Setting:

MORNING. American Consulate.
The American flag and the framed picture of President Reagan are prominently displayed.

Time: 1984

At Rise:

CONSULAR CLERK, who is different than in scene II, is sitting behind the thick glass. There is a U.S. MARINE standing close to the CLERK's window. PERSON #27 and PERSON #59, both males, are sitting in the front row. RUBEN is a few years older.

PERSON #27
Ay! I forgot!
(quickly covers his left hand with his right hand)

PERSON #59 reacts with a questioning look.

PERSON #27
(in a whisper)
My ring.

PERSON # 27 removes his wedding ring quietly, trying not to attract attention.

PERSON #59
You applied as a single person?

PERSON #27 drops the ring in his shirt pocket.

PERSON #27
I've been waiting too long.

Escena VII – De Vuelta al Final de la Cola

Ambientación:

MAÑANA. Consulado Americano. La bandera estadounidense y la imagen enmarcada del presidente Reagan se muestran prominentemente.

Fecha: Año 1984

Telón:

SECRETARIO CONSULAR diferente al de la Escena II, está sentado detrás del vidrio grueso. Hay un MARINE americano de pie cerca de la ventanilla. PERSONA #27 y PERSONA #59, ambos hombres, están sentados en la primera fila. RUBÉN es unos años mayor.

PERSONA #27
¡Hay! ¡Me olvidé!
(rápidamente cubre su mano Izquierda con su mano derecha)

PERSONA # 59 reacciona con una mirada interrogante.

PERSONA #27
(en un suspiro)
Mi anillo.

PERSONA # 27 se quita su anillo de bodas en silencio, tratando de no llamar la atención.

PERSONA #59
¿Te presentaste como soltero?

PERSONA # 27 deja caer el anillo en el bolsillo de su camisa.

PERSONA #27
He estado esperando demasiado tiempo.

RUBEN is standing at the CLERK's window. He is a few years older.

CONSULAR CLERK
Name?

RUBEN
Rubén García Martinez.

CLERK types name into the computer.

I applied about four years ago. I received a letter to come. My file number is 343455.
(RUBEN shows the letter)

CONSULAR CLERK
Yes. Mr. García Martinez we have amended your application with the correct spelling of your name. All your documents are spelled with an E in your first name now.

RUBEN
Oh!

CONSULAR CLERK
Has your civil status changed? Are you married now?

RUBEN
No.

CONSULAR CLERK
When you get married, you'll re-file your application to include your wife.

RUBEN
Okay, that should not be a problem. Can you tell me how much longer do I have to wait?

CONSULAR CLERK
We'll send you a letter twelve months before your interview.

RUBÉN esta parado en la ventanilla.

SECRETARIO CONSULAR
¿Nombre?

RUBÉN
Rubén García Martínez.

SECRETARIO CONSULAR ingresa el nombre en la computadora.

RUBÉN *(continuación)*
Presenté mi solicitud hace unos cuatro años. Recibí una carta para venir. Mi número de solicitud es 343455.
(Rubén muestra la carta)

SECRETARIO CONSULAR
Si. Sr. García Martínez hemos enmendado su solicitud con la ortografía correcta de su nombre. Ahora todos sus documentos están escritos con una E en su primer nombre.

RUBÉN
¡Oh!

SECRETARIO CONSULAR
¿Ha cambiado su estado civil? ¿Está usted casado ahora?

RUBÉN
No.

SECRETARIO CONSULAR
Cuando se case, volverá a presentar su solicitud para incluir a su esposa.

RUBÉN
De acuerdo, eso no será un problema. ¿Me puede decir cuánto tiempo más tengo que esperar?

SECRETARIO CONSULAR
Le enviaremos una carta doce meses antes de su entrevista.

RUBEN
(anxious)
But can you tell me anything?

CONSULAR CLERK
No. We have a high volume of applicants around the world and the Office of Immigration and Naturalization Services processes all applications as fast as they can. You just have to wait. Goodbye, Mr. García Martinez.

CLERK turns off his/her microphone and returns his attention to his paperwork.

Lights fade slowly.

(BLACKOUT)

(END OF SCENE)

RUBÉN
(ansioso)
Pero ¿me puede decir algo?

SECRETARIO CONSULAR
No. Tenemos un gran volumen de solicitantes en todo el mundo y la Oficina de Servicios de Inmigración y Naturalización procesa todas las solicitudes tan rápido como puede. Solo tiene que esperar. Adiós, Sr. García Martínez.

SECRETARIO CONSULAR apaga so micrófono y regresa su atención a su escritorio.

Las luces bajan lentamente.

(TELÓN)

(FIN DE ESCENA)

Scene VIII - Sugar, Please

Setting:

DAY. A market. A storefront with baskets of produce in front of the counter. The potatoes, tomatoes, and corn baskets each have a price prominently displayed. The prices are in the thousands.

Time: 1985

At Rise:

DOÑA LUPE a middle-age, working woman is tending the stand. There is a phone on the counter.

          DON FRANCISCO enters.

DON FRANCISCO
Morning, Doña Lupe! Do you have any sugar today?

DOÑA LUPE
(frustrated)
No! Wish I had! Haven't seen sugar in weeks. Not even brown sugar.

DON FRANCISCO
Gosh! I'm down to less than a cup. My granddaughter, Katia, she only takes her milk with sugar.

DOÑA LUPE
(wiping sweat from her brow)
Rice is disappearing too. If you find it, stock up.

DON FRANCISCO
I'll walk to Fernando's. See if he has any left.

          The phone rings. DOÑA LUPE answers.

Escena VIII – Azúcar, Por Favor

Ambientación:

DÍA. Un mercado. Un escaparate con canastas de productos frente al mostrador. Las canastas de papas, tomates y maíz cada una tiene un precio prominentemente exhibido. Los precios son en los miles.

Fecha: Año 1985

Telón:

DOÑA LUPE, una mujer trabajadora de mediana edad, está atendiendo el stand. Hay un teléfono en el mostrador.

          Entra DON FRANCISCO

DON FRANSICO
¡Buenos días, Doña Lupe! ¿Tiene azúcar hoy?

DOÑA LUPE
(frustrada)
¡No! ¡Desearía tener! No he visto azúcar en semanas. Ni siquiera azúcar Morena.

DON FRANCISCO
¡Dios! Tengo menos de una taza. Mi nieta Katia, solo toma su leche con azúcar.

DOÑA LUPE
(limpiándose el sudor de la frente)
El arroz también esta desapareciendo. Si lo encuentra cómprelo.

DON FRANCISCO
Voy a caminar a donde Fernando. A ver si le queda a él algo.

          Suena el teléfono. DOÑA LUPE responde.

DOÑA MARTA enters.

DOÑA MARTA
Morning, Don Francisco! Doña Lupe!

DON FRANCISCO
Good morning, Doña Marta. How are you?

DOÑA MARTA
Tired of looking for food. I've already walked four markets this morning. I can't find anything! No sugar. No rice. No flour. Nothing to eat!

> DOÑA LUPE hangs up the phone and with a small calculator and a big red magic marker she goes around crossing off the prices that are advertised and writes new higher prices on the labels.

DON FRANCISCO
No sugar here. I was going to try Fernando's.

DOÑA MARTA
He doesn't have any. I come from there.

DOÑA LUPE
There's no sugar anywhere.

DOÑA MARTA
I need sugar. I have children.

DOÑA LUPE
Try the black market.

DON FRANCISCO
At ten times the official price.

> Phone rings again. DOÑA LUPE answers.

DOÑA LUPE
¡Sí! ¡Sí! ¿Cuanto? Esta bien, está bien, lo cambio.

> Entra DOÑA MARTA.

DOÑA MARTA
¡Buenos días, Don Francisco! ¡Doña Lupe!

DON FRANCISCO
¡Buenos días, Doña Marta! ¿Cómo esta?

DOÑA MARTA
Cansada de buscar comida. Ya he caminado cuatro mercados esta mañana. ¡No puedo encontrar nada! No hay azúcar. No hay arroz. No hay harina. ¡Nada para comer!

> DOÑA LUPE cuelga el teléfono y con una pequeña calculadora y un plumón rojo y grande va tachando los precios anunciados y escribe precios más altos.

DON FRANCISCO
No hay azúcar aquí. Iba a ir donde Fernando.

DOÑA MARTA
No tiene. Vengo de ahí.

DOÑA LUPE
No hay azúcar en ninguna parte.

DOÑA MARTA
Necesito azúcar. Tengo hijos.

DOÑA LUPE
Pruebe en el mercado negro.

DON FRANCISCO
A diez veces el precio oficial.

> El teléfono vuelve a sonar. DOÑA LUPE responde.

DOÑA MARTA
I can't afford that.

DOÑA LUPE
(to the phone)
Yes! Yes! I got it.

DOÑA LUPE hangs up the phone and once again goes around changing prices with her magic marker.

DON FRANCISCO
(to DOÑA MARTA)
Last week at the hospital I heard your daughter, the nurse, left.

DOÑA MARTA
She went to Spain. To Barcelona.

DON FRANCISCO
You have family there?

DOÑA MARTA
No, no, a friend of one of her girlfriends gave her a contact. She went to work for a family. She's taking care of their two babies. Twins, I think.

DON FRANCISCO
Her little one used to play with Katia, my granddaughter.

DOÑA MARTA
Oh, my grandson is still here. She left him with me. She can't take care of a child when she's working all day.

DON FRANCISCO
Oh!

DOÑA MARTA
It was hard at first. But he's okay now. Children get over things fast.

DOÑA MARTA
No puedo pagar eso.

DOÑA LUPE
(al teléfono)
¡Sí! ¡Sí! Ya entendí.

DONA LUPE cuelga el teléfono y una vez mas va cambiando los precios con su plumón grande.

DON FRANCISCO
(a DOÑA MARTA)
La semana pasada en el hospital escuche que su hija, la enfermera, se fue.

DOÑA MARTA
Se fue a España. A Barcelona.

DON FRANCISCO
¿Tiene familia allá?

DOÑA MARTA
No, no, un amigo de una de sus amigas le dio el contacto. Fue a trabajar para una familia. Les esta cuidando sus dos bebes. Gemelos creo.

DON FRANCISCO
Su pequeño solía jugar con Katia, con mi nieta.

DOÑA MARTA
Oh, mi nieto todavía está aquí. Ella lo dejó conmigo. No puede cuidar de su hijo mientras que está trabajando todo el día.

DON FRANCISCO
¡Oh!

DOÑA MARTA
Fue duro al principio. Pero ahora esta bien. Los niños superan las cosas rápidamente.

DON FRANCISCO
(to DOÑA LUPE)

Doña Lupe, in the time I've been here you've changed the prices twice. Now,

(takes two potatoes and hands them to DOÑA LUPE to weigh)

I don't have enough for a kilo. Half will have to do.

DOÑA LUPE weighs the potatoes.

DOÑA LUPE

Half a kilo.

DON FRANCISCO quickly takes the potatoes and shoves them in his pocket.

DON FRANCISCO
(he pulls out of his wallet a bunch of bills and sets them on the counter)

Here! Before you change the price on me again. *(referring to the bills)*

I guess these are not worth much anymore.

DOÑA LUPE

The world is crazy, Don Francisco. I can't keep up with these price changes. I'm just a simple storekeeper. If my son weren't helping me every day, I'd have lost everything by now.

DON FRANCISCO
(hacia DOÑA LUPE)

Doña Lupe, en el tiempo que llevo aquí ha cambiado los precios dos veces. Ahora,

(agarra dos papas y se las entrega a DOÑA LUPE para pesar)

No tengo suficiente para un kilo. Tendrá que ser medio kilo.

DOÑA LUPE pesa las papas.

DOÑA LUPE

Medio kilo.

DON FRANCISCO
rápidamente toma las papas y las mete en su bolsillo.

DON FRANCISCO
(saca de su billetera un montón de billetes y los pone en el mostrador)

¡Aquí está! Antes de que me cambie el precio otra vez.
(refiriéndose a los billetes de dinero)

Supongo que estos ya no valen mucho.

DOÑA LUPE

El mundo esta loco, Don Francisco. No puedo estar al día con estos cambios de precio. Solo soy una simple tendedera. Si no fuese porque mi hijo me ayuda todos los días, a estas alturas ya hubiera perdido todo.

DON FRANCISCO
We've all lost so much already.

DOÑA MARTA
I'll have to wait till my daughter sends money.
(sits down and puts her bag down.)
I'm tired.

(BLACKOUT)

(END OF SCENE)

DON FRANCISCO
Ya todos hemos perdido tanto.

DOÑA LUPE

Tendré que esperar hasta que mi hija me envié dinero.
(se sienta y deja su bolso en el suelo)

Estoy cansada.

(TELÓN)

(FIN DE ESCENA)

Scene IX - Please, Turn on the Lights

SETTING:

NIGHT. MEDINA living room/kitchen Same setting as Scene II.

TIME: Three months later. 1985

AT RISE:

MEDINA front stoop from Scene III. LUCIA is frozen with her hand on the door handle.

LUCIA unfreezes. She opens the front door to the MEDINA home and enters.

DON FRANCISCO is sitting on his favorite chair.

LUCIA
Good evening, Father!
*(puts down her pouch and gives her father a kiss
on the cheek as a greeting)*

DON FRANCISCO
Lucia, what happened? You've never been this late before.

(looks up at the clock that reads 10:20pm)

It's past curfew.

LUCIA
I'm sorry. I had to work late. I got to the bus stop with enough time to catch the last bus. But the bus never came. I had to walk home.

DON FRANCISCO
Katia is already asleep.

LUCIA
I know, I'm sorry I'm late.

Escena IX – Por Favor, Ciendan as Luces

Ambientación:

NOCHE. Sala de estar/cocina. Mismo escenario que en la Escena II.

Fecha: Tres meses después. Año 1985

Telón:

Entrada de la casa MEDINA, final de la Escena III. LUCÍA esta congelada con la mano en la manija de la puerta.

Proyección: Tres meses después. LUCÍA se descongela. Abre la puerta principal de la casa MEDINA y entra.

DON FRANCISCO esta sentado en su sillón favorito.

LUCÍA
¡Buenas noches, padre!
(deja su bolsa y le da a su padre un beso en la mejilla como saludo)

DON FRANCISCO
Lucía, ¿qué paso? Nunca antes has llegado tan tarde. *(mira hacia el reloj que lee 10:20pm)* Ya empezó el toque de queda.

LUCÍA
Lo siento. Tuve que trabajar hasta tarde. Llegue a la parada de autobús con suficiente tiempo para tomar el último carro, pero el bus nunca llegó. Caminé a casa.

LUCÍA
Lo sé. Estoy tarde.

LUCÍA se sienta en el sofá y se quita las sandalias de nuevo. Mira sus pies sucios.

LUCIA plops on the sofa and takes off her sandals again. She looks at her dirty feet.

LUCIA (CONT'D)
The streets emptied early. Something is happening.

DON FRANCISCO
Thank God you're home safe.

LUCIA
There are soldiers and tanks on the streets tonight.

DON FRANCISCO
Yesterday, at my chess club there was talk. Maybe there'll be a new President in the morning.

LUCIA
Father, how long have we lived under curfew? Do you remember?

DON FRANCISCO
Almost seven years, I believe.

LUCIA
I'm forgetting how life used to be before.

DON FRANCISCO takes off his reading glasses and slowly puts them in their case.

DON FRANCISCO
Seven long years in which we've been trained to hide like cockroaches.

LUCIA
Seven years since I've been to a real party.

DON FRANCISCO
(sarcastic tone)
People converging?   Oh, no Lucía, that's not allowed.

LUCÍA (continuación)
Las calles se vaciaron temprano. Algo está pasando.

DON FRANCISCO
Gracias a Dios que estas en casa a salvo.

LUCÍA
Hay soldados y tanques en las calles esta noche.

DON FRANCISCO
Ayer, en mi club de ajedrez había comentarios. Quizás habrá un nuevo presidente por la mañana.

LUCÍA
Padre, ¿cuánto tiempo hemos vivido bajo toque de queda? ¿Te acuerdas?

DON FRANCISCO
Casi siete años, creo.

LUCÍA
Me estoy olvidando como solía ser la vida antes.

DON FRANCISCO se quita las gafas de lectura y deliberadamente las pone en su estuche.

DON FRANCISCO
Siete largos años en los que hemos sido entrenados para escondernos como cucarachas.

LUCÍA
Siete años desde que he ido a una verdadera fiesta.

DON FRANCISCO
(en tono sarcástico)
¿Personas convergiendo? Oh, no Lucía, eso no está permitido.

LUCIA
Why? Why can't people just have a little fun?

DON FRANCISCO
A party? Mi'ja, you never know what can happen when people mingle and talk. What crazy ideas they can concoct. It could incite a revolution!

DON FRANCISCO heads toward the kitchen.

LUCIA
Some days all I want is to dance... dance till daybreak.
(turns the radio dial to a 'love songs' station)

Will I ever be able to see a sunrise on the beach again?

DON FRANCISCO
Life is a journey in learning to adapt mi'ja. You have to learn to float with the wind. They want us to hide in our houses at night? We hide. The day will come when you'll be able to party all night.

LUCIA
I'll be really old by then, and I won't WANT to go to an all-night party. I won't care then. It won't matter.

(a beat)

I can't be as patient as you, Father. The years go by. Life is passing me by. It's slipping through my fingers.

DON FRANCISCO puts his hand on the pot to assess the temperature of the food.

LUCÍA
¿Por qué? ¿Por qué la gente no se puede divertirse un poco?

DON FRANCISCO
¿Una fiesta? Mi'ja nunca se sabe lo que puede pasar cuando la gente se mezcla y habla. Que ideas locas pueden complotar. Podrían incitar una revolución.

DON FRANCISCO se dirige a la cocina.

LUCÍA
Algunos días lo único que quiero es bailar hasta el amanecer.
(gira el dial de la radio a una estación con canciones de amor)
¿Algún día podré volver a ver un amanecer en la playa otra vez?

DON FRANCISCO
Mi'ja, la vida es un viaje en aprender a adaptarse. Tienes que aprender a flotar con el viento. ¿Quieren que nos escondamos en nuestras casas en la noche? Nos escondemos. Llegará el día en que podrás festejar toda la noche.

LUCÍA
Seré muy vieja para entonces, y no QUERRÉ ir a una fiesta de toda la noche. Ya no importara para entonces.

(una pausa)

No soy tan paciente como tu padre. Los años se pasan. Mi vida se me esta pasando. Se esta deslizando entre mis dedos.

DON FRANCISCO pone su mano sobre la olla para evaluar la temperatura de los alimentos.

DON FRANCISCO
I think dinner is still warm. I won't have to turn on the stove again. We haven't finished paying last month's electric bill.

> KATIA, a five-year-old child in her pajamas, appears at the doorway and comes into the living room.

KATIA
Mommy! You missed my soccer game!

LUCIA
Mi Amor! I woke you up! I'm sorry I didn't make it home in time to see you play.

> KATIA moves close to LUCIA.

KATIA
We won! Grandpa saw me make the only goal!

LUCIA
Wow! That's great!

DON FRANCISCO
Yes, Katia was the best player today. Her team is going to the next level in the championship...

> DON FRANCISCO is interrupted by a loud explosion. The lights go out. Stage goes dark.

LUCIA
Apagón! Blackout!

> There is sound of bullets.

KATIA
Mommy, I'm scared!

LUCIA
It's okay mi amor, Grandpa is going to get us a candle. ... Everything is okay.

DON FRANCISCO
Creo que la cena aun esta caliente. No tendré que prender la cocina otra vez. No hemos terminado de pagar el recibo de luz del mes pasado.

> KATIA una niña de cinco años en pijamas aparece en la puerta y entra a la sala de estar.

KATIA
¡Mamá! ¡Te perdiste mi partido de futbol!

LUCÍA
¡Mi amor! ¡Te desperté! Lo siento no llegué a casa con tiempo para verte jugar.

> KATIA va hacia LUCÍA

KATIA
¡Ganamos! El abuelo me vio hacer el único gol.

LUCÍA
¡Wow! ¡Eso es genial!

DON FRANCISCO
Sí, hoy Katia fue la mejor jugadora. Su equipo sube al siguiente nivel en el campeonato

> DON FRANCISCO es interrumpido por una gran explosión. Las luces se apagan. El escenario se apaga.

LUCÍA
¡Apagón! ¡Apagón!

> Se escuchan disparos.

KATIA
¡Mami, tengo miedo!

DON FRANCISCO lights a candle. Lights up.

DON FRANCISCO
Let's see... this is a good time to visit some old friends.

DON FRANCISCO starts making puppet shadows.

LUCIA
Katia, look! What's that on the wall?

KATIA
Umm... A bunny!

DON FRANCISCO
That was too easy. How about this one?

DON FRANCISCO makes the shadow of a swan.

KATIA
I know! I know! A duck!

LUCIA
Almost.

KATIA
Something with a long neck?

LUCIA
It's a swan.

DON FRANCISCO
(he uses his hands to follow the rhyme)
Now, let's try this.
    (he begins to sing)
This little pig went to market,

LUCIA and KATIA join in the singing.

LUCÍA
Esta bien, mi amor, el abuelo nos va traer unas velas. Todo está bien.

DON FRANCISCO enciende una vela. Se Ilumina el escenario.

DON FRANCISCO
Veamos… este es el momento de visitar algunos viejos amigos.

DON FRANCISCO comienza a hacer sombras de títeres.

LUCÍA
¡Katia, mira! ¿Qué es eso en la pared?

KATIA
Umm…. ¡Un conejito!

DON FRANCISCO
Eso fue demasiado fácil. ¿Qué tal este?

DON FRANCISCO hace la sombra de un cisne.

KATIA
¡Lo sé! ¡Lo sé! ¡Un pato!

LUCÍA
Casi.

KATIA
¿Algo con un cuello largo?

LUCÍA
Es un cisne.

DON FRANCISCO
(usa sus manos para seguir la rima)
Ahora, probemos esto,
    (empieza a cantar)

Este cerdito fue al mercado,

DON FRANCISCO
(CONT'D), LUCIA, KATIA
This little pig stayed home, and this little pig said, "wee, wee! I can't find my way home."

They ALL share a light moment.

DON FRANCISCO
All right Katia, enough playing. Remember what I told you about bedtime?

KATIA
Yes. All good players go to sleep early.

LUCIA
Let's go, *mi amor,* I'll tuck you in. You can tell me all about the game tomorrow.

KATIA
Good night, Grandpa.

LUCIA and KATIA exit with a candle.

DON FRANCISCO appears beaten. He looks up to the ceiling, questioning.

(END OF SCENE)

LUCÍA y KATIA se unen en el canto.

DON FRANCISCO, LUCIA, KATIA
Este cerdito se quedó en casa, y este cerdito dijo ¡wee, wee! No puedo encontrar mi camino a casa.

TODOS comparten un momento liviano.

DON FRANCISCO
Muy bien Katia, basta de jugar. ¿Recuerdas lo que te dije sobre la hora de acostarse?

KATIA
Sí. Todos los buenos jugadores se van a dormir temprano.

LUCÍA
Vamos, mi amor, te voy a arropar en la cama. Mañana me puedes contar todo sobre el partido.

KATIA
Buenas noches, abuelo.

LUCÍA y KATIA salen con la vela.

DON FRANCISCO parece golpeado. Mira hacia el techo cuestionando.

(FIN DE ESCENA)

Scene X - Lucia's Dream

SETTING:

NIGHT. KATIA's bedroom. The room is lighted only by the candle that LUCIA is holding.
LUCIA tucks KATIA in bed and then sits at her bedside.

LUCIA
I'm sorry, *mi amor*. Sorry I didn't make it home in time for your game.

KATIA
It's okay, Mommy.

LUCIA
You're growing up so fast.

   KATIA dozes off to sleep.

KATIA
(speaks in her sleep)
I love you, Mommy!

LUCIA
I love you too my little girl.
   (a beat)
I don't know if I can do this. I didn't think about actually saying good-bye. About being separated from you and Grandpa.

LUCIA stands.

When you were a baby, I could protect you. Nothing could harm you. ... Now that you're getting older, it's harder and harder to lie. Harder to explain why we have to hide at night, why there's no sugar for your milk, why the lights go off suddenly. ... I cannot turn on the lights for you, Katia. I cannot protect you from the monsters of the night.
   A beat.

Escena X – El Sueño de Lucía

Ambientación:

NOCHE. Dormitorio de KATIA. La habitación está iluminada solo por la vela que está sosteniendo LUCÍA.
LUCÍA mete a KATIA en la cama y luego se sienta junto a la cama.

LUCÍA
Lo siento, mi amor. Lo siento que no llegué a casa a tiempo para ver tu partido.

KATIA
Está bien, mami.

LUCÍA
Estas creciendo tan rápido.

   KATIA duerme.

KATIA
(habla mientras duerme)
¡Te amo, mami!

LUCÍA
Yo te amo también, mi pequeña.
   (una pausa)
No se si puedo hacer esto. No pensé en tener que despedirme. No pensé en estar separada de ti y el abuelo.

LUCÍA se para.

Cuando eras una bebe, te podía proteger. Nada podía hacerte daño …. Ahora, que estas creciendo es cada día más difícil mentir. Es más difícil explicar porque tenemos que escondernos en la noche, porque no hay azúcar para tu leche, porque las luces se apagan de repente. … No puedo prender las luces para ti, Katia. No puedo protegerte de los monstruos de la noche.
   Una pausa.

LUCIA (CONT'D)
When I was a child, like you, I watched on TV all the big houses and pretty families that people in the United States have. Two cars for each house, children playing on beautiful lawns, electric washing machines. I dreamed of having that life. I wanted that life. I can still remember the jingle.
(sings jingle)

"Claro, clarisimo! Use CLARO and your clothes will come out sparkling white... Claro, clarisimo! Claro, clarisimo will make your family happy."

I dreamed that one day I'd buy my mother an electric washing machine, so she wouldn't have to scrub sheets and towels by hand every week. I dreamed I'd buy my parents a nice house with a car parked in the driveway... Only one... We wouldn't have use for two cars.
(a beat)
My poor mother worked so hard. She was always exhausted at the end of 'laundry day.' After dinner she sat on the sofa to watch her *telenovela* and in minutes, she was sound asleep... so tired.
(turning toward KATIA)

You never met your grandma. She was a great woman...
(a beat)

When the blonde woman on the TV did her laundry, she just put the clothes in the washer and   sat down to read a magazine while the machine did all the work.
(sings jingle)

"Claro, clarisimo! Use CLARO and your clothes will come out sparkling white... Claro, clarisimo! Claro, clarisimo will make your family happy."

(a beat)

LUCÍA *(continuación)*
Cuando era niña, como tú, veía en la televisión todas las casas grandes y familias bonitas que tienen las personas en Estados Unidos. Dos coches en cada casa, niños jugando en bellos jardines, lavadoras eléctricas. Soñaba con tener esa vida. Quería esa vida. Hasta ahora puedo recordar el estribillo.
(canta el estribillo)

¡Claro, Clarísimo! Usa Claro y tu ropa saldrá brillantemente blanca… ¡Claro, Clarísimo! ¡Claro, Clarísimo, harán feliz a tu familia.

Soñé que algún día le compraría a mi madre una lavadora eléctrica, para que no tuviera que fregar sabanas y toallas a mano todas las semanas. Soñé que les compraría a mis padres una bonita casa con un coche en la entrada… Solo uno… no tendríamos uso para dos carros.
(una pausa)
Mi pobre madre trabajo tan duro. Siempre estaba agotada al terminar el 'día de lavandería.' Después de la cena se sentaba en el sofá para ver su telenovela y en unos minutos, estaba profundamente dormida… tan cansada.
(volteando hacia KATIA)

Nunca conociste a tu abuela. Era una gran mujer …
(una pausa)

Cuando la mujer rubia en el televisor lavaba la ropa, simplemente ponía la ropa en la lavadora y se sentaba a leer una revista, mientras que la maquina hacia todo el trabajo.
(canta el estribillo)

LUCIA (CONT'D)
Mother died without ever seeing an electric washing machine. *(a pause)* I don't want my father to die without having a nice house.

> LUCIA moves toward KATIA and caresses her face.

Katia, I promise you, you'll live in a place where you can have the lights on all night. I promise you, you'll live in a place without fear.

> LUCIA kisses KATIA and begins to exit. She sings the jingle softly as lights fade out.

"Claro, clarisimo! Use CLARO and your clothes will come out sparkling white... Claro, clarisimo! Claro, clarisimo will make your family happy."

(END OF SCENE)

LUCÍA (continuación)
¡Claro, Clarísimo! Usa Claro y tu ropa saldrá brillantemente blanca… ¡Claro, Clarísimo! ¡Claro, Clarísimo, harán feliz a tu familia.

(una pausa)

Mama murió sin ver nunca una lavadora eléctrica. (una pausa) No quiero que mi padre muera sin tener una casa bonita.

> LUCÍA se acerca a KATIA y le acaricia la cara.

Katia, te lo prometo, vivirás en un lugar donde podrás tener las luces encendidas toda la noche. Te prometo que vivirás en un lugar sin miedo.

> LUCÍA besa a KATIA y comienza a salir. Canta el estribillo suavemente mientras que las luces bajan.

¡Claro, Clarísimo! Usa Claro y tu ropa saldrá brillantemente blanca… ¡Claro, Clarísimo! ¡Claro, Clarísimo, harán feliz a tu familia.

(FIN DE ESCENA)

Scene XI - I'll Take My Chances

SETTING:

NIGHT. MEDINA living room / kitchen.

DON FRANCISCO is dishing food on plates. LUCIA enters carrying her lit candle.

LUCIA
I brought work home, but I guess it won't get done tonight.

LUCIA sits at the dinner table and sets her candle on the table.

DON FRANCISCO
I hope this one doesn't last all night. It's hard to quiet the mind when you can't see past your own hands.

LUCIA
(with quiet disappointment)
Rice and potatoes again?

DON FRANCISCO
It's all we have left until we make a payment to Doña Lupe. I added soy sauce for a different flavor. *(a pause)* I'll go back to the Bank tomorrow. ... If I get my check, I'll buy us a chicken and milk for Katia.

LUCIA
There's still some milk left.

DON FRANCISCO
Thirty long years working as a Professor for the National University and my pension check buys us a little more than a chicken!

LUCIA
Don't worry, Father. I'll get paid Friday.

Escena XI – Me Arriesgaré

Ambientación:

NOCHE. Salón / cocina de la casa MEDINA.

DON FRANCISCO está sirviendo la comida. LUCÍA entra llevando su vela encendida.

LUCÍA
Traje trabajo a casa, pero supongo que no lo podré hacer esta noche.

LUCÍA se sienta a la mesa y pone su vela sobre la mesa.

DON FRANCISCO
Espero que este no dure toda la noche. Es difícil calmar la mente cuando no puedes ver pasado tus propias manos.

LUCÍA
(con decepción)
¿Arroz y papas otra vez?

DON FRANCISCO
Es todo lo que nos queda hasta que le hagamos un pago a Doña Lupe. Le agregué salsa de soya para darle un sabor diferente. *(una pausa)* Voy a regresar al banco mañana. … Si me dan mi cheque puedo comprarnos un pollo y leche para Katia.

LUCÍA
Todavía queda un poco de leche.

DON FRANCISCO
¡Treinta largos años trabajando como profesor para la universidad y mi cheque de pensión nos compra un poco más que un pollo!

DON FRANCISCO
And next month, my whole check will only pay for half a chicken!

LUCIA
I saw your dirty overalls at the door. Were you helping somebody with their car?

DON FRANCISCO
Diego was waiting for me when I got home from the Bank. His old FIAT broke down again. Died at a red light, just after he had picked up a passenger. Poor guy. We patched the water pump and got it running.

LUCIA
Till next time.

DON FRANCISCO
So, what's new at the big architecture office today, Ms. Lead Architect? Are you still working on that new government building downtown?

LUCIA
Nothing much. Just work.
(begins clearing the table)
Father... I am leaving Sunday.

DON FRANCISCO
What do you mean?

LUCIA
I got a visa.

DON FRANCISCO
Somehow, I knew one day you too would leave. Everybody leaves.

DON FRANCISCO pours himself tea from a thermos.

Where are you going?

LUCIA is washing dishes with water from a pail.

LUCÍA
No te preocupes padre. Me pagan el viernes.

DON FRANCISCO
¡Y el próximo mes mi cheque solo pagara por medio pollo!

LUCÍA
Vi tu ropa sucia en la puerta. ¿Le estabas ayudando a alguien con su carro?

DON FRANCISCO
Diego me estaba esperando cuando llegue a casa del banco. Su viejo Fiat se malogró de nuevo. Se murió en el semáforo rojo, justo cuando acababa de recoger a un pasajero. ¡Pobre! Parchamos la bomba de agua, y el carro arrancó.

LUCÍA
Hasta la próxima.

DON FRANCISCO
Entonces, ¿Qué hay de nuevo hoy en la gran oficina de arquitectura, señora jefa arquitecta? ¿Sigues trabajando en ese nuevo edificio del gobierno en el centro?

LUCÍA
Nada. Solo trabajo.
(comienza a levantar lo platos)

Padre... me voy el domingo.

DON FRANCISCO
¿A qué te refieres?

LUCÍA
Conseguí una visa.

DON FRANCISCO
De alguna manera sabía que un día tú también te irías. Todos se van.

LUCIA
Mexico. I have a plane ticket and a visa to Mexico. From there, I don't know yet, maybe Spain... maybe the United States.

DON FRANCISCO
No visa after Mexico?

LUCIA
I have a contact that can get me entry to Spain, but I'm going to try my chances in the United States.

DON FRANCISCO
Illegally.

LUCIA
You know there's no other way.

DON FRANCISCO
Lucía, have you thought this through?

LUCIA
Yes. I've thought about it for a long time.

DON FRANCISCO
It's not easy to be illegal.

DON FRANCISCO opens the sugar bowl. There is no sugar.

LUCIA
I've been putting a little money aside every month. For the visa. Diego helped me. He introduced me to...

DON FRANCISCO
Diego! That bastard! He never told me anything.

LUCIA
He couldn't. I made him promise me he would never tell you anything. I've bought us our ticket to a better life.

DON FRANCISCO se sirve té de un termo.

¿A dónde vas?

LUCÍA está lavando los platos con agua del balde.

LUCÍA
México. Tengo un boleto de avión y visa para México. De ahí, no se todavía, quizás España… o quizás los Estados Unidos.

DON FRANCISCO
¿No tienes visa después de México?

LUCÍA
Tengo un contacto que me puede conseguir entrada a España, pero voy a tratar mi suerte en Estados Unidos.

DON FRANCISCO
Ilegalmente.

LUCÍA
Sabes que no hay otra manera.

DON FRANCISCO
Lucía, ¿has pensado bien esto?

LUCÍA
Sí, lo he pensado durante mucho tiempo.

DON FRANCISCO
No es fácil ser ilegal.

DON FRANCISCO abre el azucarero. No hay azúcar.

LUCÍA
He estado guardando un poco de dinero cada mes. Para la visa. Diego me ayudó. Me presentó a…

> Lights come back on. The radio starts playing again.

Thank God! I'll be able to get some work done.

> DON FRANCISCO blows out the candle on the table.

DON FRANCISCO
You won't get a job as an architect.

LUCIA
I know.

DON FRANCISCO
All those years studying. Lucía, you worked sooo hard to become an architect.

LUCIA
And I tried. I'm at the office twelve, fourteen hours every day and what do I have to show for all my hard work? Nothing.

> LUCIA finishes with the dishes and starts to pick up some old toys in the living room.

DON FRANCISCO
You're going to give up everything? Your career?

LUCIA
I want you to have a nice house someday.

DON FRANCISCO
I'm happy here. I don't need anything else.
(a beat)
You'll only find work that nobody else wants.

LUCIA
I'll be okay.
(a beat)

DON FRANCISCO
¡Diego! ¡Ese bastardo! Nunca me dijo nada.

LUCÍA
No podía. Le hice prometer que nunca te diría nada. Nos he comprado un boleto para una vida mejor.

> Las luces regresan. La radio vuelve a sonar.

¡Gracias a Dios! Podré hacer algo de trabajo.

> DON FRANCISCO sopla la vela sobre la mesa.

DON FRANCISCO
No conseguirás un trabajo como arquitecta.

LUCÍA
Lo sé.

DON FRANCISCO
Todos esos años estudiando. Lucía, trabajaste muy duro para hacerte arquitecta.

LUCÍA
Y lo intenté. Estoy en la oficina doce, catorce horas diarias, ¿y que tengo que mostrar por todo ese trabajo duro? Nada.

> LUCÍA termina con los platos y comienza a recoger los viejos juguetes tirados en el salón.

DON FRANCISCO
¿Vas a renunciar a todo? ¿Tu carrera?

LUCÍA
Quiero que algún día tengas una casa bonita.

Don't you wish to live in a place where you don't have to hide at night?

DON FRANCISCO
Lucía, mi'ja, you will not sit at a desk like you do here. You will not have a nice office, a secretary... people working for you. There, you'll be the person that everybody else orders around. The cleaning person.

LUCIA
I'll make more money there cleaning than here as Ms. Architect.

DON FRANCISCO
How does an architect adjust her brain to be able to clean toilets, or take care of babies for other people? How? How, Lucía?

LUCIA
It'll be just for a few years.

DON FRANCISCO
They'll look down at you. As if you were begging... as if there was something inherently bad, flawed about you, that you couldn't make it in your own country.

LUCIA
I know.

DON FRANCISCO
No, Lucía. No, you don't know. You don't know how it feels when people treat you as if you don't exist. *(a pause)* I've seen it too many times with my students that return. *(pause)* They'll break you.

> DON FRANCISCO searches in the cupboards and finds an old dusty bottle of rum. He pours himself a shot and chugs it down. He is not used to drinking.

DON FRANCISCO
Estoy feliz aquí. No necesito nada más.

(una pausa)

Solo encontrarás trabajo que nadie mas quiere.

LUCÍA
Estaré bien.

(una pausa)

¿No deseas vivir en un lugar donde no te tienes que esconderte de noche?

DON FRANCISCO
Lucía, mi'ja, no te sentarás en un escritorio como lo haces aquí. No tendrás una bonita oficina, una secretaria, ... gente trabajando para ti. Alla, serás la persona a la que todos los demás ordenan. La persona de la limpieza.

LUCÍA
Ganaré más dinero allá limpiando, que aquí como señora arquitecta.

DON FRANCISCO
Como adecua una arquitecta su cerebro para poder limpiar inodoros, o para cuidar a niños de otros? ¿Cómo? ¿Cómo, Lucía?

LUCÍA
Será solo por unos años.

DON FRANCISCO
Te mirarán con desprecio. Como si estuvieras mendigando, ... como si hubiese algo inherentemente malo, defectuoso en ti, que no pudiste sobrevivir en tu propio país.

LUCÍA
Lo sé.

> DON FRANCISCO walks to the living room and picks up a picture frame of his wife and daughter.

LUCIA
And according to you, inheritor of her intelligence.

DON FRANCISCO
Always the brightest student.

LUCIA
When I was a child, you'd always tell me that one day I would be President and right the wrongs in this country. Remember?

DON FRANCISCO
You were our dream come true.

(a beat)

What about Katia? She'll be devastated. At five, she needs her mother.

LUCIA
You saw the fear on her face tonight. We'll be separated at most a year. I'll have the money we need by then. Maybe faster. Then, you'll make the trip with her.

> DON FRANCISCO leaves his empty glass on the kitchen sink and walks to the potted avocado plant. He preoccupies himself with cleaning the dead leaves and pruning.

DON FRANCISCO
No. I'm too old to start in a new place. I'll die here, in this house, with my memories.

DON FRANCISCO
No, Lucía. No lo sabes. No sabes como se siente cuando la gente te trata como si no existieras. *(una pausa)* Lo he visto demasiadas veces en alumnos que regresan. Te romperán.

> DON FRANCISCO busca en el armario y encuentra una vieja, polvorienta botella de ron. Se sirve, y lo toma de un tiro. No está acostumbrado a tomar.

> DON FRANCISCO camina hacia la sala de estar y levanta un marco con una foto de su esposa y su hija.

DON FRANCISCO (continuación)
Eres la hija de tu madre. La misma terquedad.

LUCÍA
Y según tú, heredera de su inteligencia.

DON FRANCISCO
Siempre la estudiante mas brillante.

LUCÍA
Cuando era niña siempre me decías que algún día seria presidente y corregiría los errores de nuestro país. ¿Recuerdas?

DON FRANCISCO
Eras nuestro sueño hecho realidad.
Una pausa

¿Qué será de Katia? La va a destrozar. A los cinco años necesita de su madre.

LUCÍA
Viste el miedo en su cara esta noche. Estaremos separados a lo más un año. Tendré el dinero que necesitamos para entonces. Tal vez más rápido. Entonces harás el viaje con ella.

LUCIA
But Father, don't you understand? There's nothing here. I'm doing this for us.

DON FRANCISCO
Lucía, I'm old, I cannot bend like you think you can. Here, I can read the paper, talk to the neighbors, get angry at the government and as crazy and violent as this city is, in a foreign land I would be lost. Unable to even go to the store to buy food, unable to talk or read the paper. What kind of life is that? No, as bad as it is here, at least I know what to expect. That's something to hold on to. Here, I exist.

(BLACKOUT)

(END OF SCENE)

DON FRANCISCO deja su vaso vacío en el fregadero de la cocina y camina hacia la planta de aguacate en la No. maceta. Se ocupa en limpiar las hojas muertas y podar.

DON FRANCISCO
No. Estoy demasiado viejo para empezar en un lugar nuevo. Moriré aquí, en esta casa, con mis memorias.

LUCÍA
Pero padre, ¿no entiendes? Aquí no hay nada. Estoy haciendo esto por nosotros.

DON FRANCISCO
Lucía, soy viejo, no puedo doblarme como tu crees que puedes. Aquí puedo leer el periódico, hablar con los vecinos, enojarme con el gobierno y por más loca y violenta que sea esta ciudad, en una tierra extranjera estaría perdido. Incapaz de ir a la tienda a comprar comida, incapaz de hablar o leer el periódico. ¿Qué tipo de vida es esa? No, por terrible que sean las cosas acá, al menos sé que esperar. Eso es algo a que aferrarse.
Aquí existo.

(TELÓN)

(FIN DE ESCENA)

Scene XII - The Dream

SETTING:

MORNING. MEDINA living room / kitchen. A child's backpack is close to the door.

TIME: Sunday morning.

AT RISE:

LUCIA and DON FRANCISCO are having a final coffee. LUCIA is wearing jeans and new canvas tennis shoes.

>The doorbell rings.

LUCIA
Diego is here.

>LUCIA stands to open the door. DIEGO comes in.

DIEGO
Morning, Lucía!
(greets LUCIA with a kiss on the cheek)

>DIEGO walks to DON FRANCISCO to shake his hand.

DIEGO
Don Francisco, good morning.

DON FRANCISCO
Ahh, Judas!
(waves his hand at DIEGO in disgust)
The worst day of my life!

LUCIA
C'mon, Father, everything is going to work out fine. This is a good thing for us.

Escena XI – El Sueño

Ambientación:

MAÑANA. Salón / cocina MEDINA. La mochila de una niña esta cerca a la puerta.

Fecha: Domingo por la mañana.

Telón:

LUCÍA y DON FRANCISCO están tomando un último café. LUCÍA lleva pantalones vaqueros zapatillas de lona nuevas.

>Suena el timbre.

LUCÍA
Diego está aquí.

>LUCIA se pone de pie para abrir la puerta. Entra DIEGO.

DIEGO
¡Buenos días, Lucía!
(saluda a Lucía con un besoen la mejilla)

>DIEGO camina hacia DON FRANCISCO para estrecharle la mano.

DIEGO
Don Francisco, buenos días.

DON FRANCISCO
Ahh, ¡Judas!
(agita su mano hacia DIEGO con disgusto)
¡El peor día de mi vida!

LUCÍA
Vamos, padre, todo va salir bien. Esto es algo bueno para nosotros.

DIEGO
Where's Katia?

LUCIA
We said our goodbyes early. I took her to Doña Maria's house. It's better for her not to see me actually walk out the door. It'd be too emotional for her.

        DIEGO picks up the backpack.

DIEGO
Katia's backpack?

LUCIA
She insisted.

DIEGO
You have everything?

LUCIA
Yes. I also bought a new pair of shoes.

        LUCIA demonstrates the canvas tennis shoes she's wearing.

DIEGO
We better get going. It's a long drive to the airport. You don't want to be late.

        DIEGO exits.

LUCIA
Good-bye, Father.

DON FRANCISCO
(choking back tears)
I'll never see you again.

LUCIA
That's not true. This is just a temporary goodbye.

DIEGO
¿Dónde esta Katia?

LUCÍA
Nos despedimos temprano. La lleve a casa de Doña María. Es mejor para ella que no me vea salir por la puerta. Sería muy emotivo para ella.

        DIEGO recoge la mochila.

DIEGO
¿La mochila de Katia?

LUCÍA
Insistió.

DIEGO
¿Tienes todo?

LUCÍA
Sí. También compré un nuevo par de zapatos.

        LUCÍA demuestra los tenis de lona que lleva puestos.

DIEGO
Es mejor que nos pongamos en marcha. El camino al aeropuerto es largo. No quieres llegar tarde.

        DIEGO sale.

LUCÍA
Adiós, padre.

DON FRANCISCO
(ahogando las lágrimas)
Nunca te volveré a ver.

LUCÍA
Eso no es cierto. Esto es solo un adiós temporal.

LUCIA (CONT'D)
We'll be together in a year. Promise.

DON FRANCISCO
Que Dios te bendiga, mi'ja.

LUCIA
Love you!

    LUCIA exits.

DON FRANCISCO
(to an empty room)
And I love you more than life itself.

    DON FRANCISCO sits at the kitchen table.

    A beat.

    DON FRANCISCO stands and gets the bottle of liquor. He pours a shot and chugs it down.

    Doorbell rings.

DON FRANCISCO
Adelante! Door's open!

RUBEN
Good morning, Don Francisco! I stopped to say good-bye to Lucía.

DON FRANCISCO
You're late. She's gone.

RUBEN
Oh! ... I wanted to see her one last time.

    RUBEN just stands there awkwardly.

LUCÍA (continuación)
Estaremos juntos en un año. Te lo prometo.

DON FRANCISCO
Que Dios te bendiga, mi'ja.

LUCÍA
¡Te amo!

    LUCÍA sale.

DON FRANCISCO
(a una habitación vacía)
Y yo te amo mas que la vida misma.

    DON FRANCISCO se sienta en la mesa de la cocina.

    Una pausa.

    DON FRANCISCO se pone de pie y agarra la botella de licor. Se sirve, y lo toma de un golpe.

    Suena el timbre.

DON FRANCISCO
¡Adelante! ¡La puerta está abierta!

RUBÉN
¡Buenos días, Don Francisco! Vine a despedirme de Lucía.

DON FRANCISCO
Llegaste tarde. Ya se fue.

RUBÉN
¡Oh! … Quería verla por última vez.

    RUBÉN se queda parado torpemente.

DON FRANCISCO
Come. Sit. I don't want to be alone today.

DON FRANCISCO gets another glass for RUBEN.

RUBEN
She's really gone?

DON FRANCISCO
Yes! And I'll never see her again in this lifetime.

RUBEN
What? She told me you were going to join her in a year?

DON FRANCISCO
I just let her believe that. She was so insistent.

RUBEN
What about Katia?

DON FRANCISCO
When Lucía gets the money, I'll find somebody to take her. Maybe Diego.

RUBEN
So, where's she going?

DON FRANCISCO
North.

RUBEN
I was afraid of that.
(shaking his head)
I told her not to do it. It's a dangerous crossing.

FRANCISCO
She thinks she'll make more money in the United States than in Spain.

DON FRANCISCO
Ven. Siéntate. No quiero estar solo hoy.

DON FRANCISCO consigue otro vaso para RUBÉN.

RUBÉN
¿Realmente se ha ido?

DON FRANCISCO
¡Sí! Y nunca la volveré a ver en esta vida.

RUBÉN
¿Qué? ¿Me dijo que usted la iba a alcanzar en un año?

DON FRANCISCO
Solo le dejé creer eso. Fue tan insistente.

RUBÉN
¿Y Katia?

DON FRANCISCO
Cuando Lucía consiga el dinero, encontraré a alguien que la lleve. Tal vez Diego.

RUBÉN
Entonces, ¿a dónde va?

DON FRANCISCO
Norte.

RUBÉN
Tenía miedo de eso.
(sacudiendo la cabeza)
Le dije que no lo hiciera. Es un cruce peligroso.

DON FRANCISCO
Cree que ganará más dinero en Estados Unidos que en España.

RUBEN
When I get my visa, I'll go visit her.

FRANCISCO
Too bad she got involved with that deadbeat Carlos. That good for nothing. Katia is the only good thing that came out of that. You would have been a good son-in-law. *(a pause)* We both have lost her.

RUBEN
(looking at the avocado plant)
I remember when you brought the avocado from your office. It really hasn't grown much.

FRANCISCO
It needs to be planted in the ground. The poor thing is crammed in that pot.

RUBEN
Yeah, it looks like it's stuck.

FRANCISCO
Will you help me plant it in the backyard?

RUBEN
Sure! I'll bring a spade next week.

FRANCISCO
Katia will forget me.

RUBEN
Don Francisco, don't think about that.

FRANCISCO
I've lost my wife to cancer, my daughter to the war, and I'll soon lose Katia to a dream. She'll forget how to speak to me.

RUBÉN
Cuando obtenga mi visa, iré a visitarla.

DON FRANCISCO
Que pena que se mezcló con ese mala muerte de Carlos. Ese bueno para nada. Katia es lo único bueno que salió de eso. Tu habrías sido un buen yerno. *(una pausa)* Los dos la perdimos.

RUBÉN
(mirando la planta de aguacate)
Recuerdo cuando trajo el aguacate de su oficina. Realmente no ha crecido mucho.

DON FRANCISCO
Necesita ser plantada en la tierra. La pobre esta apretada en ese macetero.

RUBÉN
Sí, parece que está estancada.

DON FRANCISCO
¿Me ayudas a plantarla en el jardín?

RUBÉN
¡Seguro! La próxima semana traigo una pala.

DON FRANCISCO
Katia se olvidará de mí.

RUBÉN
Don Francisco, no piense en eso.

DON FRANCISCO
He perdido mi esposa al cáncer, a mi hija a la guerra, y pronto perderé a Katia por un sueño.
Ella se olvidará de como hablar conmigo.

RUBEN
A dream?

FRANCISCO
Lucia dreams for a better life.

RUBEN
I guess we all want that.

FRANCISCO
It hurts to say goodbye. To know our lives will be condensed to pictures and a few phone calls a year. *(pause)* But, I am proud of my girl... She has guts... Courage to take her life in her own hands. Our country failed her... failed us. She did not want to settle for just surviving.
  (looking directly at RUBEN)
She's not like us. Just waiting for things to happen. Just hoping things get better someday.

> Sound of an explosion rattles the window glass and a stray bullet hits a mirror/frame and shatters it.

RUBEN
On the floor!

> Both RUBEN and DON FRANCISCO hit the ground as lights dim.

(BLACKOUT)

(END OF SCENE, END OF ACT I)

RUBÉN
¿Un sueño?

DON FRANCISCO
Lucía sueña con una vida mejor.

RUBÉN
Supongo que todos queremos lo mismo.

DON FRANCISCO
Duele el decir adiós. Saber que nuestras vidas se condensarán en algunas fotos y algunas llamadas telefónicas al año. *(una pausa)* Pero, estoy orgulloso de mi hija... Tiene agallas... Coraje para tomar su vida en sus propias manos. Nuestro país le falló... nos falló. Ella no quería conformarse con esta vida.
  (mirando directamente a RUBÉN)
Ella no es como nosotros. Solo esperando a que las cosas sucedan y que las cosas mejoren.

El sonido de una explosión sacude el vidrio de la ventana y una bala perdida golpea un espejo y lo destroza.

RUBÉN
¡Al suelo!

> RUBÉN y DON FRANCISCO se tiran al suelo. Las luces bajan.

(TELÓN)

(FIN DE ESCENA, FINAL DE PRIMER ACTO)

INTERMISSION

ACT II

Scene I - Mirage in the Desert

SETTING:

DAY. The Sonoran Desert in the United States, close to the Mexican border. There are personal belongings scattered around, including LUCIA's backpack. A human skull and a few human bones can be seen on stage. On center left, there is a tree with several plastic gallons of water hanging from its branches. A white flag with the painted symbol of three blue drops of water stands high above the tree. COYOTE # 1 and COYOTE # 2 are two Hispanic looking men. They are wearing boots. SAMARITAN PAUL is an older white man. SAMARITAN CARRIE is a younger white woman. Both are wearing ball caps with the same blue drops symbol that is on the flag over the tree. They both have a light sunburn, appear sweaty, and are wearing light long sleeve shirts and boots.

TIME: 1985

AT RISE:

Dim stage.

Sound of a gunshot and a scream.

A beat.

Lights up. Three bodies lie on the ground; they appear to have been killed.

One of the bodies is LUCIA. She lies behind a dry bush, a distance separated from the other two bodies. She is wearing the same jeans and shoes as in the previous scene.

SEGUNDO ACTO

Escena I – Espejismo en el Desierto

Ambientación:

DÍA. El desierto de Sonora en los Estados Unidos, cerca de la frontera con México. Hay pertenencias personales esparcidas por todas partes, incluida la mochila de LUCIA. Un cráneo humano y algunos huesos humanos se pueden ver en el escenario. En el centro a la izquierda hay un árbol con varias galoneras plásticas de agua, colgando de sus ramas. Una bandera blanca con el símbolo de tres gotas azules de agua pintado, se encuentra en lo alto del árbol. COYOTE # 1 y COYOTE # 2 son dos hombres de apariencia hispana. Ambos llevan botas. SAMARITANO PAUL es un hombre blanco, de edad. SAMARITANA CARRIE es una joven mujer blanca. Ambos llevan gorras con el mismo símbolo de gotas azules que está en la bandera sobre el árbol. Ambos tienen una quemadura solar ligera, están sudando y usan camisetas ligeras de manga larga y botas.

Fecha: 1985

Telón:

Luz tenue.

Sonido de un disparo y un grito.

Una pausa.

Se ilumina el escenario. Tres cuerpos yacen en el suelo, parecen haber sido asesinados. Uno de los cuerpos es el de LUCÍA. Ella esta tirada detrás de un arbusto seco, a una distancia de los otros dos cuerpos. Está usando los mismos vaqueros y zapatillas que en la Escena anterior.

One body is shoe-less, and the soles of his feet are visibly burned. The other body has shoes with melted soles.

Projection:

The Sonoran Desert in Arizona, close to the Mexican border. The temperature is 110 degrees Fahrenheit.

> COYOTE # 1, who appears to have been on top of LUCIA, is pulling his pants up.

COYOTE # 1
Man! This bitch is as dry as the damn Sonoran!
> *(spits on the ground)*

> COYOTE # 2 is picking the dead bodies for jewelry, watches, etc.

COYOTE # 2
Cabrón! Who fucks a dead woman? You got any vergüenza left?
> *(disgusted)*
Apúrate! Los Federales we'll be here soon!

> COYOTE # 1 cuts the bottom of LUCIA's backpack with a blade. And finds a tight roll of hundred dollars.
>
> He flips the bills to assess the amount.

COYOTE # 1
Orale!

> COYOTE # 1 stuffs the roll of dollars in his pant pocket.

Un cuerpo no tiene zapatos y las plantas de sus pies están visiblemente quemadas. El otro cuerpo tiene zapatos con suelas derretidas.

Proyección:

El desierto de Sonora en Arizona, cerca de la frontera con México. La temperatura es de 110 grados Fahrenheit.

> COYOTE # 1, que parece haber estado encima de LUCÍA, se está subiendo los pantalones.

COYOTE # 1
¡Hombre! ¡Esta perra esta más seca que el Sonora!
> *(escupe en el suelo)*

> COYOTE # 2 robando de los cuerpos joyas, relojes, etc.

COYOTE # 2
¡Cabrón! ¿Quién se tira a una mujer muerta? ¿Te queda algo de vergüenza?
> *(disgustado)*
¡Apúrate! ¡Los Federales van a llegar pronto!

COYOTE # 1 corta la parte inferior de la mochila de
> COYOTE # 1 corta la parte inferior de la mochila de LUCÍA con una cuchilla y encuentra un rollo apretado de cienes de dólares. Evalúa la cantidad.

COYOTE # 1
¡Órale!

> COYOTE # 1 se mete el rollo de dólares en el bolsillo de su pantalón.

(laughs)
Vergüenza? Mano, we BOTH lost that a long time ago.

COYOTE # 2
Speak for yourself. I pray to La Morena every night.

COYOTE # 1
(inspecting a passport from one of the victims)
Híjole! This one was from Turkey...

COYOTE # 2
Looking for his 'American Dream.'

COYOTE # 1
Mano, el chingón was a doctor!

COYOTE # 2
And all his dreams were going to come true when he entered the promised land...
(shakes his head in disbelief)

COYOTE # 1
That's why he didn't speak while we were walking.
(puts the passport in his pocket or backpack)
I'll get something for this one.

COYOTE # 2
Orale! ... We need to go now.

> Both men go to the tree and each grab a gallon of water. They both take long sips and begin exiting.

COYOTE # 1
(toward the dead bodies)
They found their 'American Dream.'

COYOTE # 2
Better to die with one than to live without a dream.

COYOTE # 1 (continuación)
(riéndose)
¿Vergüenza? Mano, los dos perdimos eso hace mucho tiempo.

COYOTE # 2
Habla por ti mismo. Yo le rezo a La Morena todas las noches.

COYOTE # 1
(inspeccionando el pasaporte de una de las víctimas)
¡Híjole! Este era de Turquía...

COYOTE # 2
Buscando su 'sueño americano.'

COYOTE # 1
¡Mano, el chingón era doctor!

COYOTE # 2
Y todos sus sueños se iban ha hacer realidad cuando entrara a la tierra prometida.
(sacude la cabeza con incredulidad)

COYOTE # 1
Por eso no hablaba cuando estábamos caminando.

COYOTE # 1 (continuación)
(guarda el pasaporte en su bolsillo o mochila)
Conseguiré algo por esto.

COYOTE # 2
¡Órale! ... tenemos que irnos ahora.

> Ambos hombres van al árbol y cada uno toma un galón de agua. Ambos toman largos sorbos y comienzan a salir

> Both men exit. Silence for a beat. Lights dim.
>
> Lights up on SAMARITAN PAUL and SAMARITAN CARRIE who enter carrying gallons of water.

SAMARITAN PAUL
I know, this isn't the day we're supposed to check this station, but something tells me to come here today.

SAMARITAN CARRIE
(sounding exhausted)
When I volunteered to do this, I didn't realize the heat was so brutal.

SAMARITAN PAUL
Just drink water constantly and keep your skin covered. It's normal to feel heat exhaustion on your first few days. You'll get used to it.

SAMARITAN CARRIE
I'm from Wisconsin. I'll never get used to this heat.

SAMARITAN PAUL
(smiling)
I'm from Maine.

> SAMARITAN CARRIE reacts with surprise.

I've been doing this for five years... Most people don't have the slightest clue as to the amount of water they need to survive this desert.

SAMARITAN CARRIE
The bottles at the last station were split open. Was it the heat?

COYOTE # 1
(hacia los cadáveres)
Encontraron su 'sueño americano.'

COYOTE # 2
Mejor es morir con uno, que vivir sin un sueño.

> Ambos hombres salen. Silencio por un momento.
>
> Las luces bajan.
>
> Se ilumina en SAMARITANO PAUL y SAMARITANA CARRIE que entran llevando galones de agua.

SAMARITANO PAUL
Lo sé, este no es el día que debemos revisar esta estación, pero algo me dice que venga aquí hoy.

SAMARITANA CARRIE
(agotada)
Cuando me ofrecí como voluntaria para hacer esto, no me di cuenta que el calor podía ser tan brutal.

SAMARITANO PAUL
Bebe agua constantemente y mantén tu piel cubierta. Es normal sentir agotamiento por el calor en los primeros días. Te vas a acostumbrar.

SAMARITANA CARRIE
Soy de Wisconsin. Nunca me acostumbraré a este calor.

SAMARITANO PAUL
(sonriendo)
Yo soy de Maine.

SAMARITAN PAUL
No, activists. They follow us. They're as committed as we are...

> As they approach the center of stage, they discover the first two bodies.

Oh, my God!
(makes the sign of the cross)

SAMARITAN CARRIE
> kneels next to the bodies and checks for pulse.

This is why I was being called here today, to witness.

SAMARITAN CARRIE
We're too late.

SAMARITAN PAUL
If it's not the heat, it's those dammed coyotes!

SAMARITAN CARRIE
(looking at the burned soles)
Oh, my, look at these feet! They're burned!

SAMARITAN PAUL
Cheap shoes.

SAMARITAN CARRIE
(looking at the burned shoes)
The soles of these shoes are... I've never seen anything like this.

SAMARITAN PAUL
Get used to it.

SAMARITAN CARRIE
It had to be excruciatingly painful to walk on these feet. Why do people do this?

SAMARITANA CARRIE
reacciona con sorpresa.

He estado haciendo esto por cinco años... la mayoría de la gente no tiene la menor idea de la cantidad de agua que necesitan para sobrevivir este desierto.

SAMARITANA CARRIE
Las botellas de la última estación estaban cortadas, ¿Fue el calor?

SAMARITANO PAUL
No, activistas. Nos siguen. Están tan comprometidos como nosotros.

> A medida que se acercan al centro del escenario descubren los dos primeros cuerpos.

(hace la señal de la cruz)

SAMARITANA CARRIE se arrodilla junto a los cuerpos y chequea por pulso.

Es por esto que estaba siendo llamado aquí hoy, para ser testigo.

SAMARITANA CARRIE
Llegamos tarde.

SAMARITANO PAUL
¡Si no es el calor, son esos malditos coyotes!

SAMARITANA CARRIE
(mirando las plantas de pies)
¡Dios, mira estos pies! ¡Están quemados!

SAMARITANO PAUL
Zapatos baratos.

SAMARITAN PAUL
You'd have to be in their shoes. I don't pretend to understand.
(busily searching pockets)
No documents. Nothing...

SAMARITAN CARRIE
(looking at the sky)
Vultures are starting to circle.

SAMARITAN PAUL
Help me here. We need to find something to identify them....to let their families know.
(picks up a few scattered photos)
These might help. Let's walk the area and check around the shrubs.

SAMARITAN CARRIE searches behind the bushes and finds LUCIA.

SAMARITAN CARRIE
There's one more here!

SAMARITAN CARRIE kneels next to LUCIA.

LUCIA
(Moans)

SAMARITAN CARRIE
She's still alive! Bring water!

SAMARITAN PAUL grabs a bottle of water and rushes to LUCIA's side.

SAMARITAN PAUL
She's very weak. Hurry! Let's take her to the prayer house! To Dr. Wilson!

SAMARITAN CARRIE
Wait! Aren't we are supposed to turn them over to Border Patrol?

SAMARITANA CARRIE
(mirando los zapatos quemados)
Las suelas de estos zapatos están … Nunca en mi vida he visto algo así.

SAMARITANO PAUL
Acostúmbrate.

SAMARITANA CARRIE
Tiene que haber sido insoportablemente doloroso caminar en estos pies. ¿Por qué la gente hace esto?

SAMARITANO PAUL
Tendrías que estar en sus zapatos. Yo no pretendo entender.
(buscando en los bolsillos de los muertos)
Sin documentos. Nada.

SAMARITANA CARRIE
(mirando al cielo)
Los buitres están empezando a dar vueltas.

SAMARITANO PAUL
Ayúdame aquí. Necesitamos encontrar algo que los identifique … para informarles a sus familias.
(recoge algunas fotos dispersas)

Estas nos podrán ayudar. Caminemos por el área y revisemos los arbustos.

SAMARITANA CARRIE busca detrás de los arbustos y encuentra a LUCÍA.

SAMARITANA CARRIE
¡Hay una más aquí!

SAMARITANA CARRIE se arrodilla junto a LUCÍA.

LUCIA
(gemidos)

SAMARITAN PAUL
Yes. But we won't this time. We can't. We're her only chance.

SAMARITAN CARRIE
Okay. That's what they told us to do at training, but you're the boss.

SAMARITAN PAUL
I'll bring the truck closer!

        SAMARITAN PAUL exits running.

(BLACKOUT)

(END OF SCENE)

SAMARITANA CARRIE
¡Todavía está viva! ¡Trae agua!

SAMARITANO PAUL agarra una botella de agua y corre al lado de LUCÍA.

SAMARITANO PAUL
Esta muy débil. ¡Apúrate! ¡Vamos a llevarla a la casa de oración! ¡A donde el doctor Wilson!

SAMARITANA CARRIE
¡Espera! ¿No se supone que tenemos que entregarlos a la Patrulla Fronteriza?

SAMARITANO PAUL
Sí. Pero no vamos a hacer eso esta vez. No podemos. Nosotros somos su única oportunidad.

SAMARITANA CARRIE
Okay. Eso es lo que nos dijeron en el entrenamiento, pero tú eres el jefe.

SAMARITANO PAUL
¡Voy a traer la camioneta más cerca!

        SAMARITANO PAUL sale corriendo.

(TELÓN)

(FIN DE ESCENA)

Scene II -- It's a Long Wait

SETTING:

MORNING. American Consulate. The American flag and the framed picture of President George H. W. Bush are prominently displayed.

TIME: 1991

AT RISE:

CONSULAR CLERK is different than in Act I. He/she is sitting behind the glass. A U.S. MARINE is standing close to the window.

An older RUBEN with a bruised face and broken arm in a sling is standing next to the counter.

          CONSULAR CLERK
Wow! What happened to you?

          RUBEN
Car accident.

          CONSULAR CLERK
             (unconvinced)
File number?

          RUBEN
343455.

          CONSULAR CLERK inputs number.

I applied about twelve years ago and haven't heard anything. Can you please check my status?

          CONSULAR CLERK
It's a long waiting list.

Escena II – Es una Larga Espera

Ambientación:

MAÑANA. Consulado Americano. La bandera estadounidense y la imagen enmarcada del presidente H. W. Bush se muestran prominentemente.

Fecha: Año 1991

Telón:

SECRETARIO CONSULAR diferente al del Acto I está sentado detrás del vidrio grueso. Hay un MARINE americano de pie cerca de la ventanilla.

Un RUBÉN mayor con cara magullada el brazo roto en un cabestrillo está de pie junto a la ventanilla.

          SECRETARIO CONSULAR
¡Wow! ¿Qué le paso a usted?

          RUBÉN
Un accidente de carro.

          SECRETARIO CONSULAR
             (no convencido)
¿Número de solicitud?

          RUBÉN
343455

          SECRETARIO CONSULAR
             ingresa el número.

Apliqué hace como doce años y aún no he escuchado nada. ¿Podría usted chequear mi estatus?

          SECRETARIO CONSULAR
La lista de espera es larga.

People that have preferential status move faster and I see here, Mr. Garcia Martinez, that you haven't declared a preferential status.

Let's see, we probably need to update your application. Has your civil status changed?

                    RUBEN
No.

            CONSULAR CLERK
You're not married?

                    RUBEN
No.

            CONSULAR CLERK
You understand, Mr. García Martínez, you must be truthful. If we catch a lie on your application, it'll be denied.

                    RUBEN
I understand.

            CONSULAR CLERK
May I see your passport?

> RUBEN passes his passport under the glass. CONSULAR CLERK inspects the passport.

            CONSULAR CLERK
Mr. García Martínez, your passport has expired. When you first applied you were told you must maintain a valid passport at ALL times while you're in this process. This problem must be corrected immediately. And you must bring me a valid passport. Do you understand?

Las personas que tienen estatus preferencial se mueven más rápido y veo aquí Sr. García Martínez que usted no ha declarado un estatus preferencial. Veamos, probablemente necesitamos actualizar su solicitud. ¿Ha cambiado su estado civil?

                    RUBÉN
No.

            SECRETARIO CONSULAR
¿No está casado?

                    RUBÉN
No.

            SECRETARIO CONSULAR
Usted entiende Sr. García Martínez que tiene que ser honesto. Si lo atrapamos con una mentira su solicitud será rechazada.

                    RUBÉN
Entiendo.

            SECRETARIO CONSULAR
¿Puedo ver su pasaporte?

> RUBEN pasa su pasaporte por debajo del vidrio. SECRETARIO CONSULAR lo inspecciona.

            SECRETARIO CONSULAR
Sr. García Martínez su pasaporte esta vencido. Cuando presentó su solicitud por primera vez, se le dijo que debe mantener su pasaporte válido en TODO momento mientras esta en este proceso. Este problema debe ser corregido inmediatamente. Y me debe traer un pasaporte valido. ¿Entiende?

RUBEN
Yes. But can you tell me how long I have to wait?

CONSULAR CLERK
First, you need to bring in a valid passport.

RUBEN
(light frustration)
Ahh, it costs money and full day's work to renew a passport.

CONSULAR CLERK
(surprised)
Don't you know that you have to prove you have adequate financial means in order to emigrate to the United States? It's a requirement for approval.

RUBEN
Yes, yes, I'll renew my passport. But can you tell me how much longer I have to wait?

CONSULAR CLERK
We'll send you a letter twelve months before your interview.

CONSULAR CLERK turns off microphone and turns his attention to his/her computer.

RUBEN taps the glass with his knuckles.

RUBEN
Excuse me. Excuse me. Can you please…

U.S. MARINE moves quickly toward RUBEN.

RUBÉN
Si, ¿pero puede decirme cuanto tiempo tengo que esperar?

SECRETARIO CONSULAR
Primero tiene que traerme un pasaporte válido.

RUBÉN
(ligera frustración)
Ahh, cuesta dinero y un día completo de trabajo el renovar un pasaporte.

SECRETARIO CONSULAR
(sorprendido)
¿No sabe usted que tiene que demostrar que tiene los medios financieros adecuados para emigrar a los Estados Unidos? Es un requisito para ser aprobado.

RUBÉN
Sí, sí, voy a renovar mi pasaporte. ¿Pero me puede decir cuánto tiempo más tengo que esperar?

SECRETARIO CONSULAR
Le enviaremos una carta doce meses antes de su entrevista.

SECRETARIO CONSULA apaga el micrófono y dirige su atención a su computadora.

RUBÉN golpea el vidrio con los nudillos.

RUBÉN
Perdón. Perdón. Por favor, puede…

MARINE americano se acerca rápidamente a RUBÉN.

U.S. MARINE Sir! Step away from the window!	**MARINE** ¡Señor! ¡Aléjese de la ventanilla!
RUBEN is surprised.	RUBÉN se sorprende
U.S. MARINE I said, step away from the window. NOW!	**MARINE** Dije aléjese de la ventanilla, ¡AHORA!
(BLACKOUT)	(BAJA TELÓN)
(END OF SCENE)	(FIN DE ESCENA)

Scene III -- Pledge Allegiance

SETTING:

DAY. A school in a city in the United States.

TIME: 1987

AT RISE:

An eight-year-old KATIA is standing next to her desk. TEACHER is standing with her right hand on her heart.
The U.S. Pledge of Allegiance begins on the intercom.

          AUDIO
I pledge allegiance...

          TEACHER
I pledge allegiance...

                KATIA remains silent.

          AUDIO
...to the flag of the United States of America, and to...

          TEACHER
Katia, put your hand on your heart. Repeat the words!

                KATIA does not understand the TEACHER. She remains mute and does not move her hand.

          AUDIO
...the Republic for which it stands, one Nation under God, indivisible, with....

                TEACHER moves toward KATIA, takes the child's right hand and places it over her heart.

Escena III – Juramento de Lealtad

Ambientación:

DÍA. Una escuela en una ciudad de Estados Unidos.

Fecha: Año 1987

Telón:

KATIA de ocho años está de pie junto a su escritorio. La MAESTRA esta de pie con su mano derecha en el corazón. El Juramento de lealtad de Estados Unidos comienza en el intercomunicador.

          AUDIO
Prometo lealtad...

          MAESTRA
Prometo lealtad...

                KATIA permanece en silencio.
          AUDIO
...a la bandera de los Estados Unidos de America, y a...

          MAESTRA
Katia, non tu mano sobre tu corazón. ¡Repite las palabras!

                KATIA no entiende a la MAESTRA. Permanece muda y no mueve la mano.

          AUDIO
...la Republica que representa, una Nación bajo Dios, indivisible, con...

                MAESTRA se mueve hacia KATIA, y toma la mano derecha de la niña y la coloca sobre su corazón. Luego señala su oído y

Then, she points to her ear and voices the words of the Pledge, trying to get KATIA to repeat.

AUDIO
...liberty and justice for all.

TEACHER
...liberty and justice for all.

TEACHER
Katia, you're in America now. The Pledge of Allegiance is the first thing you have to learn. You have to put your right hand over your heart. That means you're serious. That you promise with all your heart. Do you understand?

KATIA nods affirmatively.

You have to learn the words. Repeat them all the time, until you learn them.

KATIA nods affirmatively.

Do you understand what I'm telling you? Comprende?

KATIA does not respond.

Let's try it. Repeat after me. I pledge allegiance...

KATIA
Ai...

TEACHER
Pledge, pled-ge.

KATIA
Plech.

Luego señala su oído y pronuncia las palabras del Juramento, tratando de que KATIA repita.

AUDIO
libertad y justicia para todos...

MAESTRA
libertad y justicia para todos...

MAESTRA
Katia estas en los Estados Unidos ahora. El Juramento de Lealtad es lo primero que tienes que aprender. Tienes que poner tu mano derecha sobre tu corazón. Eso significa que es serio. Que lo prometes con todo tu corazón. ¿Entiendes?

KATIA asiente afirmativamente.

Tienes que aprender las palabras. Repetirlas todo el tiempo, hasta que lo aprendas.

KATIA asiente afirmativamente.

¿Entiendes lo que te estoy diciendo? ¿Comprendes?

KATIA no responde.

Vamos a intentarlo. Repite después de mí. I pledge allegiance...

KATIA
Ai...

MAESTRA
Pledge, pled-ge.

KATIA
Plech.

TEACHER
Allegiance. A-lle-giance.

Lights begin to fade out.

KATIA
A-lli-gins.

(BLACKOUT)

(END OF SCENE)

MAESTRA
Lealtad. A-lle-giance.

Las luces comienzan a bajar.

KATIA
A-lli-gins.

(TELÓN)

(FIN DE ESCENA)

Scene IV - Tell Me the Truth

SETTING:

DAYBREAK. LUCIA'S apartment. A small and simple apartment in a city in the U.S.

TIME: 1994

AT RISE:

A tired LUCIA arrives from work. She is carrying a heavy shoulder bag and wearing a cleaning uniform with a big logo for "SPEEDY CLEAN" stamped on the back. From this point on LUCIA walks awkwardly because of a bad leg. She puts a kettle on the stove, removes her work shoes and puts on old slippers.

She uses a land line to call DON FRANCISCO.

DON FRANCISCO is audio only.

          LUCIA
Hi, Father! Did I wake you up?

          DON FRANCISCO (V.O.)
No, mi'ja. I was just reading. Us old people don't need much sleep. What're you doing up so early? Getting ready for work?

> LUCIA begins fixing herself a cup of tea and then gets busy preparing a lunch box for KATIA.

          LUCIA
Yes, getting ready. But I wanted to know how your doctor's visit went yesterday? What did he say?

Escena IV – Dime la Verdad

Ambientación:

AMANECER. Apartamento de LUCÍA en una ciudad de Estados Unidos. Apartamento chico y simple.

Fecha: Año 1994

Telón:

Una LUCÍA cansada llega del trabajo. Lleva un bolso pesado y un uniforme de limpieza con un gran logotipo 'Speedy Clean' estampado en la espalda. A partir de este punto LUCÍA camina torpemente debido a una pierna mala. Pone una tetera en la cocina y se quita los zapatos de trabajo y se pone unas chancletas viejas.

Ella usa un teléfono fijo para llamar a DON FRANCISCO.

DON FRANCISCO es solo audio.

          LUCÍA
¡Hola, papá! ¿Te desperté?

          DON FRANCISCO (v.o.)
No, mi'ja, solo estaba leyendo. Nosotros los viejos no necesitamos dormir mucho. ¿Qué estas haciendo tan temprano? ¿Te estas preparando para el trabajo?

> LUCÍA comienza a prepararse una taza de té y luego se ocupa de preparar una lonchera para KATIA.

DON FRANCISCO (V.O.)
He said, I'm doing fine. Just getting older.

LUCIA
Are you telling me the truth?

DON FRANCISCO (V.O.)
Of course. There's nothing for you to worry about. I am quite healthy for my age. But how are you? Tell me, what kind of work are you doing now?

LUCIA
I'm working in a large architecture office.

DON FRANCISCO (V.O.)
In an office?

LUCIA
Yes, people are really nice to me. My boss likes me so much, he's told me that when my English improves, I can move to become an architect's assistant.

DON FRANCISCO (V.O.)
That's nice, mi'ja. Soon you'll get your career back.

LUCIA
Someday. Maybe. Father, how's Ruben?

DON FRANCISCO (V.O.)
Good. He's completely recuperated from the accident.

LUCIA
That's good to hear. I worry about him.

DON FRANCISCO (V.O.)
I never understood why the two of you did not marry?

LUCIA
It's complicated. Will you give him my love?

LUCÍA
Sí, preparándome. Pero quería saber ¿cómo te fue tu visita con el médico ayer? ¿Qué te dijo?

DON FRANCISCO (v.o.)
Dijo que estoy bien. Solo envejeciendo.

LUCÍA
¿Me estás diciendo la verdad?

DON FRANCISCO (v.o.)
Por su puesto. No hay nada de que preocuparte. Estoy bastante saludable para mi edad. Pero, ¿cómo estas tú? Dime, ¿qué tipo de trabajo estás haciendo ahora?

LUCÍA
Estoy trabajando en una oficina grande de arquitectos.

DON FRANCISCO (v.o.)
¿En una oficina?

LUCÍA
Sí, la gente es muy amable conmigo. A mi jefe le gusto tanto que me ha dicho que cuando mi inglés mejore puedo subir a ser asistente de arquitecto.

DON FRANCISCO (v.o.)
Eso es bueno, mi'ja. Pronto recuperarás tu carrera.

LUCÍA
Algún día. Quizás. Papá, ¿cómo está Rubén?

DON FRANCISCO (v.o.)
Bien. Esta completamente recuperado de su accidente.

LUCÍA
Eso es bueno escuchar. Me preocupo por él.

DON FRANCISCO (V.O.)
Sure. How's my granddaughter? My little Katia?

LUCIA
She's still asleep. She misses you. Treasures every letter you send her.

LUCIA sets the lunch box on the counter and sits at the kitchen table.

LUCIA inspects her red, swollen hands and massages them with hand lotion.

DON FRANCISCO (V.O.)
She never writes back.

LUCIA
Oh, young people these days, they don't do much handwriting. They're lazy about that. But you'd be proud of her, she's captain of her soccer team this year.

DON FRANCISCO (V.O.)
Ah, I wish I could see her play.

LUCIA
Katia is fearless on the field.

DON FRANCISCO (V.O.)
That's my granddaughter!

LUCIA
You'll also be happy to know she's talking about studying medicine.

DON FRANCISCO (V.O.)
A healer! Yes! Just like my father.

LUCIA
It's in her blood.

DON FRANCISCO (V.O.)
I knew it!

DON FRANCISCO (v.o.)
Nunca entendí ¿porque ustedes dos no se casaron?

LUCÍA
Es complicado. ¿Le das mi cariño?

DON FRANCISCO (v.o.)
Seguro. ¿Cómo está mi nieta?

LUCÍA
Todavía está dormida. Te extraña. Atesora cada una de las cartas que le mandas.

LUCIA coloca la lonchera en la mesa y se sienta.

LUCIA inspecciona sus manos rojas e hinchadas y las masajea con crema de manos.

DON FRANCISCO (v.o.)
Nunca me escribe.

LUCÍA
Oh, los jóvenes de este tiempo no escriben mucho a mano. Son perezosos al respecto. Pero estarías orgulloso de ella, es capitana de su equipo de futbol este año.

DON FRANCISCO (v.o.)
Ah, desearía verla jugar.

LUCÍA
Katia no tiene miedo en la cancha.

DON FRANCISCO (v.o.)
¡Esa es mi nieta!

LUCÍA
También estarás encantado de saber que está hablando de estudiar medicina.

LUCIA
Father, are the two hundred dollars a month enough?

DON FRANCISCO (V.O.)
Yes, mi'ja, its more than enough.

>   Teenage KATIA enters. She is getting her book bag ready for school.

LUCIA
If you need more you let me know, okay?

DON FRANCISCO (V.O.)
Yes, yes. But, more importantly, when will you come home? Katia will turn fifteen soon. Her quinciañera has to be here. I want to see her become a señorita.

LUCIA
Soon. I'm working on it.

DON FRANCISCO (V.O.)
Please give me that joy.

>   LUCIA cups the phone and motions KATIA to come to the phone.

LUCIA
(whispering)
It's Grandpa. He wants to talk to you.

>   KATIA excitedly takes the phone from LUCIA.

KATIA
(on the phone)
Hola, Abuelito! Yes, yes, I'm doing well. I'm studying history, biology and computer science this semester.... Uhh, hold on.
(to LUCIA)
Mom, how do you say computer science in Spanish?

DON FRANCISCO (v.o.)
¡Una sanadora! ¡Sí! ¡Igual que mi padre!

LUCÍA
Está en su sangre.

DON FRANCISCO (v.o.)
¡Lo sabía!

LUCÍA
Papá, los doscientos dólares que te mando al mes, ¿es suficiente?

DON FRANCISCO (v.o.)
Sí, mi'ja, es más que suficiente.

>   Entra la adolescente KATIA. Está preparando su bolsa de libros para la escuela.

LUCÍA
Si necesitas mas me lo haces saber, ¿de acuerdo?

DON FRANCISCO (v.o.)
Sí, sí. Pero lo más importante, ¿cuándo vas a regresar a casa? Katia va a cumplir sus quince pronto. Su quinceañera tiene que ser aquí. Quiero verla convertirse en una señorita.

LUCÍA
Pronto. Estoy trabajando en eso.

DON FRANCISCO (v.o.)
Por favor, dame esa alegría.

>   LUCÍA cubre el auricular y le hace una seña a KATIA para que venga al teléfono.

LUCÍA
(susurrando)
Es el abuelo. Quiere hablar contigo.

> LUCIA shrugs and walks to a bookcase in the room where she picks up a dictionary and begins looking up the words.

Grandpa, did you watch the World Cup Championship game?... No, the cable we have did not carry it.   Uh huh... Uh huh... Well, uh... hold on... un momento, por favor.
(toward LUCIA)
Mom, he's speaking too fast. I don't understand a word he's saying.

> KATIA hands the phone to LUCIA and LUCIA gives KATIA the open dictionary.

LUCIA
¿Si, Papá? Si, si.

KATIA
(reading from the dictionary)
CIEN-CIAS-DE-COM-PU-TA-CION.

LUCIA
Okay... Adiós. I'll try calling tomorrow.

> LUCIA hangs up the phone.

He was saying that he had someone at the door.

KATIA
Mom, where's my lunch? I'm running late. Henry is driving me to school and...

> LUCIA grabs the Metal Stanley construction grade lunchbox that is on the counter and sets it on the table for KATIA.

Uh... What? What's that?

The Avocado Tree/ El Árbol de Aguacate 81

> KATIA toma el teléfono con entusiasmo de LUCÍA.

KATIA
(al teléfono)
¡Hola, abuelito! Sí, sí, estoy bien... Este semestre estoy estudiando historia, biología y computer science... Uhh, espera
(a LUCÍA)
Mamá, ¿cómo se dice Computer Science en español?

> LUCÍA se encoge de hombros y camina hacia el estante en la habitación de donde saca un diccionario y comienza a buscar las palabras.

KATIA (continuación)
Abuelo, viste el partido del Campeonato de la Copa del Mundo? ... No el cable que tenemos no lo llevaba. Uh, uh... Uh, uh... Bueno, uh... espera... un momento por favor.
(hacia LUCÍA)

Mamá, está hablando demasiado rápido. No entiendo una palabra de lo que está diciendo.

> KATIA le entrega el teléfono a LUCÍA y LUCÍA le da a KATIA el diccionario abierto.

LUCÍA
¿Si, papá? Sí, sí.

KATIA
(leyendo del diccionario)
Cien-cias-de-com-pu-ta-cion.

LUCÍA
De acuerdo... Adiós. Trataré de llamar mañana.

LUCIA
Your lunchbox. I bought it at a garage sale. Do you like it?

KATIA
Oh, no it's not! I'll never carry that. You want everyone at school to make fun of me?

LUCIA
Your lunch will stay hot. It's a sturdy box.

> KATIA opens the box and pulls out a Tupperware container with rice and beans.

KATIA
Beans again? You've got to be kidding me!

LUCIA
It's healthy. Good for you…

KATIA
Why can't you fix pizza? Hamburgers? We're in America, Mom!

> KATIA grabs her school bag and swings it over her shoulder.

You just don't understand anything!

> KATIA exits in a huff, leaving her lunch behind.

(BLACKOUT)

(END OF SCENE)

LUCIA cuelga el teléfono

LUCÍA
Estaba diciendo que tenía a alguien en la puerta.

KATIA
Mamá, ¿dónde está mi almuerzo? Estoy tarde. Henry me esta llevando a la escuela y…

> LUCIA agarra la lonchera de Metal Stanley de trabajador de construcción, que esta en la cocina y se la pone en la mesa para KATIA.

KATIA (continuación)
Uh… ¿Qué? ¿Qué es eso?

LUCÍA
Tu lonchera. La compré en una venta de garaje. ¿Te gusta?

KATIA
Oh, no, ¡no lo es! Nunca voy a llevar eso. ¿Quieres que todos en la escuela se burlen de mí?

LUCÍA
Tu almuerzo se mantendrá caliente. Es una lonchera fuerte.

> KATIA abre la lonchera y saca un recipiente de Tupperware con arroz y frejoles.

KATIA
¿Frejoles otra vez? ¡Tienes que estar bromeando!

LUCÍA
Es saludable. Bueno para ti…

KATIA
¿Por qué no puedes cocinar pizza?
¿Hamburguesas? ¡Mamá, estamos en Estados
Unidos!

> KATIA agarra su mochila
> escolar y se la pone al hombro.

¡Simplemente no entiendes nada!

> KATIA sale molesta, dejando
> atrás su almuerzo.

(TELÓN)

(FIN DE ESCENA)

Scene V -- Checkmate!

SETTING:

AFTERNOON. The backyard behind the MEDINA house. The avocado plant is now a large tree, loaded with fruit.

TIME: That afternoon. 1994

AT RISE:

An aged and sick DON FRANCISCO is in a wheelchair under the shade of the avocado tree playing chess with RUBEN.

RUBEN
Your turn, Don Francisco.

DON FRANCISCO
Wait! I'm thinking. I let you beat me last week, but you won't be that lucky today.

DON FRANCISCO makes a move on the table.

There!

RUBEN
It's nice back here. This avocado gives a nice shade. I really never imagined that little plant you brought home so long ago would grow this big.

DON FRANCISCO
Good dirt and strong roots.

RUBEN
And somebody that takes good care of it.

RUBEN makes a move.

Escena V – ¡Jaque Mate!

Ambientación:

TARDE. El patio trasero de la casa MEDINA. La planta de aguacate es ahora un árbol grande, cargado de fruta.

Fecha: Esa tarde. Año 1994

Telón:

Un anciano y enfermo DON FRANCISCO está en una silla de ruedas bajo la sombra del árbol de aguacate, jugando al ajedrez con RUBÉN.

RUBÉN
Su turno, Don Francisco.

DON FRANCISCO
¡Espera! Estoy pensando. Te deje ganarme la semana pasada, pero no tendrás tanta suerte hoy.

DON FRANCISCO hace una movida en el tablero.

¡Allí!

RUBÉN
Es muy agradable aquí. Este aguacate da una buena sombra. Realmente nunca me imaginé que esa pequeña planta que trajo a casa hace tanto tiempo, creciera tan grande.

DON FRANCISCO
Buena tierra y raíces fuertes.

RUBÉN
Y alguien que lo cuide bien.

RUBÉN hace un movimiento.

DON FRANCISCO
That was when we first transplanted it. Now, I can't care for my garden anymore. But the tree is strong now. Its long roots find water on their own.

RUBEN
Don Francisco, how's Lucía doing?

DON FRANCISCO
Really well. She called this morning. She was getting ready to go to her office. Her boss is going to promote her to Assistant Architect soon.

RUBEN
Wonderful! When is she coming back to visit you?

DON FRANCISCO
I'm waiting for that. She tells me it'll be soon. She's waiting on some paperwork that'll allow her to travel.

RUBEN
Have you told her you're not doing well? Does she know about the wheelchair?

DON FRANCISCO
No, no need to worry her. She has enough on her hands raising a teenager alone.

RUBEN
She would want to know.

> DON FRANCISCO makes a move.

DON FRANCISCO
I went into Katia's room this morning and found two books I was going to read to her when she was old enough... Lucía took her too young. I'm worried about her.

DON FRANCISCO
Eso fue cuando lo trasplantamos. Ahora no puedo cuidar de mi jardín. Pero ahora el árbol es fuerte. Sus raíces largas encuentran el agua por si solas.

RUBÉN
Don Francisco, ¿cómo está Lucía?

DON FRANCISCO
Muy bien. Llamo esta mañana. Se estaba preparando para ir a su oficina. Su jefe la ascenderá a asistente de arquitecto pronto.

RUBÉN
¡Maravilloso! ¿Cuándo va a regresar a visitarlo?

DON FRANCISCO
Estoy esperando eso. Me dice que será pronto.

RUBÉN
¿Le ha dicho que su salud no está bien? ¿Sabe de la silla de ruedas?

DON FRANCISCO
No, no hay necesidad de preocuparla. Tiene suficiente entre sus manos criando a una adolescente sola.

RUBÉN
Ella querría saberlo.

> DON FRANCISCO hace un movimiento.

DON FRANCISCO
Fui a la habitación de Katia esta mañana y encontré dos libros que iba a leerle cuando tuviera la edad suficiente…. Lucía se la llevó demasiado joven. Estoy preocupado por ella.

RUBEN
Oh?

DON FRANCISCO
She's not getting a good, solid education.

> RUBEN reacts with a questioning look.

She's not learning about us, about her family.

RUBEN
Well, she's learning all the things she needs in the new country she lives in now.

DON FRANCISCO
You don't understand. I'm talking about OUR stories. The stories your grandpa told you when you were a kid. Remember?

RUBEN
Yeah, some.

DON FRANCISCO
Katia is growing up with no stories. With no history.

RUBEN
Katia will be fine, Don Francisco. You told me last time that Lucía said Katia speaks perfect English. No accent. JUST THAT will open doors for her.

DON FRANCISCO
Speaking English is not everything.

RUBEN
(lighthearted)
It sure helps a lot.

DON FRANCISCO
Katia discovered the world in Spanish. She has memorized the words in English.

RUBÉN
¿Oh?

DON FRANCISCO
Ella no está recibiendo una educación buena y sólida.

> RUBÉN reacciona con una mirada interrogante.

No esta aprendiendo sobre nosotros, sobre su familia.

RUBÉN
Bueno, ella está aprendiendo todas las cosas que necesita en el nuevo país donde vive ahora.

DON FRANCISCO
No entiendes. Estoy hablando de NUESTRAS historias. Las historias que tu abuelo te contó cuando eras niño. ¿Recuerdas?

RUBÉN
Sí, algo.

DON FRANCISCO
Katia esta creciendo sin historias. Sin pasado.

RUBÉN
Katia estará bien Don Francisco. Usted me dijo la última vez que Lucía le dijo que Katia habla inglés perfectamente. Sin ningún acento. SOLO ESO le abrirá puertas.

DON FRANCISCO
Hablar inglés no es todo.

RUBÉN
(liviano)
Pero ayuda un montón.

RUBEN
She speaks both languages.

DON FRANCISCO
Even if she speaks a foreign language now, her roots are here. She'll struggle until she understands that. Generations of Medinas on this land will call her back.

> RUBEN makes a move on the board.

RUBEN
I bet you didn't expect that!

DON FRANCISCO
This morning, Lucía told me Katia wants to be a doctor. That's my father's spirit manifesting itself. We come from a long line of curanderos, of healers.

RUBEN
Don Francisco, Katia's future will be better than if she'd stayed here. She'll be fine.

DON FRANCISCO
(worried)
No, I'm afraid my little one will wander for a long time. Searching for her way home.

RUBEN
Maybe she IS home. Maybe this is not home anymore.

RUBEN (CONT'D)
After all, she's an American now.

DON FRANCISCO
The saddest thing is to lose our young... our new generations.

DON FRANCISCO
Katia descubrió el mundo en español. Ella a memorizado las palabras en inglés.

RUBÉN
Habla ambos idiomas.

DON FRANCISCO
Incluso si ahora habla un idioma extranjero, sus raíces están aquí. Ella tendrá dificultad hasta que entienda eso. Generaciones de Medinas en esta tierra la llamaran de vuelta.

> RUBÉN hace un movimiento en el tablero.

RUBÉN
¡Apuesto a que no esperaba eso!

DON FRANCISCO
Esta mañana, Lucia me dijo que Katia quiere ser doctora. Ese es el espíritu de mi padre manifestándose. Venimos de una línea larga de curanderos, de sanadores.

RUBÉN
Don Francisco, el futuro de Katia será mejor que si se hubiera quedado aquí. Ella estará bien.

DON FRANCISCO
(preocupado)
No, me temo que mi pequeña vagará durante mucho tiempo. Buscando su camino a casa.

RUBÉN
Tal vez ella ESTÁ en casa. Tal vez, este ya no es su casa. Después de todo ella es ahora una Americana.

DON FRANCISCO
Una sin raíces.

DON FRANCISCO moves the last piece on the board.

Checkmate!

RUBEN
(smiles)
Not again! I've only beat you once!

DON FRANCISCO
(laughing)
And that was because I was under the weather.

DON FRANCISCO starts setting the chess pieces on the table again.

RUBEN
I was at the Consulate this morning.

DON FRANCISCO
Really? You're still following up with that? I thought you'd given up long time ago.

RUBEN
No... I check on my progress every couple years. It's a very slow-moving list. But I have a feeling I'm really close now. That any day, I'll get the letter for my interview.

DON FRANCISCO
Things are better here. There's no curfew...

RUBEN
They're better than when Lucia and Diego left, but things haven't changed for me.

DON FRANCISCO
How long have you been at the school now?

RUBEN
I'm not at the school anymore. I'm driving Diego's taxi full time now.

DON FRANCISCO mueve la última pieza en el tablero.

¡Jaque Mate!

RUBÉN
(sonriendo)
¡No otra vez! ¡Solo le he ganado una vez!

DON FRANCISCO
(riendo)
Y eso fue porque estaba un poco enfermo.

DON FRANCISCO comienza a arreglar las piezas en el tablero de nuevo.

RUBÉN
Estuve en el Consulado esta mañana.

DON FRANCISCO
¿Sí? ¿Todavía sigues con eso? Pensé que ya lo habías abandonado hace tiempo.

RUBÉN
No… reviso mi progreso cada par de años. Es una lista que se mueve muy despacio. Pero tengo la sensación que ahora estoy cerca. Que cualquier día recibiré la carta para mi entrevista.

DON FRANCISCO
Las cosas están mejor aquí. Ya no hay toque de queda.

RUBÉN
Están mejor de cuando Lucía y Diego se fueron, pero las cosas no han cambiado para mí.

DON FRANCISCO
¿Cuánto tiempo tienes en el colegio?

DON FRANCISCO
What happened?

RUBEN
After the accident, I had some problems with the school administration.

DON FRANCISCO
Oh!

RUBEN
I just can't make ends meet.

DON FRANCISCO
Can't you find a job in another school?

RUBEN
No, I am blacklisted.

                A pause.

DON FRANCISCO
Rubén, you're a nice, well-educated man. I'm surprised that after all these years, you haven't found a good woman to marry. Life is easier when you have somebody to share it with.

RUBEN
I had somebody many years ago.

DON FRANCISCO
Lucía is not coming back.

RUBEN
Lucía has always been my best friend. *(a pause)* The person I loved was murdered.

                Both men look at each other for a beat.

DON FRANCISCO
Ricky?

RUBÉN
Ya no estoy en el colegio. Ahora estoy conduciendo el taxi de Diego a tiempo completo.

DON FRANCISCO
¿Qué pasó?

RUBÉN
Después del accidente tuve algunos problemas con la administración del colegio.

DON FRANCISCO
¡Oh!

RUBÉN
Simplemente no me alcanza para el final de mes.

DON FRANCISCO
¿No puedes encontrar un trabajo en otra escuela?

RUBÉN
No. Estoy en la lista negra.

                Una pausa.

DON FRANCISCO
Rubén eres un hombre agradable y bien educado. Me sorprende que después de todos estos años no hayas encontrado una buena mujer con quien casarte. La vida es más fácil cuando tienes a alguien con quien compartirla.

RUBÉN
Tuve alguien hace muchos años.

DON FRANCISCO
Lucía no va a volver.

RUBEN
Yes.

DON FRANCISCO
I'm sorry, I didn't know. *(A pause)* You're a good man, Rubén.

        DON FRANCISCO finishes setting the chess table.

Another game?

(BLACKOUT)

(END OF SCENE)

RUBÉN
Lucía siempre ha sido mi mejor amiga. *(una pausa)* La persona que amaba fue asesinada.

        Ambos hombres se miran el uno al otro por un momento.

DON FRANCISCO
¿Ricky?

RUBÉN
Sí.

DON FRANCISCO
Lo siento, no lo sabía. *(una pausa)* Eres un buen hombre Rubén.

        DON FRANCISCO termina de arreglar las piezas de ajedrez.

¿Otro juego?

(TELÓN)

(FIN DE ESCENA)

Scene VI -- It's All About Image

SETTING:

NIGHT. Sweatshop. There is a clock on the wall. The time is 7:45 p.m. There is a rolling rack of finished prom dresses on the side.

TIME: 1997

AT RISE:

LUCIA, noticeably older, is working on a sewing machine station. She is finishing a dress. Co-worker GLORIA is working on the next station.

The sound of more sewing machines hum in the background.

LUCIA
I'm just about finished with this sleeve. I only have the hem to finish.

GLORIA
I'm almost done too.

LUCIA
(looking at the clock)
It's almost eight. I want to get home to have dinner with my daughter. We just don't do that anymore. Back home my father would always wait up for me to have dinner together. Didn't matter if I got home really late. He always waited.

GLORIA
Nobody waits for anybody here. My children fix their own dinner, their own lunch. And they eat when they
feel like it.

Escena VI – Todo es Imagen

Ambientación:

NOCHE. Taller de costura. Hay un reloj en la pared. La hora es 7:45 p.m. Hay un colgador rodante de vestidos de fiesta terminados en el costado.

Fecha: 1997

Telón:

LUCÍA, notablemente mayor, está trabajando en una estación de máquina de coser. Está terminando un vestido. La compañera de trabajo, GLORIA está trabajando en la estación siguiente.

El sonido de más máquinas de coser zumba en el fondo.

LUCÍA
Estoy a punto de terminar con esta manga. Solo tengo el dobladillo por terminar.

GLORIA
Yo también casi he terminado.

LUCÍA
(mirando el reloj)
Son casi las ocho. Quiero llegar a casa para cenar con mi hija. Ya no hacemos eso. En casa, mi padre siempre me esperaba para cenar juntos. No importaba si llegaba a casa super tarde. Él siempre me esperaba.

GLORIA
Aquí nadie espera a nadie. Mis hijos se arreglan su propia comida, su propio almuerzo. Y comen cuando tienen ganas.

LUCIA
I miss sitting at the table and sharing a plate of potatoes and rice.

GLORIA
Potatoes and rice?

> LUCIA finishes the sleeve, pulls the dress from the machine and shakes it.

LUCIA
It was dinner when there was nothing else left in the pantry. Funny, how I miss that now.

GLORIA
You don't miss the potatoes and the rice. You miss your father and dinner time.

LUCIA
Maybe. I just know my daughter is growing up fast and I'll miss her when she goes off to college.

GLORIA
College?

LUCIA
Yes. My girl is a really good soccer player and a straight A student. She got a scholarship to college. I'm really proud of her.

GLORIA
Humm.

> LUCIA stands up and stretches. Her back hurts.

LUCIA
Gloria, how did you end up here?

LUCÍA
Echo de menos el sentarme en la mesa y compartir un plato de papas y arroz.

> LUCÍA termina la manga, saca el vestido de la máquina y lo sacude.

GLORIA
¿Papas y arroz?

LUCÍA
Era la cena cuando no quedaba mas en la despensa. Gracioso, como extraño eso ahora.

GLORIA
No echas de menos las papas y el arroz. Echas de menos la hora de la cena con tu padre.

LUCÍA
Quizás. Solo se que mi hija está creciendo rápido y la voy a extrañar cuando se vaya a la universidad.

GLORIA
¿Universidad?

LUCÍA
Sí. Mi hija es una buena jugadora de futbol y una buena estudiante. Recibió una beca para la universidad. Estoy muy orgullosa de ella.

GLORIA
Humm.

> LUCÍA se para y se estira. Le duele la espalda.

LUCÍA
Gloria, ¿cómo terminaste aquí?

GLORIA
My cousin recommended me. You know you have to have connections…

LUCIA
No, no, I mean how did you end up in this country?

GLORIA
That's a long story. *(a pause)* I came for just 'a few years,' and a few years turned into ten, then fifteen, twenty, and here I am. Twenty-four years. Still here.

LUCIA
I told myself the same thing, 'Just for a few years.' It's now eleven years and eight months.

> LUCIA puts the dress back on the machine and starts hemming. We hear the sound of her machine for a beat.

The other day I realized I've been absent from all the birthdays, weddings, funerals in my family for over a decade. … I feel my memories are blurring.

GLORIA
Your family is here.

> LUCIA reacts with a questioning look.

Let go.

LUCIA
It's not that easy.

GLORIA
The daughter, the sister, the girlfriend, all those that you were, stayed behind. Stayed home. Far away, they will never be again.

GLORIA
Mi primo me recomendó. Sabes que tienes que tener conexiones.

LUCÍA
No, no, quiero decir, ¿cómo terminaste en este país?

GLORIA
Esa es una historia larga. *(una pausa)* Vine por 'solo unos años,' y unos años se convirtieron en diez, después quince, veinte, y aquí estoy. Veinticuatro años. Todavía aquí.

LUCÍA
Yo me dije lo mismo, 'solo por unos años.' Ahora son diez años y ocho meses.

> LUCÍA vuelve a poner el vestido en la máquina y comienza a doblar. Escuchamos el sonido de su máquina por un momento.

El otro día me di cuenta de que he estado ausente de todos los cumpleaños, bodas funerales de mi familia por más de una década. … Siento que mis memorias se están borrando.

GLORIA
Tu familia esta aquí.

> LUCIA reacciona con una mirada cuestionadora.

Déjalo ir.

LUCÍA
No es tan fácil.

GLORIA
La hija, la hermana, la enamorada, todas esas que fuiste, se quedaron atrás.

LUCIA
You make it sound like it's as easy as taking your coat off. Don't you think about your family?

GLORIA
(shrugs)
I don't dwell on it. We make new families... My children are Americans. Their families will grow here.

       A beat.

LUCIA
Have you been back to visit?

GLORIA
What kind of question is that? You know there's no way out of our gilded cage.

LUCIA
What if your father or mother were to pass?

GLORIA
They both have. And each time I've grieved from a distance.

LUCIA
I don't know. I don't think I could do that.

    GLORIA stands to hang the finished dress she's been working on. She begins putting plastic wrap over the gowns that are finished.

GLORIA
Lucia, all your friends and family back home would DIE for a chance to be in your shoes right now. True?

GLORIA (continuación)
Se quedaron en tu casa. Muy lejos, nunca volverán a ser.

LUCÍA
Lo dices como si fuera tan fácil como quitarte un abrigo. ¿Tú no piensas en tu familia?

GLORIA
(se encoge de hombros)
No pienso en ello. Hacemos nuevas familias … mis hijos son todos Americanos. Sus familias crecerán aquí.

       Una pausa.

LUCÍA
¿Has regresado a visitarlos?

GLORIA
¿Qué tipo de pregunta es esa? Sabes que no hay salida de nuestra jaula dorada.

LUCÍA
¿Qué pasaría si tu padre o tu madre falleciera?

GLORIA
Ambos han fallecido. Y cada vez los he llorado desde la distancia.

LUCÍA
No sé. No creo que pueda hacer eso.

    GLORIA se pone de pie para colgar el vestido terminado en que ha estado trabajando. Comienza a envolver con plástico los vestidos terminados.

LUCIA
I guess.

GLORIA
You send some money home every month and they think you've made it big. True?

LUCIA
Yes.

GLORIA
Well, doesn't that make you feel good? Everybody that knew you back home envies your lucky stars.

LUCIA
But they're no lucky stars.

GLORIA
Who cares about that? ... The truth would be a disappointment. It's all about the illusion. Like this dress, these ruffles, it'll make some girl believe that she's beautiful for a night. That's all that matters.

A beat

LUCIA
I used to believe I could work my way out of poverty... This job pays a little more than the cleaning job I used to have.

GLORIA
This is better than cleaning. The chemicals were hard on my hands.

LUCIA
You know, I once was an Architect.

GLORIA
For real? You went to the University?

GLORIA
Lucía, todos tus amigos y familia en casa MORIRIAN por la oportunidad de estar en tus zapatos en este momento. ¿Verdad?

LUCÍA
Sí.

GLORIA
Bueno, ¿eso no te hace sentir bien? Todos los que conocías en tu casa envidian tus estrellas de la suerte.

LUCÍA
Pero no hay estrellas de la suerte.

GLORIA
¿A quien le importa eso? ... La verdad sería una decepción. Todo es la ilusión.
Como estos vestidos, estos volantes, harán que alguna chica crea que es hermosa por una noche. Eso es todo lo que importa.

Una pausa.

LUCÍA
Solía creer que trabajando podía salir de la pobreza. Este trabajo paga un poco mas que el trabajo de limpieza que tenía.

GLORIA
Esto es mejor que limpiar. Los productos químicos eran duros en mis manos.

LUCÍA
Sabes, un tiempo fui una arquitecta.

GLORIA
¿De verdad? ¿Fuiste a la universidad?

LUCÍA
Sí, por seis largos años.

LUCIA
Yes, for six long years.

GLORIA
Graduated and all?

LUCIA
With honors.

GLORIA
Now that's why you overthink everything. Books were never my thing. I dreamed that one day I would model beautiful dresses with silver needle heels.

> GLORIA parades like a model on a runway.

LUCIA
(laughs)
A runway model.

GLORIA
I had the looks and the curves.

LUCIA
Nice!

> BOSS enters. He is a middle-aged man.

> GLORIA stops in her tracks and hurries to hang the dress on the rack.

BOSS
Are you two finished yet?

GLORIA
Almost. Lucía is finishing the hem of the last one.

GLORIA
¿Graduada y todo?

LUCÍA
Con honores.

GLORIA
Ah, por eso es que sobre piensas todo. Los libros nunca fueron lo mío. Yo soñaba que un día iba a modelar bellos vestidos con tacones de aguja plateados.

> GLORIA desfila como una modelo en una pasarela.

LUCÍA
(se ríe)
Una modelo de pasarela.

GLORIA
Tenía el cuerpo y las curvas.

LUCÍA
¡Bonita!

> JEFE entra. Es un hombre de edad mediana.

> GLORIA se detiene y se apresura a colgar el vestido.

JEFE
¿Ustedes dos, ya terminaron?

GLORIA
Casi. Lucía está terminando el dobladillo del último.

JEFE
Bien. Van a recogerlos mañana a primera hora.
(hacia GLORIA)

BOSS
Good. They'll be picked up first thing in the morning.
(toward GLORIA)

Gloria, you can go. I'll see you tomorrow.
(toward LUCIA)

You, I need to see you in my office before you leave.

                    BOSS exits.

LUCIA
What do you think he wants?

GLORIA
(nervously)
I don't know.

                    GLORIA gathers her things to leave.

Congratulations on your daughter's scholarship. Just remember, she's waiting for you at home. Good night!

                    GLORIA exits.

                    Stage dark on work area and lights up on BOSS's office.

                    BOSS is sitting behind a desk in a small, cluttered office. A family picture is on the desk.

                    LUCIA enters.

LUCIA
You wanted to see me, sir?

BOSS
How long have you been with us, Lucía?

JEFE *(continuación)*
Gloria, tú puedes irte. Te veo mañana.
(hacia LUCÍA)

Tú, necesito verte en mi oficina antes de que te vayas.

                    El JEFE sale.

LUCÍA
¿Qué crees que quiere?

GLORIA
(nerviosa)
No lo sé.

                    GLORIA reúne sus cosas para irse.

GLORIA *(continuación)*
Felicitaciones por la beca de tu hija. Solo recuerda, ella te esta esperando en casa. ¡Buenas noches!

                    GLORIA sale.

                    Escenario oscuro en el área de trabajo se ilumina en la oficina del JEFE.

                    JEFE está sentado detrás de un escritorio en una oficina pequeña y desordenada. Una foto de su familia esta sobre el escritorio.

                    LUCÍA entra.

LUCÍA
¿Quería verme, señor?

JEFE
¿Cuánto tiempo llevas con nosotros, Lucía?

LUCIA
It'll be three months at the end of this week.

BOSS
Three months! That's a long time. I think you deserve some rest time.

LUCIA
Rest? Are you firing me, sir? Did I do something wrong? Please, I really need the work.

BOSS
No, I'm not firing you. I just want you to take some rest time. Don't come to the shop tomorrow.

LUCIA
Will I get paid for the work I've done till today?

BOSS
Yes, of course. I wouldn't cheat you out of your money. You disappoint me, Lucía. What a terrible thing for you to think.

LUCIA
When can I come back?

BOSS
I'll call you when we need you back.

LUCIA
Is there anything I can do to get my job back?

BOSS moves closer to LUCIA.

BOSS
Well, since you ask, I can think of a few things you can do.

LUCÍA
Serán tres meses al final de esta semana.

JEFE
¡Tres meses! Ese es un tiempo largo. Creo que mereces un tiempo de descanso.

LUCÍA
¿Descanso? ¿Me está despidiendo señor? ¿Hice algo equivocado? Por favor, realmente necesito este trabajo.

JEFE
No, no te estoy despidiendo. Solo quiero que te tomes un tiempo de descanso. No vengas a trabajar mañana.

LUCÍA
¿Me pagaran por el trabajo que he hecho hasta hoy?

JEFE
Sí, por supuesto. No te engañaría de tu dinero. Me decepcionas Lucía. Que cosa tan terrible piensas.

LUCÍA
¿Cuándo puedo volver?

JEFE
Te llamaré cuando te necesitemos de vuelta.

LUCÍA
¿Hay algo que pueda hacer para recuperar mi trabajo?

JEFE se acerca a LUCÍA.

JEFE
Bueno, ya que lo preguntas, puedo pensar en algunas cosas que puedes hacer.

LUCIA bites her lip and stands still.

BOSS moves closer and starts massaging her breasts and then forcefully pushes her down to her knees.

Lights out.

BOSS
Be really nice to me, bitch.

(END OF SCENE)

LUCÍA se muerde el labio y se queda quieta.

El JEFE se acerca comienza a masajearle sus senos y luego la empuja con fuerza para que se arrodille.

Luces apagadas.

JEFE
Se muy amable conmigo, perra.

(FIN DE ESCENA)

Scene VII-- Learning to Drive

SETTING:

NIGHT. LUCIA's apartment.

TIME: That evening. 1997

AT RISE:

KATIA is working on her homework. A box of partially eaten pizza is on the kitchen table.

LUCIA, looking defeated, enters.

KATIA jumps from the sofa to greet LUCIA.

KATIA
Mom! I'm so glad you're finally home! I've been waiting for you. I have to tell...

LUCIA
Not now, Katia. I'm really tired today.

KATIA
Katie, Mom. Katie. How many times do I have to tell you that I'm not Katia. I'm Katie.

LUCIA
You'll always be Katia.

KATIA
Ahh! You just don't understand anything!

> LUCIA puts her bag down, removes her coat and heads for the shower.

Escena VII – Aprendiendo a Conducir

Ambientación:

NOCHE. Apartamento de LUCÍA

Fecha: Esa noche. Año 1997

Telón:

KATIA esta trabajando en su tarea. Una caja de pizza parcialmente consumida está en la mesa de la cocina.

KATIA salta del sofá para saludar a LUCÍA.

KATIA
¡Mami! ¡Estoy feliz que finalmente llegaste a casa! Te he estado esperando. Tengo que contarte..

LUCÍA
Ahora no, Katia. Estoy muy cansada hoy.

KATIA
Katie, mami. Katie. Cuantas veces tengo que decirte que no soy Katia. Soy Katie.

LUCÍA
Siempre serás Katia.

KATIA
¡Ahh! ¡No entiendes nada!

> LUCÍA deja su bolso, se quita el abrigo y se va a ducharse.

> KATIA se va a la cocina y empieza a comer un pedazo de pizza.

KATIA goes to the kitchen and starts eating a piece of pizza.

After a long shower LUCIA enters with a robe and slippers.

KATIA (CONT'D)
That was a really long shower.

LUCIA
I am tired. Lemme rest for a minute.

LUCIA sits on the sofa, hugs a pillow, puts her feet up and closes her eyes.

A beat.

KATIA
Okay, did you rest enough?

LUCIA
(with eyes still closed)
What is it?

KATIA
I found the car I want to buy!

LUCIA
(opens her eyes, surprised)
A car?

KATIA
Yes, it's red. Exactly like I dreamed it!

LUCIA
What?

KATIA
It's a surprise! I've been saving all of my baby-sitting money for the last year for this. Henry and I are going to go see it tomorrow.

Después de una ducha larga, LUCIA entra con una bata y chancletas.

KATIA (continuación)
Esa fue una ducha realmente larga.

LUCÍA
Estoy cansada. Déjame descansar un minuto.

LUCIA se sienta en el sofá, abraza su almohada, levanta los pies y cierra sus ojos.

Una pausa.

KATIA
Okay, ¿ya descansaste lo suficiente?

LUCÍA
(con los ojos aun cerrados)
¿Qué es?

KATIA
¡Encontré el carro que quiero comprar!

LUCÍA
(abre los ojos, sorprendida)
¿Un carro?

KATIA
Sí. Es rojo. ¡Exactamente como los soñé!

LUCÍA
¿Qué?

KATIA
¡Es una sorpresa! He estado ahorrando todo el dinero que he recibido cuidando niños en el último año. Henry y yo lo vamos a ir a ver mañana.

LUCIA
Katia, are you crazy? You don't know how to drive!

KATIA
Oh! That's not a problem.

(she mimics driving)

Henry has been teaching me. I'm a fast learner. And I can get my driver's license in two weeks. When I turn seventeen. Henry is going to take me to take the test.

It'll be perfect!

LUCIA stands and begins to pace.

LUCIA
You can't get a driver's license.

KATIA
Why? You're not going to let me? ... You won't have to put in any money. I am paying for everything.

LUCIA
What about insurance? You have to buy insurance. Have you thought about that?

KATIA
Yes! I'll start tutoring after school. I can tutor math and biology. I figured that plus my weekend babysitting should be enough to pay for insurance and gas. Think about it, Mom, when my soccer team goes to tournaments we can drive, and it'll be cheaper... It's going to be awesome!

LUCÍA
Katia, ¿estás loca? ¡No sabes conducir!

KATIA
Oh! Eso no es un problema.

(imita conducir)

Henry me ha estado enseñando. He aprendido rápido. Y puedo conseguir mi licencia de conducir en dos semanas. Cuando cumpla diecisiete años. Henry me va a llevar a tomar el examen. ¡Va a ser perfecto!

LUCIA se pone de pie y comienza a caminar.

LUCÍA
No puedes conseguir una licencia de conducir.

KATIA
¿Por qué? ¿No me vas a dejar? ... No tendrás que poner dinero. Yo estoy pagando por todo.

LUCÍA
¿Qué es del seguro? Tienes que comprar seguro. ¿Haz pensado en eso?

KATIA
¡Sí! Voy a comenzar a dar clases particulares después del colegio. Puedo enseñar matemáticas y biología. Pensé que eso, más el cuidar niños los fines de semana será suficiente para pagar el seguro y la gasolina. Piénsalo, mama, cuando mi equipo de futbol vaya a los torneos podemos conducir, y será mas barato... ¡Va a ser increíble!

LUCIA
Katia, you can't get a driver's license.

KATIA
(hurt)
Mom, why are you being so mean? I thought you'd be happy for me. I never cause you any trouble. My grades are always good.

LUCIA sits.

KATIA (CONT'D)
I'll be able to drive you to the beach. See a sunrise. Like you've always talked about wanting to do. We'll do it, Mom.

LUCIA
Come here.

KATIA moves to sit next to LUCIA.

Katia, I'm not being mean. I just don't want you to get hurt. I'm trying to protect you.

KATIA
Mom, I'm older now. You know I'm very responsible. I'll be a really responsible driver. You'll never have to worry about me.

LUCIA
I know, mi amor. I know that you would be a very responsible driver. But you cannot get a driver's license.

KATIA
Why?

LUCIA
You need to show papers for that.

LUCÍA
Katia no puedes obtener una licencia de conducir.

KATIA
(herida)
Mamá, ¿porque estas siendo tan mala? Pensé que estarías feliz por mí. Nunca te causo problemas. Mis notas siempre son buenas.

LUCÍA se sienta.

KATIA (continuación)
Podré llevarte a la playa. Ver un amanecer. Lo que siempre haz hablado de querer hacer. Lo haremos, mami.

LUCÍA
Ven aquí.

KATIA se mueve para sentarse junto a LUCÍA.

Katia, no estoy siendo mala. Simplemente no quiero que te lastimes. Estoy tratando de protegerte.

KATIA
Mama, ahora soy mayor. Tu sabes que soy muy responsable. Voy a ser una conductora muy responsable. Nunca vas a tener que preocuparte de mí.

LUCÍA
Lo sé, mi amor. Se que serías una conductora muy responsable. Pero no puedes conseguir una licencia de conducir.

KATIA
¿Por qué?

KATIA
(confused)
What? Pedro and Cecilia have theirs and they're like us. What are you talking about?

LUCIA
The laws changed. When Pedro and Cecilia got their licenses, they didn't have to show papers.

KATIA
(springs off the sofa)
No! That can't be!

LUCIA
I'm sorry, mi'ja.

KATIA
No... it can't be. All my friends are getting their licenses. Everybody knows I've been saving for a car... What am I going to say now? ... Nobody in school knows. I've never told anybody.

LUCIA
Just tell them that I didn't let you get the car. Blame it on me.

KATIA
No driver's license. ... Mom, what's going to happen? What's going to happen to me? ... And what about Henry? I've never told him anything.

LUCIA
Calm down, mi'ja. We'll figure something out.

KATIA
Figure something out! Mom! What are you saying? You know you can't fix this!

LUCIA
You don't need to tell Henry anything.

LUCÍA
Para eso necesitas mostrar papeles.

KATIA
(confundida)
¿Qué? Pedro y Cecilia tienen las suyas, y son como nosotras. ¿De que estas hablando?

LUCÍA
Las leyes cambiaron. Cuando Pedro y Cecilia obtuvieron sus licencias, no tenían que mostrar papeles.

KATIA
(salta del sofá)
No, ... no puede ser. Todos mis amigos están consiguiendo sus licencias. Todos saben que he estado ahorrando para un carro. ¿Qué voy a decir ahora? Nadie en el colegio sabe. Nunca le he dicho nada a nadie.

LUCÍA
Solo diles que no te dejé comprar el auto. Échame a mi la culpa.

KATIA
Sin licencia de conducer. ... Mamá, ¿qué va a pasar? ¿Qué me va a pasar? ... ¿Y qué va a pasar con Henry? Nunca le he dicho nada.

LUCÍA
Cálmate mi'ja. Encontraremos una solución.

KATIA
¡Solución! ¡Mamá! ¿Qué estás diciendo? Sabes que no puedes arreglar esto.

LUCÍA
No necesitas decirle nada a Henry

KATIA
He'll ask non-stop until he gets an answer. He'll figure it out.

LUCIA
Tell him I am afraid of cars. That I absolutely will not let you drive a car. That my brother, your uncle, died in a bad car accident.

KATIA
(facial reaction)
My uncle?

LUCIA
Yes.

KATIA
We've been planning this for a long time. With a car I'll be able to visit him in college next semester.

LUCIA
You can still find a way to visit him. Nothing has changed.

KATIA
Why Mom? Why? ... I just want to be like everybody else... I hate this! I hate this life!

KATIA runs out of room.

(BLACKOUT)

(END OF SCENE)

KATIA
Me cuestionará sin parar hasta obtener una respuesta. Él lo averiguará.

LUCÍA
Dile que le tengo miedo a los carros. Que absolutamente no te dejaré conducir un automóvil. Que mi hermano, tu tío, murió en un terrible accidente automovilístico.

KATIA
(reacción facial)
¿Mi tío?

LUCÍA
Sí.

KATIA
Hemos estado planeando esto por mucho tiempo. Con un auto lo puedo visitar en la universidad el próximo semestre.

LUCÍA
Todavía puedes encontrar una manera de visitarlo. Nada ha cambiado.

KATIA
¿Por qué mamá? ¿Por qué? ... Solo quiero ser como todos los demás. ¡Odio esto! ¡Detesto esta vida!

KATIA sale corriendo.

(TELÓN)

(FIN DE ESCENA)

Scene VIII -- Goodbye

SETTING:

MORNING. LUCIA's apartment.

TIME: Several months later. 1997

AT RISE:

LUCIA is in the living room.

Phone rings.

RUBEN is audio only.

> RUBEN (V.O.)
> Lucía, he's gone.

> LUCIA
> Oh, God!

> RUBEN (V.O.)
> It was in his sleep. It was peaceful... I'm sorry, Lucía.

LUCIA sits and hugs a pillow, holding back crying.

> LUCIA
> Thank you, my friend.

> RUBEN (V.O.)
> I wish I could give you a hug.

> LUCIA
> Me too.

> RUBEN (V.O.)
> I've started making arrangements. When will you arrive?

LUCIA struggles with a painful decision in her head.

Escena VIII – Adiós

Ambientación:

MAÑANA. Apartamento de LUCÍA.

Fecha: Varios meses después. Año 1997

Telón:

LUCÍA esta en la sala de estar.

Suena el teléfono

RUBÉN es solo audio.

> RUBÉN (v.o.)
> Lucía, se ha ido.

> LUCÍA
> ¡Oh, Dios!

> RUBÉN (v.o.)
> Fue mientras dormía. Se fue tranquilo… Lo siento, Lucía.

LUCÍA se sienta y abraza una almohada, conteniendo el llanto.

> LUCÍA
> Gracias, amigo.

> RUBÉN (v.o.)
> Quisiera poder darte un abrazo.

> LUCÍA
> Yo también.

> RUBÉN (v.o.)
> He comenzado a hacer arreglos. ¿Cuándo llegarás?

LUCÍA lucha con una decisión dolorosa en su cabeza.

RUBEN (CONT'D)
Everybody in the neighborhood will be waiting with a hug. You know everybody loved your father. There are a lot of decisions that need to be made. Who do you want as pallbearers? The funeral home is waiting for... Lucía, are you still there?

LUCIA
Yeah.

RUBEN (V.O.)
I'm sorry, I know it's a lot to process right now. I'll hold things off till you arrive. When do you think you will be here? Tomorrow? Or Friday?

LUCIA
I ... I can't Ruben.

RUBEN (V.O.)
What do you mean?

LUCIA
I … can't… I can't leave.

> A beat.

RUBEN (V.O.)
I understand.

LUCIA
I'll send money.

RUBEN (V.O.)
I'll take care of everything.

LUCIA
Please make sure it's a beautiful casket... and that there're lots of flowers.

RUBEN (V.O.)
I will. Don't worry.

RUBÉN (v.o.)
Lucía, Lucía, ¿estas ahí?

LUCÍA
Yo… no puedo. No puedo ir.

> Una pausa.

RUBÉN (v.o.)
Entiendo.

LUCÍA
Enviaré dinero.

RUBÉN (v.o.)
Yo me encargaré de todo.

LUCÍA
Por favor, asegúrate que sea un hermoso ataúd… y que haya muchas flores.

RUBÉN (v.o.)
Lo haré. No te preocupes.

LUCÍA
Amaba su jardín.

RUBÉN (v.o.)
Sí. Pasé muy buenos momentos con el bajo el árbol de aguacate.

LUCÍA
¿Su pequeña planta se convirtió en un árbol?

RUBÉN (v.o.)
Sí. Un bello árbol. Todos los años está cargado de fruta. Y todos los años le ayudaba a recoger la fruta y llevarla al Centro Comunitario. Lo donaba todo.

LUCÍA
Rubén, no sabía a lo que estaba renunciando cuando me fui.

LUCIA
He loved his garden.

RUBEN (V.O.)
Yes. I spent some good times with him under the avocado tree.

LUCIA
His little plant grew into a tree?

RUBEN (V.O.)
Yes. A beautiful one. Every year it's loaded with fruit. And every year I'd help him pick the fruit and take it to the Community Center. He donated it all.

LUCIA
Ruben, I didn't know what I was giving up when I left.

RUBEN (V.O.)
He waited for you to come home. I think that hope is what kept him alive the last few years. Hoping to see you and Katia one more time.

LUCIA
I didn't know. I didn't understand. I didn't realize how much I stole from him.

RUBEN (V.O.)
Lucía, what do you want me to do with your father's things? With your things?

LUCIA
I don't know. I don't know if I'll ever be able to come back.

LIGHTS start dimming.

RUBÉN (v.o.)
Espero a que volvieras a casa. Creo que esa esperanza es lo que lo mantuvo vivo los últimos anos. Esperando verte a ti y a Katia una vez más.

LUCÍA
No lo sabía. No lo entendí. No me di cuenta de cuanto le robé.

RUBÉN (v.o.)
Lucia, ¿qué quieres que haga con las cosas de tu papá? ¿Con tus cosas?

LUCÍA
No lo sé. No sé si alguna vez podré volver.

Las luces comienzan a bajar.

RUBÉN (v.o.)
Sé que querría que guardaras al menos sus libros y sus fotos. Guardaras sus memorias …. tus memorias.

(TELÓN)

(FIN DE ESCENA)

RUBEN (V.O.)
I know he would have wanted you to save at least his books and his pictures. Save his memories... your memories, Lucia.

(BLACKOUT)

(END OF SCENE)

Scene IX -- The End of the Road

SETTING:

MORNING. American Consulate.

The American flag and the framed picture of President George W. Bush are prominently displayed. A U.S. MARINE stands close to the CLERK's window.

TIME: 2004

AT RISE:

A much older RUBEN is standing at the counter. A young, cheerful CONSULAR CLERK is behind the glass.

          CONSULAR CLERK
Number?

          RUBEN
343455

          CLERK inputs number.

          RUBEN
          (excited, shows a letter)
I received this letter, to come today.

          CONSULAR CLERK
Yes, Mr. Garcia Martinez, we need to inform you that the office of Immigration and Naturalization Services has ceased to exist. Now, all matters of immigration to the United States are being handled by the Office of Homeland Security.

Escena IX – El Final del Camino

Ambientación:

MAÑANA. Consulado Americano.
La bandera estadounidense y la imagen del presidente George W. Bush se muestr prominentemente. Un MARINE esta parado cerca de la ventanilla.

Fecha: Año 2004

Telón:

Un RUBEN mucho mayor esta parado en la ventanilla. Un joven y alegre SECRETARIO CONSULAR está detrás del vidrio.

          SECRETARIO CONSULAR
¿Número?

          RUBÉN
343455

          SECRETARIO CONSULAR
          ingresa el número.

          RUBÉN
          (entusiasmado muestra una carta)
Recibí esta carta para venir hoy.

          SECRETARIO CONSULAR
Si, Sr. García Martínez, necesitamos informarle que la oficina de Servicios de Inmigración y Naturalización ha dejado de existir. Ahora todos los asuntos de inmigración a los Estados Unidos están siendo manejados por la oficina de Seguridad Nacional.

RUBEN
What does that mean?

CONSULAR CLERK
It means that your application is being transferred to Homeland Security and I am going to assign you a new number. Let's see... your file number is now 100-391-672.

RUBEN
I don't understand. That's a bigger number. Did I get pushed further down the waiting list?

CONSULAR CLERK
No, no, nothing has changed. Your application is still on the same spot in the waiting list.

RUBEN
I've been waiting a long time.

CONSULAR CLERK
(looking at the computer screen)
Yes, looking at your wait time. I suspect you're almost there.

RUBEN
Almost? What does that mean?

CONSULAR CLERK
It means that we should update your file today. To get you ready to come interview soon. Let's see, do you have an updated health certificate?

RUBEN
I had one done when I applied.

RUBÉN
¿Qué significa eso?

SECRETARIO CONSULAR
Significa que su solicitud ha sido transferida a Seguridad Nacional y le voy a asignar un nuevo número. Veamos… su numero de archivo es ahora 100-391-672.

RUBÉN
No entiendo. Ese número es mas grande. ¿Me empujaron mas abajo en la lista de espera?

SECRETARIO CONSULAR
No, no, nada ha cambiado. Su solicitud esta en el mismo lugar en la lista de espera.

RUBÉN
He estado esperando mucho tiempo.

SECRETARIO CONSULAR
(mirando la pantalla de la computadora)
Sí, mirando su tiempo de espera, sospecho que ya casi esta ahí.

RUBÉN
¿Casi? ¿Qué significa eso?

SECRETARIO CONSULAR
Significa que debemos actualizar su archivo hoy. Para prepararlo para su próxima entrevista A ver, ¿tiene su certificado de salud actualizado?

RUBÉN
Tenia uno cuando presente mi solicitud.

CONSULAR CLERK
We need a current one in the file. It can't be over a year old. You must have a complete physical, and it must now include an HIV test. Can you get that done?

RUBEN
I'll go to the hospital tomorrow.

CONSULAR CLERK
Interpol clearance and national police clearance certificates?

RUBEN
I had those done when I applied.

CONSULAR CLERK
Once again, they're too old. You need to get current certificates. There's now an additional FBI clearance, but that will be done internally.

RUBEN
Okay.

CONSULAR CLERK
Has your civil status changed?

RUBEN
No.

CONSULAR CLERK
Do you have a common-law partner?

RUBEN
No.

CONSULAR CLERK
Children?

RUBEN
None.

SECRETARIO CONSULAR
Necesitamos uno actual en el archivo. No puede tener más de un año. Debe tener un examen físico completo, y ahora debe incluir una prueba de Sida. ¿Puede hacer eso?

RUBÉN
Iré al hospital mañana.

SECRETARIO CONSULAR
¿Certificados de Interpol y de la policía nacional?

RUBÉN
Lo hice cuando presente mi solicitud.

SECRETARIO CONSULAR
Una vez más, son demasiado viejos. Necesita obtener certificados actuales. Ahora hay una autorización adicional del FBI, pero eso se hará internamente.

RUBÉN
Okay.

SECRETARIO CONSULAR
¿Su estado civil ha cambiado?

RUBÉN
No.

SECRETARIO CONSULAR
¿Tiene una pareja con quien no tiene un matrimonio oficial?

RUBÉN
No.

SECRETARIO CONSULAR
¿Hijos?

RUBÉN
Ninguno.

CONSULAR CLERK
No children?

RUBEN
No.

A beat.

CONSULAR CLERK
We'll also need to see your tax filings for the last five years. And a letter from your current employer.

RUBEN
I'm self-employed.

CONSULAR CLERK
Oh! ... I see here that when you applied you listed a school as your employer. You're no longer working there?

RUBEN
No. I'm a taxi driver now.

CONSULAR CLERK
Well, that's a bit of a problem. We need to have proof of financial resources. Self-employed does not make it. *(a pause)* Do you have anybody in the United States that can guarantee you? Somebody that can support you financially in the event that you can't?

RUBEN
Umm.... I have a good friend, Lucía Medina. She lives there.

CONSULAR CLERK
Is Ms. Medina gainfully employed?

RUBEN
Yes. She works.

SECRETARIO CONSULAR
¿Ningún hijo?

RUBÉN
No.

Una pausa.

SECRETARIO CONSULAR
También necesitaremos ver sus declaraciones de impuestos de los últimos cinco años. Y una carta de su actual empleador.

RUBÉN
Trabajo independientemente.

SECRETARIO CONSULAR
¡Oh! ... veo aquí que cuando puso su solicitud puso usted un colegio como su empleador. ¿Ya no trabaja ahí?

RUBÉN
No, ahora soy taxista.

SECRETARIO CONSULAR
Bueno eso es un poco problemático. Necesitamos tener pruebas de recursos financieros. Ser trabajador independiente no califica. (una pausa) ¿Tiene alguien en los Estados Unidos que pueda garantizar por usted? ¿Alguien que le pueda apoyar financieramente en caso de que usted no pueda?

RUBÉN
Umm... Tengo una buena amiga, Lucía Medina Ella vive allí.

SECRETARIO CONSULAR
¿La señora Medina tiene un empleo remunerado?

RUBÉN
Sí. Ella trabaja.

CONSULAR CLERK
Then. Ms. Medina has to write a letter on your behalf. She must state that she will be financially responsible for you, in the event that you are unable to support yourself.

RUBEN
She won't have a problem doing that for me.

CONSULAR CLERK
Okay, Mr. García Martinez, you have a lot of work to do. When the time comes, the interview will be conducted here. It'll be a three-hour interview.

RUBEN
Three hours!

CONSULAR CLERK
It's a detailed interview. Be prepared to answer some very personal questions. Do you have any questions now?

RUBEN
No.

CONSULAR CLERK
Oh! Did I mention that your sponsor... this Ms. ... Medina, she has to be a U.S. citizen. Is she a citizen?

RUBEN
I... don't know.

CONSULAR CLERK
If she's not a citizen, you'll have to find somebody else.

RUBEN
Oh, Okay.

SECRETARIO CONSULAR
Entonces la señora Medina tiene que escribir una carta en su nombre. Ella debe declarar que será financieramente responsable de usted, en caso de que usted no pueda mantenerse por sí mismo.

RUBÉN
Ella no tendrá problema de hacer eso por mí.

SECRETARIO CONSULAR
Okay, Sr. García Martínez, tiene bastante trabajo que hacer. Cuando el momento llegue, la entrevista será aquí. Será una entrevista de tres horas.

RUBÉN
¡Tres horas!

SECRETARIO CONSULAR
Es una entrevista detallada. Prepárese para responder a preguntas bastante personales. ¿Tiene alguna pregunta ahora?

RUBÉN
No.

SECRETARIO CONSULAR
¡Oh! mencione que su patrocinador… esta señora… Medina, tiene que ser una ciudadana Americana. ¿Es una ciudadana?

RUBÉN
Yo… no sé.

SECRETARIO CONSULAR
Si ella no es ciudadana, tendrá que buscar a alguien mas.

RUBÉN
Oh, okay.

CONSULAR CLERK
Mr. Garcia Martinez, it's always a pleasure to work with people that do things the right way. On behalf of the United States of America, I thank you for your patience.

> RUBEN walks away from the window and sticks his manila envelope in the trash bin as he exits.

(BLACKOUT)

(END OF SCENE)

SECRETARIO CONSULAR
Sr. García Martínez siempre es un placer trabajar con personas que hacen las cosas correctamente. En nombre de los Estados Unidos de América, le agradezco su paciencia.

> RUBEN se aleja de la ventanilla y mete su sobre de manila en el contenedor de basura cuando sale.

(TELÓN)

(FIN DE ESCENA)

Scene X -- The Avocado Tree

SETTING:

DAY. LUCIA's apartment.

AT RISE: LUCIA is sitting in the living room looking at a picture of DON FRANCISCO.

                LUCIA
I miss you. I'm sorry, Father.

                KATIA enters carrying a backpack.

                LUCIA
What's with the backpack? Are you going somewhere?

                KATIA
Away from this town.

                LUCIA
What?

                KATIA
I'm leaving. I bought papers with the money I'd saved for the car.

                LUCIA
You did what?

                KATIA
Got a driver's license and a social security card.

                LUCIA
Katia, what're you doing? You're going to get in trouble!

                KATIA
You're worried I'm breaking the law? Really?

Escena X – El Árbol de Aguacate

Ambientación:

DÍA. Apartamento de LUCÍA.

Telón: LUCÍA esta sentada en la sala de estar mirando una foto de DON FRANCISCO.

                LUCÍA
Te extraño. Lo siento, papá.

                KATIA entra con una mochila.

                LUCÍA
¿Qué hay con la mochila? ¿Vas a alguna parte?

                KATIA
Lejos de esta ciudad.

                LUCÍA
¿Qué?

                KATIA
Me voy. Compré papeles con el dinero que había ahorrado para el carro.

                LUCÍA
¿Hiciste qué?

                KATIA
Obtuve una licencia de conducir y una tarjeta de seguro social.

                LUCÍA
Katia, ¿qué estas haciendo? ¡Te vas a meter en problemas!

                KATIA
¿Te preocupa de que este infringiendo la ley? ¿De a verdad?

LUCIA
You're still a teenager! You can't just go. You're not eighteen!

KATIA
Seventeen, eighteen. Who cares. My new driver's license says I'm twenty-one. Legally an adult.

LUCIA
Katia, you're over-reacting. You haven't thought this through. What about your future? College? Your dream to become a doctor? You have a scholarship!

KATIA
Not anymore.

> KATIA hands LUCIA an opened envelope.

LUCIA
What's this? From the University?
(opening the letter)
What does it say? You know my English is bad.
(returns letter to KATIA)

KATIA
They're taking back my scholarship.

LUCIA
What? Why?

KATIA
It's only for citizens.

LUCIA
Oh, no! Is there anything we can do? Anybody we can talk to?

KATIA
No.

LUCÍA
¡Todavía eres una adolescente! No te puedes simplemente ir. ¡No tienes dieciocho años!

KATIA
Diecisiete, dieciocho. A quien le importa. Mi nueva licencia de conducir dice que tengo veintiuno. Legalmente una adulta.

LUCÍA
Katia, estas reaccionado de forma exagerada. No has pensado esto. ¿Qué es de tu futuro? ¿La universidad? ¿Tu sueño de ser médico? ¡Tienes una beca!

KATIA
Ya no.

> KATIA le entrega a LUCÍA un sobre abierto.

LUCÍA
¿Qué es esto? ¿De la universidad?
(abriendo la carta)
¿Qué dice? Sabes que mi inglés es malo
(devuelve la carta a KATIA)

KATIA
Me están quitando mi beca.

LUCÍA
¿Qué? ¿Por qué?

KATIA
Es solo para ciudadanos.

LUCÍA
¡Oh, no! ¿Hay algo que podamos hacer? ¿Alguien con quien podamos hablar?

KATIA
No.

KATIA stuffs a few more items in her backpack.

LUCIA
There's got to be something we can do! They can't do this to you!

KATIA
They can. And they have.

A beat.

LUCIA
Katia, listen, we can do it. You can still go to the University. Study. I'll help you with the tuition.

KATIA
Mom, be real. We could never afford to pay tuition.

LUCIA
I'll get a second job, and you can work after school. Take a second shift.

(she picks up a hollow statue of a Virgin and pulls 100 dollar bills from the inside)

I've been putting aside a little money every month for you. For your education. This'll help you get in. We can make it. You'll become a doctor!

KATIA
Keep it. You've worked hard for it.

LUCIA
It's for you! For us!

KATIA guarda algunos artículos mas en su mochila.

LUCÍA
¡Tiene que haber algo que podamos hacer! ¡No te pueden hacer esto!

KATIA
Pueden. Y lo han hecho.

Una pausa.

LUCÍA
Katia, escucha, podemos hacerlo. Tu todavía puedes ir a la universidad. Estudiar. Yo te voy a ayudar con la matrícula.

KATIA
Mamá, se real. Nunca podríamos pagar la matrícula.

LUCÍA
Conseguiré un segundo trabajo, y tú puedes trabajar después de tus clases. Tomar un segundo turno.

(agarra una estatua hueca de una Virgen y saca billetes de cien dólares de dentro)

He estado guardando un poquito de dinero cada mes para ti. Para tu educación. Esto te ayudará a entrar. Podemos hacerlo. ¡Vas a ser doctora!

KATIA
Guárdalo. Has trabajado duro para eso.

LUCÍA
¡Es para ti! ¡Para nosotras!

KATIA
Mom, even if somehow we managed, I'd become a doctor that could never practice. What would be the point of that?

A beat.

LUCIA
Mi'ja, one day they'll pass that law that gives children like you papers. Just wait!

KATIA
You're dreaming, Mom. It's not going to happen.

LUCIA
Katia, you can't just give up!

KATIA
And what do you suggest I do?

A beat.

LUCIA
What about Henry? Are you leaving him too?

KATIA
No. He already did that. Saved me the trouble.

LUCIA
He left you? Why?

KATIA
Why? Because I can't lie like you. And because his father pointed out to him that no one has ever been elected to Congress with an illegal resident as a gardener. He'll never have a chance with a spouse.

KATIA
Mamá, incluso si de alguna manera lo lográramos, me convertiría en una médico que nunca podría ejercer. ¿Para que vale eso?

Una pausa.

LUCÍA
Mi'ja un día aprobarán esa ley que da a los niños como tú, papeles ¡Solo espera!

KATIA
Estas sonando, mama. No va a suceder.

LUCÍA
Katia, ¡no puedes simplemente rendirte!

KATIA
¿Y qué sugieres que haga?

Una pausa.

LUCÍA
¿Y que es de Henry? ¿Lo estas dejando a él también?

KATIA
No. Él ya lo hizo. Me ahorró el problema.

LUCÍA
¿Te dejó? ¿Por qué?

KATIA
¿Por qué? Porque no puedo mentir como tu. Y porque su padre le señaló que nadie ha sido elegido al Congreso con un jardinero indocumentado. Nunca tendría una oportunidad con un cónyuge indocumentado.

LUCIA
I thought his parents liked you?

           KATIA reacts with a "whatever" motion.

Weren't you always helping him with his papers?

KATIA
I guess he'll have to learn to do his own work now.

LUCIA
I thought he loved you.

KATIA
He loved Katie, Mom.

           A beat.

LUCIA
Forget Henry. You're beautiful and bright...

KATIA
Mom! Mom! Stop!

LUCIA
You'll be a great doctor…

KATIA
(interrupting LUCIA)
You don't get it do you? A career. I'll never have that. I'll never be a doctor. I've accepted that. You have to learn to accept it, too. *(a beat)* My time in school was a dream.

LUCIA
You're young, and it all feels dark right now, but someday the tide will turn.

LUCÍA
¿Pensé que les gustabas a sus padres?

           KATIA reacciona con un movimiento de indiferencia.

¿No era que siempre lo estabas ayudando con sus papeles?

KATIA
Supongo que ahora tendrá que aprender a hacer su propio trabajo.

LUCÍA
Pensé que te amaba.

KATIA
Amaba a Katie, mamá.

           Una pausa.

LUCÍA
Olvídate de Henry. Eres hermosa y brillante.

KATIA
¡Mamá! ¡Mamá! ¡Para!

LUCÍA
Serás una gran médico.

KATIA
(interrumpiendo a LUCIA)
No lo entiendes, ¿verdad? Una carrera. Nunca tendré eso. Nunca voy a ser médico. Yo lo he aceptado. Tú tienes que aprender a aceptarlo también. *(una pausa)* Mi tiempo en el colegio fue un sueño.

LUCÍA
Eres joven, y todo se ve oscuro en este momento, pero un día la suerte va a cambiar.

KATIA
Turn? When will it turn, Mom? *(a pause)* I've lived most of my life here. This is all I know. English is all I speak... but I will never, NEVER be able to call this my country... Why did you bring me here?

LUCIA
Katia, I did it for you! I wanted you to have a chance for a better life.

KATIA
I wish you never had.

> KATIA puts on her coat.

LUCIA
I wanted you to live without fear.

KATIA
It's too hard to watch my friends get accepted to college. ... I'll be okay, Mom. Bye, for now.

> KATIA gives a rigid LUCIA a good-bye hug and exits. LUCIA sits on the sofa burdened.

LUCIA (V.O.)
I cannot turn on the lights for you Katia... I cannot protect you from the monsters of the night.

> LIGHTS dim on LUCIA.
> LIGHTS on the avocado tree.

KATIA
¿Cambiar? ¿Cuándo va a cambiar, mama? *(una pausa)* He vivido casi toda mi vida aquí. Esto es todo lo que conozco. Inglés es lo único que hablo... pero nunca, NUNCA podré llamar este mi país... ¿Por qué me trajiste aquí?

LUCÍA
Katia, ¡lo hice por ti! Quería que tuvieras una oportunidad a una vida mejor.

KATIA
Desearía que nunca lo hubieras hecho.

> KATIA se pone su saco.

LUCÍA
Quería que vivas sin miedo.

KATIA
Es demasiado difícil ver a mis amigos ser aceptados a la universidad. Voy a estar bien, mamá. Adiós, por ahora.

> KATIA le da un abrazo rígido a LUCÍA y sale. LUCIA se sienta en el sofá agobiada.

LUCÍA (v. o.)
No puedo encender las luces para ti Katia. No puedo protegerte de los monstruos de la noche.

> Las luces bajan en LUCÍA.

LIGHTS up on LUCIA's apartment. An older KATIA enters wearing a "READY CLEAN" smock and carrying a lunch box. The smock is a different color than what LUCIA wore previously. KATIA sets the lunch box on the table and removes an avocado pit.
KATIA sets the pit on a pot and then sets the pot on the windowsill.

(BLACKOUT)

(END OF SCENE. END OF ACT II. END OF PLAY.)

Las luces iluminan el árbol de aguacate.

Luces en el apartamento de LUCÍA. Una KATIA mayor entra usando un uniforme de "READY CLEAN" y cargando una lonchera. El uniforme es de diferente color al que usaba LUCÍA anteriormente. KATIA pone su lonchera en la mesa y saca una pepa de aguacate.

KATIA pone la pepa del aguacate en una maceta y la pone en el alfeizar de la ventana.

(TELÓN)

(FIN DE ESCENA.
FINAL DE SEGUNDO ACTO. FIN.)

HER OWN DEVICES FOREWORD

Her Own Devices by Lindsay Adams Kennedy is a story that explores the complex interplay between the mind and the body, and the power of imagination to shape our reality. In an unspecified time and place, Madeleine, a young girl born with a mysterious and powerful autoimmune disorder, has spent her entire life in a lab as a test subject, with her doctors still no closer to finding a cure. Meanwhile, every night the King of Germs visits her in her dreams and tries to touch her with his contaminating hand. She enlists the help of her imaginary friend, the Robot, to fight him off and soon must make a choice whether to leave the only home she's ever known. *Her Own Devices* is a world of robots and nightmares, lab coats and Samba dances that explores the power of imagination in a young girl who refuses to be defined by her disability. It is a poignant reminder of the resilience of the human spirit, and the importance of holding onto hope even in the darkest of times.

Her Own Devices was first workshopped through KCPublic's Theatre Lab as a staged reading in March 2018 at the Uptown Arts Bar. The play had its world premiere production a year later in May 2019, in partnership with Charlotte Street Foundation at their former studio space, Capsule. The original production was directed by Elizabeth Bettendorf Bowman with the following cast:

MADELEINE: Tehreem Chaudhry
GEORGE: Briana Marxen-McCollum
BOYLE/KING OF GERMS: Ryan Fortney
ROBOT: Kaitlin Gould
ALAYNA/HORDE OF HANDS: Deanna Barron

Her Own Devices

A Play

By: Lindsay Adams Kennedy

CAST OF CHARACTERS

MADELEINE: 11. Female. Any Race. She may be played by an adult.

GEORGE: Madeleine's doctor. 25-35. Female. Any Race.

BOYLE: Madeleine's doctor. 30-40. Male. Any Race.

ROBOT: Madeleine's imaginary friend. Ageless. Genderless.

KING OF GERMS: Non-speaking. A spectre that haunts Madeleine's dreams. Doubled with Boyle.

ALAYNA: Madeleine's mother. 25-29. Female. Any Race.

HORDE OF HANDS: Non-speaking. The King of Germs' minions. A movement ensemble of actors/dancers, they are like a single organism, moving as one. They can be doubled with George and Alayna. If not doubled, two actors/dancers are needed, but more may be cast as wanted.

NOTE ON DIALOGUE:

A slash (/) in dialogue indicates that the next line should overlap starting at the slash. Madeleine's monologues early in the play should be anything but heavy. She loves words, they are her nearest and dearest friends in her cell, and she finds joy and vibrancy in wordplay. Her very first monologue, for example, is just an introduction. You or I would say, "Hello, nice to meet you." Instead, Madeleine says, "I am Tarzan." Do not try to play the drama of the situation. The words are Madeleine's, and like her they are brilliant and funny and curious and sometimes surprisingly matter-of-fact.

NOTE ON CASTING:

Any race does not mean white. The cast of this play should be diverse.

SETTING:

An Observation Lab and a Cell.

TIME:

The Close Future.

SCENE 1

A ray of light falls on Madeleine, sitting cross-legged with her eyes closed.

She is surrounded by darkness.

She talks to us.

MADELEINE

I am Tarzan. I am transplant.
I am the boy in the bubble.
I am insignificant. I signify nothing. I am nothing.
I am full of the sound and the fury of these four white sanitized walls.
I am raised in the wild of their viewing station.
I went from a womb to a plastic tub.
I am tainted.

Madeleine opens her eyes and looks around.
A song like Elvis Presley's "Surrender" plays.

I know you're here.

The circle of light widens, revealing the rest of her cell. To one side there is a pile of robotic equipment and pieces of metal. In any other circumstances it could be called a pile of debris, but all the pieces are shiny and seem new.

To the other side, the King of Germs is revealed, dressed in a dark coat that falls to his feet.

He doesn't speak.

MADELEINE (CONT'D)
Don't touch me. Stay away. Leave me alone.

He bows to her.

He holds his hand out, asking her to dance.

His fingers are syringes.

She steps back.

He reaches his arm around her.

Without touching, they dance a samba of sorts.

The dance gains urgency, becoming more and more frenetic.

Madeleine breaks away.

He holds out his hand to her again.

She shakes her head.

He beckons her back.

No!

He dances alone now, all by himself.

For the Grand Finale, he knee slides toward her.

Madeleine backs away.

His heart breaks. He clutches it, falling back wounded.

A heartbeat. Insistent. The song underscores its beating.

Human hands appear all around Madeleine, reaching out to touch her.
Falling, leaping, crawling to escape them, she falls to the ground.

As they close in around her, she screams.

The lights shift and she is awake, clutching a tiny toy robot, featureless and round.

George is revealed standing outside the cell behind glass.

GEORGE
Madeleine. Hello. Are you alright?

Madeleine sees and hears George but chooses to ignore her.

MADELEINE
I don't know who I am.

GEORGE
You were screaming.

MADELEINE
Is that normal?

They tell me that everyone is trying to find who they are.

That that's a thing that people do? Like they lost themselves somehow.

GEORGE
I guess it's only fair I tell you my name, since I know yours.
You can call me George.

MADELEINE
Maybe that's why they watch me?

GEORGE
I just wanted to introduce myself.

MADELEINE
They figured out who they are so now they want to figure me out too.

But they won't. I won't let them.

GEORGE
Madeleine, I'm not trying to... That's not why I'm here.

MADELEINE
They think I'm crazy. But I'm not.

I'm smarter than all of them.

GEORGE
Nobody thinks you're crazy.

MADELEINE
They always lie to me too.

Like I can't tell.

GEORGE
I'm not lying. I don't think you're crazy.

MADELEINE
(to George for the first time)
You don't know anything.

GEORGE
Then explain it to me. What was the nightmare about?

MADELEINE
Him.

GEORGE
Who's him?

Madeleine, was it a monster?

MADELEINE
Soon, I won't need any of you anymore.

GEORGE
What do you mean?

> Madeleine turns away from George.

Look, Madeleine. I'm going to go.

Just for a second, so that I can call someone to come help you.

MADELEINE
Help me? He never helps.

GEORGE
I'll be right back, alright?

...

I promise.

Will you be alright by yourself?

MADELEINE
I'm never by myself.

GEORGE
...

I'll be right back.

> George exits.

MADELEINE
They say they want to help.

Help with needles and walls and lasers and scanners and watching watching watching....
Sometimes I wonder what's wrong with all these people that they don't have anything better to do than watch me.

Adults are strange. Sometimes I watch. I can watch too.

I pick a spot and stare at it. Until they ask me what's wrong. What I'm looking at.

And I just tell them nothing.

> She stares intently at a spot.
>
> Boyle enters outside the cell.

BOYLE
Madeleine.

MADELEINE
What?

BOYLE
Please stop staring at the wall.

MADELEINE
But I'm not staring at the wall.

BOYLE
Then what are you staring at?

MADELEINE
Nothing.

> Then he breathes slowly. Like he's barely restraining a sigh.

BOYLE
Madeleine.

MADELEINE
Yes.

BOYLE
You have to stop narrating our conversations.

MADELEINE
He said with a furrowed brow.

BOYLE
(firmly)
Stop.

MADELEINE
But I understand them better that way.

BOYLE
They're going to think you're crazy.

MADELEINE
I'm not crazy.

BOYLE
I hope they agree about that.

MADELEINE
They?

BOYLE
Since you're awake.

Time for your morning checkup.

> Scanners turn on and go off in the cell. The light runs up and down Madeleine.

Arms out.

MADELEINE
What do you think?

BOYLE
About what?

MADELEINE
Me.

BOYLE
Touch your hands to your forehead.

MADELEINE
Do you think I'm crazy?

BOYLE
I need you to look at the finger I'm holding up.

Concentrate on it. Hold it.

MADELEINE
Do you think I'm crazy?

BOYLE
No crazier than us.

MADELEINE
Crazy. Is that the medical term for that condition?

BOYLE
You are so very funny, Madeleine.

MADELEINE
Then again. Crazy is a very subjective term.

BOYLE
Talking to yourself is generally considered crazy.

Across the board.

> The scanners retreat.

Alright.

Everything is looking good.

MADELEINE
You sure about that?

BOYLE
Your morning rations are right here.

> Boyle places food into the chute. His side closes.

A whir as the item's plastic cover is sanitized.

Madeleine's side opens.

Be back later. Don't get into any trouble when I'm gone, okay?

He exits.

MADELEINE
He says that every time. He thinks it's funny. It's not.
He doesn't know I have a plan.

BOYLE
(over loudspeaker)
You know that I can still hear you. What are you talking about?

MADELEINE
Things. You wouldn't understand.

BOYLE
(over loudspeaker)
Okay, then. Who are you talking to?

MADELEINE
I have been working and working and it's ready.

Looks at the toy robot.

Well, almost.

BOYLE
(over loudspeaker)
Madeleine.

MADELEINE
I won't get in any trouble. Okay?
That was a lie. I'm definitely going to get into trouble. But I'm not going to tell him that.

I hate him.

BOYLE
(over loudspeaker)
The talking to yourself thing. It's gotta stop. I'm just a click away. If you need anything.

MADELEINE
I know.

BOYLE
(over loudspeaker)
Just stop talking to yourself.

MADELEINE
Don't worry. I'll tell the voices in my head to be quiet.

BOYLE
(over loudspeaker)
Madeleine ...

MADELEINE
Kidding. But I'm not kidding.

I see things differently than some people.

I see pieces.

I see how things fit and how they break and how really everything is just working to keep the pieces fitting.

People don't seem to understand any of that. But I understand.

That's how I made you.

She goes to the pile of machinery and fits the toy robot into a perfectly shaped nook at the top of the pile.

Now you're finally ready.

MADELEINE (CONT'D)
After all the work putting you together.
Every last piece fits.

And all I have to do is wind you up and
you'll be here to help me. To protect me. She
starts to crank a piece that is sticking out.

> Almost like winding a clock
> or a music box.

They're there. All around me.

The pathogens. They're just waiting. Waiting
for me to mess up.

But now I have backup. And now I'll be safe.
Right?

> A voice comes from the pile
> of machinery.

ROBOT
Beep. Boop. Blop.

MADELEINE
Exactly.

> She finishes cranking. The
> pile moves. An arm appears,
> then a head. The crumpled-
> up pile transforms into a
> humanoid robot.

I have always been left to my own devices.

Mostly because devices are the only things
that won't kill me.

Do you want to know a secret? I have never
sneezed ever. Never ever.

I have always wondered what it would be
like to sneeze.
> Ha-choo Ha-choo.

Bless you.

ROBOT
Thanks.

MADELEINE
Do you know what sterile means?

It means dead.

It means nothing can grow in here. It means
anything else in here...

> Mimes death, one hand
> across neck.

I am the destroyer of worlds.

The only way I'm alive is if everything else
in here is dead.

I don't exist outside of these walls, but
everything else doesn't exist in here, so I
guess it all evens out.
Kinda. Sorta. Not really.

ROBOT
Ster-ile.

MADELEINE
Sterilization.

ROBOT
Ster-il-i-za-tion.

MADELEINE
Noun.
The process by which all living
microorganisms including bacterial spores
are killed.

ROBOT
Oh.

MADELEINE
It's also four syllables.

ROBOT
Oh.

MADELEINE
That's why you're here.

ROBOT
I am here.

MADELEINE
Not because of the syllables.

Because of the germs. They want revenge.

They're coming to get me because of all their brethren I've accidentally killed.

I need backup when that happens.

ROBOT
It happens.

MADELEINE
That's where you come in. I need help to defeat them.

ROBOT
Who are you?

MADELEINE
Oh, I didn't introduce myself.
I'm Nobody! Who are you?

ROBOT
Nobody?

MADELEINE
Wait, you're Nobody too? That's going to get confusing.

They call me Madeleine.

ROBOT
Madeleine.

MADELEINE
I guess you can too.

BOYLE
(over loudspeaker)
Madeleine, who are you talking to?

MADELEINE
Nobody.

BOYLE
(over loudspeaker)
That's reassuring.

SCENE 2
The Observation Lab.

Boyle and George sit at computers.

There is a minifridge and a mountain of paperwork.

Madeleine can be faintly seen moving around her cell.

They have monitors around the space to watch Madeleine, as well as a window that looks into the cell.

They are able to watch and listen to Madeleine, but she is unable to see or hear those in the Lab, unless they talk to her over the loudspeaker.

Boyle grabs a yogurt from a minifridge and starts eating.

GEORGE
I didn't mean to cause a problem.

BOYLE
You didn't.

GEORGE
I just didn't know what to do.
She wasn't responding to me so I thought I should notify you.
I mean it is procedure.

BOYLE
Sure. Procedure. Right.

GEORGE
It just seemed irregular.

BOYLE
I wish.
But no, she actually does it pretty often.

GEORGE
Interesting.

BOYLE
Not really, but you're new.

GEORGE
So, she routinely talks to herself?

BOYLE
Uh-huh.

GEORGE
Anything else I should know?

BOYLE
Well, she doesn't sleep well.

GEORGE
Yeah, I picked up on that.

BOYLE
Nightmares. Been getting worse just recently.

GEORGE
Have you prescribed anything?

BOYLE
(shakes head)
They want us to let it play out.
I'll go in with you for the next check-up.
Try and ease the transition.
A mouthful of yogurt.
What?

GEORGE
I wasn't expecting...this.

BOYLE
I know what you were expecting.

High Security Lab, all the rigorous interviews, and now this is the pay-off.

GEORGE
Yes, well, I just thought that the lab would be larger.

BOYLE
She's the only one left.

There's no need for Nexcorp to keep the whole facility running.

GEORGE
I guess, yeah, I was just surprised.

BOYLE
The glamorous thrill of the job wears off quick, huh.

GEORGE
No, I just meant...Never mind.
Oh. I was doing some research, looking at earlier records and there's a lot I can't open. Will I be getting access to the blood work, then?
If I'm going to be doing the check-ups.

BOYLE
Oh no. That's classified. You'd need a higher clearance.

GEORGE
Will I be getting that, eventually?

Just because that's sort of my focus.

BOYLE
Don't get ahead of yourself.

GEORGE
I'm sorry, I didn't mean to...

Just a thought.

BOYLE
You'll learn pretty quick to keep those to yourself around here. That's what I do.

GEORGE
Okay. But that's why I got hired. I thought... Because of my doctoral research in this field.

BOYLE
Partially. But there are a lot of factors in that decision.
We have a very specific... type that we look for.

GEORGE
Which is?

BOYLE
Classified.

GEORGE
Of course.

BOYLE
Right now, you just need to follow the process. Get used to the routine.

GEORGE
Sure. That's...
Of course what I'll do. I'll get it memorized.

BOYLE
Just follow the schedule.

GEORGE
I have some questions about that-

BOYLE
It's been working for eleven years. No need to reinvent the wheel here.

GEORGE
Sorry. Uh. Does she ever smile?

BOYLE
What?

GEORGE
I've been watching her for hours. She hasn't really smiled.

BOYLE
Hmmm.

GEORGE
So does she?

BOYLE
I don't know. Probably.

GEORGE
You're not sure.

BOYLE
I mean, no, I'm sure she does sometimes.

GEORGE
(Judgment starts to creep in.)
You just haven't noticed either way?

BOYLE
Look. Some advice.
Don't let yourself get sucked in, obsessing over her and her…
 Boyle makes a vague hand gesture at the cell.
Like, I get it, it's easy cause there's nothing else to do but-

GEORGE
That's my job, though.

BOYLE
No, it's not.

GEORGE
Excuse me?

BOYLE
Listen. We aren't here to save Madeleine.
We're here to find a cure for all of them out there.
All the ones that weren't lucky enough to have a facility to protect them.
So don't make it about her.

GEORGE
But she is how we do that, right? So it does matter, how she's feeling.

BOYLE
My point is you're here as a scientist, not a shrink.
So monitoring the effects of her condition, yes, that matters.
But how she feels on any given day...
 Dismissive hand gesture.
Eh. Not so much.

GEORGE
Okay... But-

BOYLE
Here's the real job description.
You monitor her, do the timed check-ins, and report it to me.
Then, all the information gets sent out to someone much higher on the food chain.
You're pretty much a glorified babysitter to that bonkers little girl.
Honestly, she doesn't really need one. Not like there's anywhere else she can go, but...
There it is.

GEORGE
There it is.

BOYLE
Sorry, sweetie. Didn't mean to burst your bubble.

GEORGE
(For the first time, we see a serious flash of annoyance.)
Don't worry. You didn't.

BOYLE
Take up Tetris. It's gonna be your best friend in here.

He finishes his yogurt and shoots it into the trash can.

SCENE 3
The Cell.

MADELEINE
My body hates me.
I don't mean like in videos how two girls say that to each other.
Like after they throw up or run on those weird ramp machines, they look into a mirror and say that to themselves.
They put plastic in their bodies with needles. They are liars. They are stupid and I hate them.

ROBOT
I hate them.

MADELEINE
You do too?

ROBOT
I think.

MADELEINE
Do you?

Robot shrugs.

I can actually say that my body hates me.

My immune cells are incompetent and attack the other cells in my body because they are VERY BAD AT THEIR JOB.

ROBOT
VERY BAD!

MADELEINE
Exactly. So essentially my cells are trying to destroy each other, because they see each other as a threat. Waged in a civil war, brother killing brother.
Even though they all just want to help.
It's quite sad actually.

ROBOT
Quite sad.

MADELEINE
I'm glad you're here.

ROBOT
I am here.

MADELEINE
You can't ever leave.

ROBOT
Leave?

MADELEINE
No. Don't.

ROBOT
Beep.

MADELEINE
No.

ROBOT
Beep.

MADELEINE
No.

ROBOT
(running out of charge)
Beeeeeeeeeep.

MADELEINE
Oh, not again.

She cranks the Robot.

Are you sleepy?

ROBOT
Sleepy?

MADELEINE
Me neither.
Do you want to read a story then?

ROBOT
Story.

MADELEINE
I read on this tablet because pages of books carry residue and germs and death.
I've always wondered what flipping the pages of a book feels like.
Or what touching someone's cheek feels like?

> *She turns her head to look at the Robot.*
>
> *The Robot turns its head to look at her, mirroring her movement.*

May I...touch your face?

ROBOT
Your face.

MADELEINE
Is that a yes?

ROBOT
Yes?

MADELEINE
(touches Robot's face)
Oh. It's cold.

ROBOT
What is cold?

BOYLE
(over loudspeaker)
Are you cold in there?
Should I raise the room temperature?

MADELEINE
No. It's fine.

BOYLE
(over loudspeaker)
Okay.

ROBOT
What is cold?

MADELEINE
Your face.

ROBOT
I'm sorry.

MADELEINE
That's alright.

> *Madeleine nods her head.*
>
> *The Robot does the same.*
>
> *It turns into a game.*
>
> *Every time she moves it mirrors her. She quickly leans to one side. Then the other.*
>
> *She speeds up her movements. Still it mimics her.*
>
> *They walk around each other in sync.*
>
> *George enters the Observation Lab. She sees Madeleine playing.*
>
> *She watches for a moment, then exits the Observation Lab.*

Your turn.

ROBOT
Your turn.

MADELEINE
No, I'm going to follow you now.

ROBOT
Follow.

MADELEINE
(pointing to Robot)
You.

ROBOT
(pointing to Madeleine)
You.

Madeleine positions the Robot to point to itself.

MADELEINE
You.

ROBOT
(a discovery)
Me.

MADELEINE
Yes.

The Robot starts to move, creakily. Madeleine mimics it.

George enters the space outside Madeleine's cell and continues to watch, unnoticed.

The Robot slowly turns. Madeleine turns, trying to keep an eye on it the whole time.

It turns again faster this time.

They spin around together and Madeleine starts laughing.

ROBOT
(attempting to mimic her laughter)
Haw. Nye. Hah. Hwa.

GEORGE
Madeleine.

MADELEINE
(without thinking)
What?

GEORGE
Oh, so you're talking to me now?

MADELEINE
I was busy before.

GEORGE
Really? Doing what?

MADELEINE
Nothing.

GEORGE
I don't think that's true.

MADELEINE
What you think doesn't matter.

GEORGE
Excuse me?

MADELEINE
Hasn't he told you yet?
He tells everyone that.

GEORGE
How do you-

MADELEINE
You'll be gone soon too. None of you last very long.

GEORGE
What do you mean?

MADELEINE
The doctors. None of you stay long. Except for him. I don't know why. They don't say goodbye. They just disappear.

MADELEINE (CONT'D)
I'm trying to understand the pattern, but I don't.
I don't have this one yet, but I always understand them eventually.
Maybe when you leave it'll fall into place.
And everything will make sense.

GEORGE
Maybe.
But I don't plan on leaving anytime soon.

MADELEINE
I don't think it'll be up to you.

GEORGE
You think a lot.

MADELEINE
There's not much else to do in here.

GEORGE
You have things to read and watch. To play with.

MADELEINE
Yes, all the things.

GEORGE
Do you like your room?

MADELEINE
I was actually in the middle of something.

GEORGE
So was I.
But I interrupted my busy schedule to come and talk to you.

MADELEINE
Your busy schedule watching me.

GEORGE
We call it monitoring, actually.

MADELEINE
Same thing.

GEORGE
Not exactly. Monitoring means you get paid for it.

MADELEINE
Why are you talking to me?

GEORGE
My mother always told me that there are two things you should never do alone, drink or laugh.

MADELEINE
Why are you talking to me?

GEORGE
It felt strange.
Me sitting around in silence watching you down here laughing.
Doesn't that seem silly to you?

Madeleine shrugs and turns away.

Oh, are you ignoring me again now?

MADELEINE
I'm busy.

GEORGE
But I thought you were doing nothing.

MADELEINE
I was thinking.

GEORGE
Did I interrupt?

MADELEINE
Yes.

GEORGE
Do you know what I think?

MADELEINE
No, that's impossible.

GEORGE
I think you're very smart. And you know it.

ROBOT
You know it.

MADELEINE
(to Robot)
Shhh.

GEORGE
No, Madeleine. You don't get to shush me.
I'm an adult.

MADELEINE
I didn't.

GEORGE
Don't try to play games with me.

ROBOT
(suddenly interested)
Games? Play. With them!

MADELEINE
No.

GEORGE
I'm not the enemy here.
We aren't as different as you think.

MADELEINE
That's what all the doctors say.
And it's never true.

BOYLE
(over loudspeaker)
George. Can I see you up here?

GEORGE
Yes, yes of course.

BOYLE
Quickly.

GEORGE
I'll talk to you later, Madeleine.

George exits.

ROBOT
Later.

Lights dim on Madeleine and the Robot.

Lights up on the Observation Lab.

BOYLE
Isn't it a bit early for a check-up?

GEORGE
Actually I wasn't…it wasn't a check-up.

BOYLE
Then why were you down there?
You can tell me if she did something wrong.

GEORGE
What?

BOYLE
Don't protect her.

GEORGE
I'm not. We were just talking.
There wasn't an emergency. No behavioral issues, really. Just...

BOYLE
Just.

GEORGE
She was laughing.

BOYLE
What?

GEORGE
Running around in circles.
Laughing at the top of her lungs.

BOYLE
Wow. She's getting worse.

This was not what George meant.

Boyle starts loading up the minifridge with yogurt.

Oh, hey, do you need to put anything in here?

GEORGE
Well...

BOYLE
Cool, thanks. I'll just fill it on up then.

George sits down and flips through the charts.

Oh and...can you print out the first three pages of the monthly report?

GEORGE
Why? Just...wondering.

BOYLE
Her mother's coming in today.

GEORGE
Wait. I thought that was...wasn't that next week?

BOYLE
It was, but she started getting pushy about seeing her.
You know, typical.

GEORGE
Well, it makes sense.

BOYLE
She has scheduled appointments for a reason. Don't even know why she keeps coming at all.

Boyle opens a yogurt.

GEORGE
She's Madeleine's mother.

BOYLE
That's what she always tells me. Over and over again.
You'll understand what I mean. When you monitor the visit today.

GEORGE
Whoa, I'm really not sure I'm ready to-

BOYLE
Of course, you are. I mean, you're a...

He gestures vaguely with the yogurt in his hand.

GEORGE
What?

BOYLE
Hopefully you can deal with her.

GEORGE
Is there anything I should know?

BOYLE
The initial training process ran you through procedures, right?

GEORGE
More or less, but-

BOYLE
Cool, then. You should be good to go.

GEORGE
And she'll be here?

BOYLE
Hour or so.

GEORGE
Thanks for the heads-up.

BOYLE
No problemo.
Keep an eye on her, last visit she tried to get into our records.
Be sure to monitor the visit closely.

GEORGE
Of course.

BOYLE
She's been known to say things to Madeleine that...

GEORGE
Yes?

BOYLE
Things that upset her.
If she starts talking to Madeleine about whether or not she wants to be here, cut her off.
Tell her she's running out of time.
It's for Madeleine's own good.

GEORGE
Right.

BOYLE
I'll check back in with you later. I got a funding meeting, you know.

GEORGE
Sure.

BOYLE
Just get her the paperwork and get her out.

GEORGE
Alright.

BOYLE
And tell her no more rescheduling visits.
She can learn how to follow the rules.

GEORGE
Got it.

Boyle shoots his yogurt at the trash can, but it rolls off the rim and lands on the floor.

George and Boyle look at the yogurt.

They look at each other.

BOYLE
Well, I'm late for my meeting.

Boyle exits.

SCENE 4

The Cell.

Madeleine and the Robot are watching something on her tablet.

Alayna enters the space outside Madeleine's cell.

ALAYNA
Hi Madeleine.

MADELEINE
Hello.

ALAYNA
I missed you.

MADELEINE
Yes.

ALAYNA
Very much. How is everything?

MADELEINE
Everything?
I don't really think we have time to talk about everything.

ALAYNA
How are you?

MADELEINE
Just peachy.

ALAYNA
Where do you pick this stuff up?

MADELEINE
Surfing. Not like on the ocean, like on the Web.

ALAYNA
I got that.

MADELEINE
Good.

ALAYNA
So you like going online?

MADELEINE
Yes.

ALAYNA
Because you can learn from it?

Madeleine shrugs.

MADELEINE
I guess.

ALAYNA
What have you been learning?

MADELEINE
Things, things, things.

ALAYNA
What kinds of things?

MADELEINE
Lots of things. That's why I said it three times.

ALAYNA
Okay.
Anything in particular?

Robot raises its hand as if waiting for Madeleine to call on it.

MADELEINE
(to Robot)
Yes?

It points to itself, very pleased about answering the question.

ALAYNA
Such as?

MADELEINE
Building a robot.

ALAYNA
Wow. That's really...unexpected.
Was that hard?

MADELEINE
Kinda.

ALAYNA
I have no idea how to do that. Wouldn't even know where to start.
You're such a smart kid.

MADELEINE
Don't worry. It's not just you.
I'm smarter than most people.

ALAYNA
Are you doing well?

MADELEINE
Well. Adjective.
In good health; free or recovered from illness.
So. That would be a no.

ALAYNA
I mean, have they been treating you well in here? The doctors.

MADELEINE
Poking and prodding me.

ALAYNA
What?

MADELEINE
I think I'm in trouble.

ALAYNA
What do you mean?

Madeleine looks up at the cameras.

MADELEINE
Nothing.

ALAYNA
Are you sure?

Madeleine shrugs.

Okay.
Are you comfortable? In here?

MADELEINE
Sure.

ALAYNA
Do you like it here, then?

ROBOT
I am here.

MADELEINE
Sure, I guess.

ALAYNA
So... you don't ever want to leave?

MADELEINE
Why would I want to leave?

GEORGE
(over loudspeaker)
You have one minute left.

MADELEINE
Why are you saying that? I'm safe here.

ALAYNA
I just miss you so much, with you being here and-

MADELEINE
You said that already.

ALAYNA
I want to make sure you understand.

MADELEINE
Understand what?

GEORGE
(over loudspeaker)
Time to start wrapping up.

MADELEINE
I don't need your help understanding things.

ALAYNA
I know, Maddy, I just meant...

MADELEINE
That's not my name.
Don't call me that.
I don't like that.

ALAYNA
I'm sorry. I'm sorry.
I love you, okay? Just know that.

Madeleine shrugs. Alayna puts her hand up against the glass that separates them.

So, I'll see you next month for sure.

A long silence as she waits for a response, any response.

Bye Madeleine.

Alayna exits to the Observation Lab, where George is waiting.

The Cell goes black.

GEORGE
Hello, you must be Alayna?

ALAYNA
I know you were watching us. So you know who I am.

GEORGE
Yes. Um. Next month the visit is scheduled for the fifteenth. Same time as usual.

ALAYNA
So you're the new coat.

GEORGE
Sorry, what?

ALAYNA
The new person they hired. George. That's you?

GEORGE
Yes, I'm George.

ALAYNA
Thought you'd be a man.

GEORGE
Nope.

ALAYNA
Hmm.
So I'm sure Boyle warned you about me.

GEORGE
No. Of course not.

ALAYNA
Sure.

GEORGE
Here are some of the vitals and information on how Madeleine's doing.
She's been good. Really good.

George hands Alayna the pages.

ALAYNA
Don't lie to me.
She wouldn't even look at me.

GEORGE
Children like Madeleine, growing up in this kind of environment, interact differently with the... "outside" / world.

ALAYNA
You don't have to explain it to me.
I know all of you think I'm stupid, but I'm not.
You've been here what, a week? I've been coming here eleven years.
So trust me, I know.
I don't need another doctor telling me it's not my fault she doesn't love me.

GEORGE
Your relationship may be different / than what you expected, but-

ALAYNA
Don't tell me about my relationship with my child.
You don't know anything about me.

GEORGE
I'm only trying to help.

ALAYNA
No. You're trying to get me out of the room.
If you wanted to help you would let me see my daughter more than ONCE A MONTH.

GEORGE
That was part of your agreement.

ALAYNA
Is that what they told you?

GEORGE
Look, I just want figure out what's wrong with Madeleine.
Just like you do. That's why we're here.

ALAYNA
We're here because I was exactly what Nexcorp was looking for.
Poor and scared and sixteen.
All that and with a baby that came out with some nameless condition I couldn't afford any kind of treatment for.

GEORGE
Nexcorp offered you a new life. You and Madeleine.

ALAYNA
They destroyed my family.

GEORGE
You know what's going on out there. You've seen the numbers with this disease. Most kids don't get the chance she has.

ALAYNA
Let me guess. You think you're here to save the world, don't you?

GEORGE
Nexcorp is trying to find a cure. They're trying to help.

ALAYNA
Help? They don't care about helping.
It was never about helping Madeleine.

GEORGE
What else would it be about?

ALAYNA
Nexcorp isn't here to save all the sick kids.
They're here to make money.

ALAYNA (CONT'D)
And when they find a cure. Get what they want out of my daughter.
They won't hesitate for a second to pull the plug on this program.

GEORGE
We're here to help Madeleine.

ALAYNA
Whatever helps you sleep at night.

GEORGE
Look, I am not the person with the answers here. I honestly have no idea what you're talking about.

George presses a button and talks into a speaker.

Boyle to the Observation Lab, please.

ALAYNA
Nexcorp turned my daughter into a lab rat.

GEORGE
Your daughter would be dead if it weren't for this program.

ALAYNA
She might as well be.

GEORGE
Because she doesn't call you mommy?

Boyle enters the lab.

ALAYNA
Because she isn't happy. She doesn't want this.

Boyle announces his presence.

BOYLE
She can end the trial anytime, according to the Escape Clause, Section / 5 of the contract.

ALAYNA
But she doesn't understand that. You've never made that clear to her.

BOYLE
We've never told her she couldn't leave.

ALAYNA
That's not the same thing.

BOYLE
Then why don't you tell her?

ALAYNA
I can't. You know I can't.

BOYLE
That's right. You made the decision. You signed the papers.

ALAYNA
She only wants to stay because you brainwashed her.
She doesn't understand. She's just a child.

BOYLE
And what about the other children Alayna?

...

That's what I thought.
You have to stop talking to her about leaving, Alayna.
I am really on my last...
My last...

Gestures looking for the right word.

GEORGE
Straw?

BOYLE
Yes. That.
My last straw. You understand me?
I've tried to be patient with you.
And you just throw that patience right back in my face.
Nexcorp will not have any more scenes from you, do you understand me?

...

I'd really hate to have to restrict your visits.

ALAYNA
You wouldn't dare.

...

You can't.

BOYLE
Actually, yeah we can.

ALAYNA
No, the contract-

BOYLE
Read the small print.
If Nexcorp decides you're hazardous to the operation, we can stop the visits.
And we will.
See… you seem to think these visits are something that's owed to you. That's a mistake.
These visits are something we're kind enough to allow you.
A little gratitude would be in order.

ALAYNA
Gratitude?! For what? For experimenting on my daughter?
For infecting everything around you?

BOYLE
Excuse me?

ALAYNA
You heard what I said.

BOYLE
Look, I don't have time today for your conspiracy theories, Alayna.

ALAYNA
You think you can threaten anyone that gets in your way.

BOYLE
Don't think of it as a threat… think of it as a warning.

ALAYNA
I'll go public.

BOYLE
George, take your break.

GEORGE
What?

BOYLE
It's time for a break.

GEORGE
Right now? But, uh....

BOYLE
We take Federal Work Regulations very seriously here at Nexcorp.

GEORGE
Oh, really?

BOYLE
Just go.

GEORGE
Oh-kay.

George awkwardly grabs her things and exits.

ALAYNA
Looks like that managed to get your attention.

BOYLE
I'd think very carefully before you say anything else, Alayna.
Some things you can't take back, and there are those in Nexcorp less forgiving than me. Face it. You can't go to the press, because you don't have anything, and we both know it.

ALAYNA
I know what you did to her.
You infected my daughter.

BOYLE
I'm at a loss as to what else you could be talking about.

ALAYNA
Your last employee didn't take being fired very well.
He contacted me. Told me all the things you weren't sending me in the reports.
How Madeleine's started getting nightmares...

BOYLE
It's a phase.

ALAYNA
After you had given her, what you told him was a routine injection.
And then suddenly her scans looked different.

BOYLE
So, I gave her a shot. That doesn't prove anything.
And you're basing all this off a disgruntled ex-employee. How's that gonna look?

ALAYNA
I don't think you want people sniffing around here with questions about how you're running this facility.

BOYLE
I don't think you want the judgement of the world raining down on you for selling your kid to Nexcorp.

ALAYNA
That's not what happened.
He told me that the cells in her bloods were changing, Like mutating.

BOYLE
Mutating? I like sci-fi novels as much as the next guy, / but really?

ALAYNA
Okay, maybe I'm not a scientist or anything. But I know that something's off.

BOYLE
There is no giant conspiracy going on here.

ALAYNA
Then why won't you tell her she can leave?

Tell her right now.

BOYLE
What?

Alayna puts her hand over the intercom button.

ALAYNA
If there's no reason she can't leave. You can just tell her right now.

BOYLE
I'm not going to do that.

ALAYNA
If you won't I will.

BOYLE
Look I don't have to tell anyone about this.
This once, to show my good will, I'll give you a break.
I'll chalk it up to a momentary hysteria, and I won't report you threatening me.

ALAYNA
You can throw all the lawyers you want at me. I don't care.
That's the problem with taking everything from me...
There is nothing left for you to threaten me with.

BOYLE
You can't tell her that she can leave.

ALAYNA
Why not?

BOYLE
Because she can't.

ALAYNA
Why / can't she?!

BOYLE
Because.
Because something happened.
The auto immune disorder she has...changed.

Alayna takes her hand off the button.

It can transmit to other people.

ALAYNA
Which means?

BOYLE
You have to stop talking about leaving.

ALAYNA
It'll spread.

BOYLE
Yes, and quickly.
Outside a sanitized cell, anyone who catches it, could, probably will, die.

ALAYNA
This just...happened?

BOYLE
There may be a correlation between the change and the shot...
We don't know.

ALAYNA
You don't know.

BOYLE
That's what I said.

ALAYNA
You're a monster.

BOYLE
If it helps you to think about this in simple terms. That's fine.
I'm really past caring what you think about me.
As long as you understand that Madeleine has to stay in her cell.
At this moment, there is NOTHING you can say that changes that fact.

ALAYNA
...

I want to see my daughter.

BOYLE
What's new-

ALAYNA
More than once a month.

BOYLE
Suppose…it's possible for me to suggest increased visits…
For the sake of the experiment, of course. I'm putting a lot out on the line, asking for that.

ALAYNA
So what?

BOYLE
I might expect, in turn, a little mano a mano.

ALAYNA
Like?

BOYLE
You're poking around, talking to ex-employees, distressing Madeleine…
It's causing me a lot of problems. So. If I get you more visits, you stop being such a royal pain in my ass every time you visit.

ALAYNA
If you let me-

BOYLE
Seriously. Can you manage that?

ALAYNA
If I get more visits, I can try.

BOYLE
Oh, and you also won't discuss anything you know about Nexcorp with the press.
Because that would end very badly for you. Very badly.

ALAYNA
You don't have children, do you?

BOYLE
I fail to see how that's relevant to this discussion. Now, I'd like to get back to work.

ALAYNA
What about the visits?

BOYLE
After I get the okay, I'll let you know when.

ALAYNA
If I don't hear from you-

BOYLE
You'll do what?
…

It'll be in the next week. I'll contact you. Now get out of my lab.

Alayna starts to leave.
Turns.

ALAYNA
I can't believe I ever trusted you.

Alayna exits.

Silence.

Boyle pulls out a yogurt and begins eating his feelings.

He hits the buzzer and, through a mouthful of yogurt, speaks.

BOYLE
George. Lab. Now

George enters.

GEORGE
Hi, you wanted me?

BOYLE
Yeah, sit down.

She does.

Look, George.

GEORGE
I'm sorry.

BOYLE
You had one job.

GEORGE
I know.

BOYLE
What did I tell you?
...
Not a rhetorical question.

GEORGE
To get her the paperwork and-

BOYLE
Get her out.

GEORGE
Yes.

BOYLE
I just got called out of a meeting with my boss.

GEORGE
I'm sorry.

BOYLE
Do you want to explain that to him?
I didn't think so.
I'm not sure this is working out.

GEORGE
What?

BOYLE
There's no shame in just…

Vague hand gesture to indicate quitting.

You know.

GEORGE
I know that. But that's not-

BOYLE
If it's too much for you to handle, I can see if we have something else.
More your speed.

GEORGE
I can do this job. I can handle this.

BOYLE
Then you need to get with the program. A-SAP.

GEORGE
I will. Absolutely.

BOYLE
Because so far-

GEORGE
I know it hasn't been great.

BOYLE
I'm not really feeling it.

GEORGE
I will 100 percent be onboard with the program, I promise.

BOYLE
To the letter.

GEORGE
Yes.

BOYLE
Seriously.
No more chats with Madeleine. You go down there for three things, you get me? One. If her vitals are off, or something like that. Alright. Two. The daily checkups.

...

GEORGE
And?

BOYLE
And what?

GEORGE
You said thr--nothing. I thought you were gonna say something else.

BOYLE
Listen to what I am saying.

GEORGE
I am.

BOYLE
I need you focused, and I need you to not...
> Looking for the right word.

To stop, um...being so interested.

GEORGE
I shouldn't be interested in Madeleine.

BOYLE
Not personally, no.

GEORGE
I'm not.

BOYLE
You don't seem disinterested. Stay disinterested. You have to. Trust me. I learned it the hard way.

GEORGE
I recognize that.

BOYLE
Just if you need to talk to her about something. Do it over the buzzer. Okay? Like I do.
Um. Cool. I feel like you know what you need to do moving forward.
Right?

GEORGE
I think so. Yes.

BOYLE
I really don't like doing this. Okay?
Being all...

> Vague gesture.

Don't make me do it again.

GEORGE
You won't have to.

BOYLE
Sure. I'm sure. I need to… get back to…
Can you finish out the shift in here? Debrief what happened.

GEORGE
Of course.

BOYLE
Don't forget. This is bigger than Madeleine.

GEORGE
I know.

> Boyle exits.
>
> George sits down and starts to type into a computer.
>
> She stops, slumps, and puts her face in her hands.
>
> Finally, George turns to look at Madeleine.
>
> In the cell, Madeleine and the Robot are playing some bizarre version of patty-cake Madeleine made up. It mostly involves them high-fiving each other with both hands as quickly as possible.
>
> They tire of this.

MADELEINE
Did the woman leave? Did she leave?

George presses the buzzer to talk to Madeleine.

GEORGE
Are you talking to me, Madeleine?

MADELEINE
Who else would I be talking to?

ROBOT
Me.

MADELEINE
Shhhh. She doesn't know that.

GEORGE
Sorry, what are you asking?

MADELEINE
Did the woman leave?

GEORGE
The woman?

MADELEINE
The one who calls herself my mother.

GEORGE
She is your mother.

ROBOT
Mother?

MADELEINE
Mothers are supposed to be someone you like.

GEORGE
Not always.
She'll be coming again next month.

MADELEINE
Fine.

George releases the buzzer.

She pauses.

She puts her hand over the buzzer, as if about to push it again.

GEORGE
What am I doing?

George moves away.

A breath.

A decision.

She goes back to the buzzer and pushes it.

Are you happy?

ROBOT
Happy?

MADELEINE
What do you mean?

GEORGE
Are you happy in here?

MADELEINE
No, what do you mean by happy?

GEORGE
Just happy. I don't know how to...
Like, living here, do you like it?

MADELEINE
I have to be in here.

ROBOT
We are here.

MADELEINE
Because going outside. Outside is bad.

ROBOT
Outside. NO.

GEORGE
But do you like being here?

MADELEINE
I...I...

ROBOT
What?

GEORGE
You don't have to have an answer.

MADELEINE
Yes, I do.

GEORGE
Have an answer? Or yes, you like living here?

MADELEINE
Yes. To both. Yes. I think.

GEORGE
It's not about thinking. It's about how you feel.

MADELEINE
I don't understand this conversation.
I don't like this conversation.

I DON'T WANT TO TALK TO YOU.

GEORGE
I'm sorry.

MADELEINE
The woman who comes, she comes and talks to me.
And then she cries, and I don't like it, I want her to stop, to stop crying.
She asked me do I want to leave, and I don't understand that question.
I don't understand it.
Of course, I don't want to leave.
I would die.
Why would I want to die?

MADELEINE (CONT'D)
And I ask why she says that, and she says she's just trying to make me understand. And I say understand what and she says-

GEORGE
Madeleine, I just want to make sure you know this is your life.

MADELEINE
I know it's my life.

GEORGE
You can decide things.

MADELEINE
Who else's life would it be?
That just doesn't make any sense.

GEORGE
Never mind.

MADELEINE
You don't make any sense.

GEORGE
Madeleine.

MADELEINE
She says in frustration.

GEORGE
Please don't.

MADELEINE
Her frustration builds.

GEORGE
No, Madeleine. I'm not frustrated. I'm just... I'm tired.
It's been a long day.

MADELEINE
Are some days longer than others? How do you know when they are? How do you keep track?

GEORGE
I mean that I have a lot of work to do.

MADELEINE
Oh.

GEORGE
You can buzz me. If you want.

MADELEINE
I don't want to buzz you.

GEORGE
That's your prerogative. But I'll be here.

ROBOT
I am here.

> As George takes her hand off of the button, the Cell goes dark.

GEORGE
Maybe later.

> George goes back to her work. She starts reading through the reports.
>
> She stops and goes back to another paper on her desk and compares the two, looking disturbed.
>
> She continues to go through the reports.

SCENE 5

The Cell.

> Madeleine and the Robot.

MADELEINE
Sometimes I feel like I have no body.
Like I sit here until my legs are numb, and it feels like they disappear and then I stare at the wall, and I stare and stare and it's like I'm floating. Like I'm suspended by a string that goes all the way up into the ceiling. Into the ceiling over this ceiling whatever that is. And it's like I don't exist.
I don't feel the eyes on me or the cameras with the eyes that follow me.
Not anymore.
It's just me and the string.

> She closes her eyes.

And it's...peaceful.

ROBOT
Me too?

MADELEINE
And you. You can float with me.
They want to be part of it. But they aren't.
They can't be.

ROBOT
To be.

MADELEINE
Or not.

ROBOT
To beep.

MADELEINE
To sleep.

ROBOT
Sleeping?

MADELEINE
I don't think you can actually.

ROBOT
I want to sleep.

MADELEINE
No, you don't.

ROBOT
I don't?

MADELEINE
Sleep means dreaming and dreams are when he comes.
He knows that's when I'm the weakest.
That's why he's there.

ROBOT
He's there.

MADELEINE
Always.
I try to never close my eyes, because he knows. He comes and I can't stop him.
Whenever I close my eyes he's always there.

> As if he has been summoned, the King of Germs appears. The Robot sees him.

ROBOT
He's there.

MADELEINE
Exactly.

ROBOT
He's there.

MADELEINE
That's what I said.

                    ROBOT
What I said!

                    MADELEINE
I said it first.

                    ROBOT
He's there.

                    MADELEINE
Are you glitching?

                    ROBOT
No glitch.

> Madeleine tenses up as she hears the same song as before start to play, something like Elvis Presley's "Surrender."

                    MADELEINE
Shhhhh.

> She puts her finger to the Robot's mouth.

                    ROBOT
Shhhh.

> The Robot does the same to her.

                    MADELEINE
He's here.

> Robot puts its arms in the air, in exasperation, as if to say, "That's what I just said."
>
> The King of Germs clears his throat, trying to get her attention.
>
> She turns.

No. Go away. Go AWAY!

                    ROBOT
Away away away away.

> Madeleine starts crying.
>
> The King of Germs performs a magic trick for Madeleine, making an absurdly large, red handkerchief appear out of nowhere.
>
> He offers it to her. The Robot steps in front of Madeleine, shielding her.
>
> The King of Germs holds the handkerchief out to one side and flicks his wrist, rippling the fabric.
>
> The Robot charges at him, but the King of Germs sidesteps at the last moment.
>
> The King of Germs moves toward Madeleine, who is curled up and shaking.

BEEBEEP.

> The King of Germs turns as the Robot charges him again. He sidesteps and the Robot misses again.

Sqreeekkk.

> In the Observation Lab, George is typing into her computer.
>
> We see Madeleine in the screen behind her, laying on the ground, shaking, in the fetal position.
>
> She appears alone in her cell, crying.
>
> A heartbeat. The Hands appear.
>
> They restrain the Robot.
>
> George turns around to get something out of the file cabinet and sees Madeleine on the screen.
>
> The sound of a heartbeat builds toward a crescendo.
>
> The King of Germs moves toward Madeleine, still trying to give her the handkerchief.

GEORGE
(over the loudspeaker)
Madeleine?

Madeleine, is everything all right?!

The Observation Lab goes dark as the King of Germs keeps moving closer to Madeleine.

George's voice cuts through the music.

Wake up, Madeleine. Madeleine!

MADELEINE
Go away! Don't touch me!

George appears outside Madeleine's cell.

GEORGE
Madeleine!

The King of Germs and the Hands disappear.

Your heartbeat was elevated off the charts. What were you dreaming about? Was it another nightmare?

MADELEINE
Am I dreaming?

GEORGE
No, you were dreaming. But not anymore. Now you're back and you're safe.

MADELEINE
I'm safe.

GEORGE
That's right.

MADELEINE
He's not here, he's not here.

GEORGE
Who isn't?

MADELEINE
He's gone.

GEORGE
Who's gone?

MADELEINE
Nobody.

GEORGE
If it was nobody, why were you cowering in the corner?

...

Look, I need your help, Madeleine.

ROBOT
Help?

MADELEINE
You do?

GEORGE
Uh-huh. See, I got in trouble.

MADELEINE
I get in trouble all the time.

GEORGE
Yeah, but I got in really big trouble.

MADELEINE
Why?

GEORGE
I messed up.

MADELEINE
Well, don't do that then.

GEORGE
(laughs a little in spite of herself)
Thanks, Madeleine. I'll remember that.

MADELEINE
If you need someone to help.
You could get a robot.

GEORGE
What?

MADELEINE
Mine isn't that good, but...we're working on that.

GEORGE
Your robot.
Is that who you talk to?

MADELEINE
Why are you asking?

GEORGE
I'm just curious.

MADELEINE
Did HE want to know? Did he ask you to ask me? You're on HIS side, aren't you?

GEORGE
I'm not on anyone's side. I'm disinterested.

MADELEINE
If you're disinterested, why did you ask?

GEORGE
No... disinterested means... It doesn't mean I'm not interested.
It means I'm impartial. Like I-

MADELEINE
I'm not stupid.

GEORGE
Of course not.

MADELEINE
I know what impartial means.

ROBOT
She knows what impartial means!

MADELEINE
Impartial. Adjective.
Not partial or biased; fair; just.

GEORGE
Madeleine. I was just wondering who you were talking to.

MADELEINE
Nothing.

Nothing. Nothing.

GEORGE
You don't have to tell me. It can be your secret.

MADELEINE
Nothing.

GEORGE
Okay.

George exits. Madeleine pushes the Robot over.

ROBOT
Beep.

MADELEINE
I don't wanna hear it.

ROBOT
Bloooooop.

Madeleine relents.

MADELEINE
Hello?

She pokes the Robot, waiting for a response.

ROBOT
Hello.

Robot pokes her back.

MADELEINE
Ouch.

ROBOT
Ouch.

MADELEINE
You were supposed to help me. To protect me from... HIM.
From the King of Germs.
You didn't do anything.

ROBOT
Do anything?

MADELEINE
Yes. Like stop him.

ROBOT
Stop him.

MADELEINE
We have to figure something out.

A   plan.

Together.

ROBOT
Together.

Lights down.

SCENE 6

The Observation Lab.

> Boyle watches Madeleine.

BOYLE
They've got bets running on you.
You know that?
Grown people taking bets on how much longer you'll last before something gets to you.

Like the rest. This can't be the future.

...

Or maybe you'll win.
Maybe you'll live in here for the rest of your life or 'til you crack.
You have no idea how much is riding on you, do you?
You're the last one, our last chance.

...

Shit.

She's got me talking to myself now.

> Boyle gets a yogurt out and looks at it, then returns it to the minifridge.
>
> He goes to a hiding place where he keeps a stash of junk food. He grabs a handful of SnoBalls and starts eating.
>
> Lights up on the Cell.
>
> The Robot is doing push-ups with Madeleine sitting on its back.
>
> Boyle starts playing Tetris, the glow of the brightly colored shapes reflected in his glasses.
>
> The Robot practices punching into Madeleine's hands.
>
> There are several packets of SnoBalls strewn about Boyle as he fails a level of Tetris.

BOYLE
Oh, come on!

> Madeleine and the Robot high five and the Robot begins mirroring her.
>
> Boyle sighs. He goes over to the buzzer.

BOYLE
(over the loudspeaker)
You can play tomorrow, Madeleine.

It's time to sleep now.

> The Observation Lab goes dark.

ROBOT
Sleep now.

MADELEINE
Alright then.

ROBOT
Alright then.

> Madeleine closes her eyes, and "Surrender" begins to play.

MADELEINE
Oh no.

ROBOT
Oh no.

> Robot continues to mimic her, thinking this is all part of the game.

MADELEINE

He's here.

ROBOT

He's here.

MADELEINE

Stop it.

ROBOT

Stop it.

MADELEINE

I'm serious.

ROBOT

I'm serious.

MADELEINE

This isn't a game.

ROBOT

This isn't-

> The King of Germs appears behind the Robot and taps him on the shoulder, like he is cutting in on a dance.
>
> The Robot turns and sees him.

ROBOT
(intimidated)

Meep!

> The King of Germs holds out his hand to Madeleine. The Robot shakes its head.
>
> The King of Germs steps toward Madeleine.
>
> The Robot blocks him. They have a stare down.

ROBOT
(intimidatingly)

BLOOOP.

> The King of Germs tries to move the Robot out of the way, but the Robot doesn't give an inch.
>
> It shakes its head again.
>
> The King of Germs tries to move the Robot again, harder this time. His hands bounce right off the Robot.
>
> The Robot pushes him with one hand, palm spread, in the center of his chest. The King of Germs goes flying back.
>
> They fight, Madeleine's fevered impression of fisticuffs. While they fight, their shadows seem to fill the stage.
>
> The Robot gains the upper hand and is about to punch out the King of Germs when...

SCENE 7

A Buzzer Sound. The Cell.

BOYLE
(over the loudspeaker)
Good morning, sleepy head.

Madeleine wakes up to Boyle's voice.

Rise and shine.
Sooooo, what do we want to listen to today?
...
Rainy day it is then.

The sound of rain starts.

Madeleine rubs her eyes. The Robot mimics her.

ROBOT
Blooooooop.

Boyle enters with his clipboard and pen.

BOYLE
Time for your check-up.

MADELEINE
Go away.

BOYLE
How I've missed these little chats.
Arms Out.

After a brief moment of hesitation, Madeleine follows his instructions. The scanners turn on.

Touch your hands to your forehead.
I need you to look at the finger I'm holding up.

Concentrate on it. Hold it.

Great.

Here are your rations.

Boyle places food into the chute. His side closes. A whir as the item's plastic cover is sanitized. Madeleine's side opens.

It's all looking good.

MADELEINE
Except for the whole thing where my immune system doesn't work, and I die if I leave.

BOYLE
Yeah, except for that.... Wait, what did you say?

MADELEINE
My immune system doesn't work.

BOYLE
Other than that.

MADELEINE
Nothing.

Boyle marks something on the clipboard, then absentmindedly puts his pen in his mouth.

Why are you eating your pen?

BOYLE
I'm not.

MADELEINE
Then why are you chewing on the pen?

BOYLE
It's just an absentminded thing.

MADELEINE
Why is the pen in your mouth though? Did you forget it was there?

BOYLE
No. There's no reason, okay?

MADELEINE
Then why would you put it in your mouth, that's gross.

BOYLE
Look. It's my mouth.

...

It's out of my mouth. Are you happy now?

MADELEINE
I don't know.

Madeleine starts talking to Robot.

Why do they ask me that?

BOYLE
Don't get into any trouble when I'm gone, okay?

Okay?

MADELEINE
(to Robot)
They are so strange.

BOYLE
Madeleine.

MADELEINE
They make me listen to the sound of rain I can't feel and then they ask me if I'm happy.

BOYLE
Stop that, Madeleine. I mean it.

ROBOT
Happy?

MADELEINE
Happy.

ROBOT
Happy!

Boyle shakes his head and exits.

MADELEINE
What does that even mean?

ROBOT
I don't know. You tell me.

MADELEINE
I don't know either.

ROBOT
Why not?

MADELEINE
I don't know.

ROBOT
You don't know.

MADELEINE
Yes.

ROBOT
(a taunt)
You don't know. You don't know.

Madeleine pulls a piece of machinery out of its leg, and it falls over.

Ow.

MADELEINE
I'm not even sorry.

> *She drops the piece in front of it. Still lying on its side, the Robot picks up the piece and lets out a mournful...*

ROBOT
Doop.

MADELEINE
Stop repeating me.

ROBOT
I wasn't. I wanted to...

> *It pauses, not knowing the word.*

MADELEINE
Apologize?

ROBOT
A-pol-o-gize.

MADELEINE
Verb. Express regret for something that one has done wrong.

ROBOT
Done wrong.

MADELEINE
Example: After the Robot was mean to Madeleine, it made sure to apologize so she didn't dismantle it.

ROBOT
Very sorry. Much apologize.

> *The Cell goes dark.*

> *George enters the Observation Lab to find Boyle surrounded by SnoBall wrappers.*

GEORGE
Good morning.

> *She throws her bag into a chair and takes out her lab coat.*

> *She puts it on.*

What, no yogurt today?

BOYLE
(looks at her like she's crazy)
What?

GEORGE
Nothing.

BOYLE
I have to...I'll be back.

GEORGE
I'll be here.

> *Boyle exits, leaving his computer on.*

> *George goes over to it, searching for something stored there.*

Where are you, where are you?
Hello. I got you.

> *She finds it.*

> *The Observation Lab goes dark, as lights come up on the Cell. Madeleine is sitting and staring straight ahead.*

> *The Robot is still fumbling, trying to fix itself.*

MADELEINE
They have lamps in here.
To keep me warm. To give me the vitamins.
Do you have the vitamins?
Vitamins are important. Necessary. That's what they say.
Light gives you vitamins apparently.

> *She looks up. She puts out her arms.*

I don't feel the light hitting me. People say they can feel the sun. Hitting them.

MADELEINE (CONT'D)
I don't feel anything.
You'd think I could feel it if the light is hitting me and giving me vitamins.
But I don't feel the difference.
It seems like sunlight should hurt, doesn't it?
I mean, the sun is approximately 10,000 degrees Fahrenheit. Sunlight is just radiation.

I thought radiation was a bad thing, but they seem to like this kind.

...

I don't feel anything.

ROBOT
Don't. Feel. My leg.

MADELEINE
Here.

Madeleine clicks the part back into place. The Robot manages to sit up.

She puts her arms back out again, waiting.

Nope. Still nothing.

ROBOT
Nothing.

MADELEINE
I'm not sure I'm happy.

ROBOT
Not happy.

MADELEINE
You're not happy either?

ROBOT
(trying to cheer her up)
Play?

MADELEINE
Yes. Let's play.
You hide.
I'll find you.

ROBOT
Find me?

MADELEINE
Always.

Go!

She puts her hands over her eyes.

The robot looks around the space, searching for somewhere to hide.

It finds a spot, but doesn't quite fit, so a piece of it is sticking out.

Madeleine opens her eyes and spots it without even moving.

I see you.
Again.

She puts her hands over her eyes.

It finds a new spot, but it still isn't very good.

Madeleine spots it again quickly.

Got you again.

The Robot is frustrated.

ROBOT
Rah. Rer. Ruh.

MADELEINE
Come on. Try again.

The Robot looks for another spot, but there isn't one.

It goes up to the glass and looks out.

MADELEINE (CONT'D)
Ready?

> Madeleine takes her hands off her eyes.

You aren't even hiding.

ROBOT
No hiding.

MADELEINE
Why not?

ROBOT
Hiding. Bad.

MADELEINE
No, it isn't.

ROBOT
I want to go outside.

MADELEINE
But you can't go outside.

ROBOT
Why not?

MADELEINE
Because I can't go outside.

ROBOT
Why not?

MADELEINE
Because I can't.
Because I'll die.

ROBOT
Why?

MADELEINE
Because I will.
Because the immune syst....I've told you this before.

ROBOT
What does death feel like?

MADELEINE
I don't know.

ROBOT
Can I die?

MADELEINE
Now you're just not even thinking before you speak.
I programmed you better than this.

ROBOT
Don't crank me. Don't.

MADELEINE
What?

ROBOT
I don't want to wake up.

MADELEINE
What do you mean wake up? You're a robot you can't sleep.

ROBOT
I don't want to wake up.

MADELEINE
You cease. You stop working. You don't sleep.

ROBOT
I want to stop working. Yes.

MADELEINE
But you won't. I made you fit together I made you perfectly. Not like me.

ROBOT
Perfectly? I want to break. Why can't I break?

MADELEINE
I suppose you can. I've just never tried.

ROBOT
Break me.

MADELEINE
No.

ROBOT
Beep.

MADELEINE
No.

ROBOT
Blep.

MADELEINE
You can't leave me here with them.

ROBOT
Blop.

MADELEINE
I won't let you.

Madeleine cranks the Robot, and it recharges. It shakes its head at her, disappointed.

Do you want to read?

ROBOT
(turning away from her)
Beep.

MADELEINE
Do you want to watch something?

ROBOT
Beep.

MADELEINE
Do you want to play?

ROBOT
Beep.

MADELEINE
Do you want to-

ROBOT
BEEP.

MADELEINE
Fine then. Just go!
I don't need you anyway!

She pulls the robot doll out of the Robot, violently.

The Robot creaks, and freezes in place for a moment, then falls to the ground.

She sits, rocking and cradling the doll.

MADELEINE
I am Tarzan....
I am Tarzan...

She cannot get the rest out.

I am tainted.

Lights fade on the cell.

I am poked and prodded and packaged in white.
I erase. I eradicate.
I am the thing that is watched.
I am blight.

All we can see is her face.

I am...
I am...
    Nobody.

Lights out on the Cell.

SCENE 8

The Observation Lab.

Boyle is eating yogurt.

George is watching Madeleine, through the monitors.

Madeleine is laying on the ground. She has clearly been deteriorating.

BOYLE
The meetings have been going well.

GEORGE
That's good.

BOYLE
The lab is going to still need your position and you've been doing well, George. Talking over the buzzer.
I've noticed.
You listened and you...

He waves his hand around, the word doesn't come. He pushes on.

My recommendation is that we keep you on past the trial period.

GEORGE
Oh. Uh. Thanks.

BOYLE
Of course of course.

He somewhat awkwardly gives her pat on the shoulder.

Good work. Yeah.

GEORGE
I wasn't expecting...
I've been trying to stay on top of everything here.
But with her like this now...

BOYLE
Nothing you can do.
She'll be just fine. She goes through phases like this sometimes.
Don't worry about it.

GEORGE
Sure.

BOYLE
She'll bounce right back. Always does.
I'll be back for the night shift. Gonna get some shuteye.

GEORGE
You go on. I'll hold down the fort.

Boyle shoots the yogurt at the trash can. It is a swoosh shot, landing cleanly into the can.

He tries to restrain his glee.

BOYLE
I'll see you.

He exits.

George lets go of the breath she has been holding.

She second-guesses herself, just for a second.

Then she pushes those thoughts away and decisively exits the

Observation Lab, moving to just outside Madeleine's cell.

GEORGE
Good morning, Madeleine.

Madeleine doesn't answer but looks away.

Please talk to me.

We don't have much time.

MADELEINE
Yes, we do.

All the time.
All the things.
All in my padded room.

GEORGE
I want to talk to you about something specific.

MADELEINE
Specific.
Adj. In Biology: of, relating to, or connected with a species.
Also Noun. Archaic. a medicine or remedy effective in treating a particular disease.
The word specific has many meanings.
It isn't very specific, is it?

GEORGE
Boyle will be coming back soon.

MADELEINE
Where did he go?

GEORGE
It doesn't matter.

MADELEINE
But I want to know.

GEORGE
He's in a meeting. The point is it's just us.

MADELEINE
No, it isn't.
Wrong. You're wrong.
He knows.

GEORGE
Who else is here?
Madeleine. Is there someone else here? You can tell me.

> Madeleine shakes her head.

MADELEINE
He'll come.

GEORGE
You keep talking about Him.
Who is that?

MADELEINE
The King of Germs.

GEORGE
Is that the one in your dreams. The King of Germs?

> Madeleine nods.

Has he...always been with you?

> Madeleine shakes her head. Madeleine points to the cameras.

Do you mean the cell, is he in the cell with you?

> Madeleine shakes her head, then points to the cameras again.

GEORGE
The cameras. What about the cameras?

MADELEINE
Behind the cameras.

GEORGE
You mean Boyle.
Don't you?

    Madeleine looks away.

Is he why you're so afraid?

MADELEINE
It itches so badly on my arm.

GEORGE
What did he do to you?

MADELEINE
He tells me not to get into trouble.
But he is the trouble.
I hate him.

GEORGE
I know.

MADELEINE
He hurt me.
He won't let me sleep.

GEORGE
I want to help you with the King of Germs.
Please let me help you.

MADELEINE
You can't.

GEORGE
Why not?

MADELEINE
He made the King of Germs.
And he put him under my skin and into my brain and I can't get rid of him now.
No matter how hard I try. He always comes back.
I didn't like it. I didn't like him touching me with his glove.

GEORGE
And that's when the nightmares started.
Why didn't you tell anyone? Your mother?

MADELEINE
I've been telling you over and over.
You just weren't listening.

GEORGE
Is there anything you'd like to... What would you say if your mother was here?

    Silence.

Madeleine.

MADELEINE
What? That's what I would say.

GEORGE
Nothing? You'd have nothing at all to say to her?

MADELEINE
Yes.

GEORGE
You know that your mother has been trying to stop him.

MADELEINE
Didn't make any difference.

GEORGE
She just didn't know how.

MADELEINE
She should have tried harder then. She should have been smarter like me.

GEORGE
I don't think that's fair, Madeleine.

MADELEINE
Nothing is in here. Adults never listen.

GEORGE
That's not it. She just didn't understand what you were trying to tell her.
Just because we're grown up, doesn't mean we always know what to do.
Even Moms, they don't always know what to do.

MADELEINE
Well, they should. What else are they there for?

GEORGE
When I was about your age.
We started doing experiments and things at school. And I really liked that.
My brother had a toy microscope. He never used it, so I would go foraging for leaves and bugs and specimens in our backyard.
Every day after school, I would spend hours staring at all those things.
Getting to know them, what they really were.
Seeing how all the sections went together.

MADELEINE
Like my Robot.

GEORGE
Yes, like that.
Then one day my mom told me, "If you keep squinting into that microscope all day, your eyes'll stick like that and nobody'll want to look at you."

MADELEINE
That's not true. Your mom's a liar.

GEORGE
Yes, she was.
But she was trying to protect me, in her own way.
And I know she did it because she wanted to help me. ...
Your mother loves you. She is still trying to help you.

Madeleine shrugs.

MADELEINE
If you say so.

GEORGE
Am I a liar?

Madeleine shrugs.

Have I ever lied to you?

Madeleine shakes her head.

Well, there you go. ...

I'm going to tell you something else that's true. Something they didn't tell you.
You weren't the only one, Madeleine.

MADELEINE
What?

GEORGE
You weren't the only one they've held in the facility.
They kept you all separate, isolated.
But there were others. Other children.

MADELEINE
Where are they now?

GEORGE
What?

MADELEINE
The children.

GEORGE
They're gone.

MADELEINE
Gone? Where?

GEORGE
They...They died, Madeleine.

MADELEINE
Oh.

GEORGE
I'm so sorry.

MADELEINE
Why? You didn't kill them. It was the germs, wasn't it?

GEORGE
Yes.

MADELEINE
They always find a way, eventually.
The King of Germs got to them.
He got to them already and that's why he wants me.
That's why he's after me.

GEORGE
No, it wasn't the King of Germs.
What happened to them wasn't an accident.

MADELEINE
What?

GEORGE
Well, some of them, their immune systems failed, yes.

Some of them just couldn't take it anymore.

But the rest of them left.

MADELEINE
How?

GEORGE
They walked out of their rooms.

MADELEINE
Why? Did they think they were fixed?

GEORGE
No... I think they wanted to go outside.

MADELEINE
They walked out?

GEORGE
Yes.

MADELEINE
Did something malfunction?

GEORGE
No.

MADELEINE
But that means...that I can...

George nods.

I can't leave. They won't let me.

GEORGE
Yes, you can. Nexcorp was required to put it in the contract. The "Escape Clause." So they weren't technically imprisoning you.

MADELEINE
Why are you saying this?
You're supposed to keep me here. That's your job.

GEORGE
Not anymore.

MADELEINE
Is this a test? Are you testing me?

GEORGE
No, Madeleine, no more tests.
I'm telling because I think you have the right to know.
Even though I'm sooooo gonna to get fired for doing this.

MADELEINE
You're still in trouble?

GEORGE
I'm definitely going to be.

MADELEINE
Are you going to fight him?

GEORGE
I'm going to try.

MADELEINE
Here take this.

> She holds the robot toy out to George.

GEORGE
I can't do that...

MADELEINE
It'll protect you. Please.

You need it more than me.

> Madeleine places the toy robot into the chute.

> Her side closes. A whir as the item is sanitized.

> George's side opens and she takes it.

MADELEINE
Keep it close.

GEORGE
I will.
You have a choice, Madeleine.
Promise me you'll think about it.

> Madeleine nods.

> As George exits, we catch a glimpse of the King of Germs; he has been in the Cell this whole time without either of them noticing.

> He steps back into the shadows.
> Madeleine sits and speaks to us.

MADELEINE
I am alone.
I am incubator
under my nails and in my cells
And spread out against the glass
growing growing growing
Sicker.
I AM NOT TARZAN.
I do not have an island.
I do not belong here.
In the room they come and go
In the world they come and go.
and go and go and go
Like that's something that I can do.
Like I can lose myself.
While they are measuring me with ticks and hands and changing coats.
But there were more.
More lights.
More cells.

> Alayna appears in the last position that Madeleine saw her. Hand out as if against the glass.

ALAYNA
M a-de-leine.

> Alayna steps forward. Hand still out.

MADELEINE
Why are you here?
You don't usually show up here.
This is my place.

I didn't invite you here.
I didn't ask you here.
Any of you. Not here. I'm alone!

(This might be to us as well.)

I'm alone!

> Madeleine looks. Alayna takes another step toward her.

ALAYNA
Ma-de-leine.

MADELEINE
(as if the words can make Alayna disappear)
I. Am. Alone.

> Madeleine gets up annoyed that apparently Alayna isn't going anywhere.

ALAYNA
Ma-de...

> Alayna's battery runs out and she freezes.
>
> Madeleine looks at her for a moment.
>
> A decision. She cranks her like the Robot.
>
> Alayna awakes.

MADELEINE
I am alone.

ALAYNA
Alone.

MADELEINE
Alone.

ALAYNA
I am here.

MADELEINE
Are you?

> Alayna shrugs.

MADELEINE (CONT'D)
I don't understand.
Why do you put your hand against the glass?
All the times.
Like you never felt it before.

ALAYNA
I... felt...

MADELEINE
You lean against it
Like you are falling
Like the glass will hold you
Like it holds me.

ALAYNA
Hold me.

MADELEINE
Are you happy?

ALAYNA
Happy.

MADELEINE
I'm not.

> Alayna sputters as her battery runs out again.

ALAYNA
Hold me
then leave
miss you
I meant
sorry
Goodbye

> Alayna freezes.
>
> Madeleine moves to her and mimics her pose, like the game she used to play with the Robot.

MADELEINE
Goodbye.

Alayna disappears.
Madeleine returns to talking to us.

MADELEINE (CONT'D)
In a minute there is time for revisions
For decisions.
Decisions. Noun. The action or process of deciding something or resolving a question.
Decide. Verb. To make a choice from a number of alternatives.
Number. Noun. a quantity.
Quantity. Noun. a considerable amount of something.
One two three four five six seven more
More than me.
So many more
the lights will run out
where do I go
In a minute
In a minute

...

there is no time

Madeleine moves to the wall of her cell.

She reaches out.

She puts her hand against the glass.

It's cold.

Lights down on Madeleine in her cell.

SCENE 9
The Observation Lab.

George is at her computer. Boyle enters.

BOYLE
How was the night?

GEORGE
It went better than expected.

BOYLE
Uneventful?

GEORGE
She didn't have nightmares if that's what you're asking.

Boyle hits the intercom. A buzzer sounds.

BOYLE
Good morning, sleepy head.

Lights up in the Cell. Madeleine wakes up to Boyle's voice.

Rise and shine.

GEORGE
How long?

BOYLE
How long what?

GEORGE
How much longer did you negotiate?

BOYLE
15 more years of funding.

Madeleine sits up.

GEORGE
Those are some deep pockets right there.

BOYLE
Nexcorp is committed to helping Madeleine.

GEORGE
Sure they are.
I looked at her blood samples.

BOYLE
What?

GEORGE
They ones I didn't have clearance for.

BOYLE
How did you see those? You weren't supposed to-

GEORGE
And wow, I found some interesting disparities.

Madeleine rubs her eyes.

BOYLE
There's a simple explanation.

GEORGE
That's why no one stays in my position long. The moment they start asking questions, you get rid of them.

BOYLE
We have to protect the experiment.

GEORGE
Except your experiment is a human being, Boyle, a child.
Alayna said some things that...
After that I started snooping.

GEORGE (CONT'D)
By the way, when you work in a high security lab, you should probably sign out on your computer when you leave the office.

BOYLE
This is what you were doing? This whole time.
Going behind my back.
I'm not sure what you think you know, but-

GEORGE
I went through all of them, Boyle.

BOYLE
You don't understand.

GEORGE
I understand completely.
Madeleine remembers last night's dream.

> She looks at her palm.

BOYLE
No you don't. You didn't have to make the hard decisions.
I did what I thought was best.
Nexcorp won't let her go now.
There are consequences that you cannot begin to imagine...
Sorry, but there is more at stake here than your feelings.

GEORGE
Oh nonono. My "feelings" aren't the problem here. You are.

BOYLE
I'm helping people. That's all I've been trying / to do.

> Still sitting, Madeleine reaches out her hand, mimicking her mother's gesture.

GEORGE
So what? That gives you the right to use her like a lab rat?

BOYLE
Yes. It does. Because Madeleine's not the only kid that needs a cure.
If it had worked, you'd be calling me a hero right now.
I thought the injection could heal her and the other kids...
All of them were dying.
They would have shut the lab down if we didn't show some progress. Shut her down.
The results were positive on the other animals we tested it on.
There was some risk involved, but I had to try.

GEORGE
Maybe you can't find a cure. Maybe none of us can. Maybe there is no cure.

BOYLE
There is a cure.

There has to be a cure.

GEORGE
You've been doing this for 11 years, and you still have no idea what it is.

BOYLE
You're done here. I hope you know that.

I hope this was worth it to you.

GEORGE
We're all done here.

BOYLE
What does that mean?

> George looks away.
>
> Madeleine speaks to the audience.

MADELEINE
Is it all futile?

The conversations continue in the two separate spaces.

BOYLE
I said, what does that mean?

MADELEINE
Futilely. Adverb. To no avail; to be unsuccessful in comprehending.

Example: They had gone to a great deal of expense for nothing.

GEORGE
I told her that she could leave.

BOYLE
Are you insane?

GEORGE
She doesn't want to be fixed. She just wants to be free.

BOYLE
She can't leave, she would infect all of us.

GEORGE
What?

BOYLE
The injection effectively weaponized her condition.
Remember, her auto immune disorder?

THE ONE WE HAVE NO CURE FOR.

GEORGE
I didn't...I didn't know.

MADELEINE
Nothingness or "non-existence": First recorded circa 1631.
What does that say about people?

MADELEINE
That that's the first time they thought to consider that?

BOYLE
Nexcorp will destroy you for this.

GEORGE
No. If we live through whatever she has now. Nexcorp is done. And so are you.

BOYLE
Is that a threat?

GEORGE
Think of it as a warning.

The Observation Lab goes dark.

Madeleine sits in her pool of light.

MADELEINE
There were more.

ROBOT
More.

The Robot appears, standing behind her.

Madeleine turns and sees it.

MADELEINE
You're here. You're still here.

ROBOT
Still here.

The Robot places a hand over her heart. We hear the sound of her heartbeat.

The sound of other heartbeats join Madeleine's.

MADELEINE
They are. Here. Now. I can hear them.
The beating, beating thumpity hearts of the children.

MADELEINE (CONT'D)
That beat away in their mother's arms.
That failed in the test tube that I lived in.
I follow, I fade.

> *A song like Elvis Presley's "It's Now or Never" begins to play, blending together with the heartbeat.*

It's him. It's them.

> *She sees the King of Germs standing outside the cell with the horde of hands. There are people attached to the hands. They all wave at her.*

You've been waiting for me to come.
You're the others, aren't you? The ones like me? Before.

> *He nods.*

I didn't realize. I'm sorry about hating you.

> *He shrugs, holds out his arms to her, and waits.*
>
> *Madeleine looks at the Robot.*
>
> *The Robot takes her hand.*

ROBOT
Together.

MADELEINE
(to audience)
Good-bye.

> *As Madeleine and the Robot step out of the cell toward the King of Germs, everything slows down, and the stage goes black.*

End of Play.

BLACK PARENT UNION FOREWORD

At its core, *Black Parent Union* by Gary Enrique Bradley-Lopez is a play about the enduring strength of the human spirit and the transformative power of solidarity. High school parents of black students at the Johnson Hill School District have gathered around their children who took part in an in-school protest against discrimination from their white peers, teachers, and administration. Utilizing the tools of community organizing, agitation, and tension, difficult decisions are made for the students. It is a call to action for all of us to join together and fight for a more just and equitable world, where every child, regardless of their race or background, has the opportunity to succeed and thrive.

The staged reading of *Black Parent Union* kicked off KCPublic's 5th season in October 2022 and was presented at Fountain City Winery in our most attended Theatre Lab to date.

BLACK PARENT UNION

A Play

By: Gary Enrique Bradley-Lopez

Cast

Julius - Black, Early 30's - Late 30's

Melissa – Black, Late 40's - Early 60's

Taylor - Black, Late 40's - Early 60's

Broderick - Black, Late 40's - Early 60's

Ricee – Black, Early 20's - Late 20's

Elizabeth – White, Mid 30's - Mid 40's

Cedric – Black, Mid 50's - Mid 60's

Cameron/Librarian/Superintendent - White, over 30

ACT ONE

PROLOGUE

A spotlight hits center stage where CAMERON, a reporter for KCHB 12, steps into the spotlight with a mic from the news stations and holds his cellphone in the other hand which he scrolls. He puts the phone in his pocket, then puts his finger on his ear, shakes his head nodding yes, then goes live.

CAMERON

This has not been an easy week for students, particularly African American students, and administration at Johnson Hill High. After a series of racial incidents—from black face snapchats, the use of the n-word on TikTok by non-African American students, racist prom-posals, teachers repeating the n-word to students of color, and coaches assisting racist cultures in practices—racial tensions across the student body have divided the Johnson Hill High School. Students have lashed out across social media and one student in particular says that "Administration has been made aware of all the incidents; however, they take no action and if anything, participate in the actions as well." Today a group of students who were finally fed up organized a protest that lasted the whole day until administration finally took back control. Since then, the superintendent has mentioned that he has been made aware about the incidents that have taken place at Johnson Hill. He said the students who organized the protest have been identified and were sent home early; however, no decisions have been made about

CAMERON (CONT'D)
any disciplinary actions. *(looks at phone)* Just in - parents will be notified about what the consequences will be in a meeting tonight. This is due to being unable to control the student protest at the same time as deciding disciplinary actions. Students have made it a point to make their voice heard. Now we wait to see what happens next. Whether consequences or progress, we will continue to provide coverage on this story. This is Cameron Woods with KCHB 12.

Lights out.

SCENE ONE

That night, walking through the door to the hallway from the principal's office are JULIUS, MELISSA, RICEE (pronounced Ricky), and TAYLOR, parents of the five students who organized the protest.

JULIUS
Two weeks, two weeks of suspension and one week of in-school suspension is wrong, especially since basically half of the student body participated.

TAYLOR
I never would've known my daughter of being capable of doing anything like this.

JULIUS
I'd say be proud.

RICEE
You would.

MELISSA
You know, Julius, I appreciate you standing up for our kids back there. I'm Melissa by the way.

JULIUS
All this shit is on social media. What our kids have experienced is in plain sight and nothing is happening other than our kids being disciplined because they reacted, it's wrong.

RICEE
What y'all expect, it's a mostly white school.

JULIUS
Ricee, right?

RICEE
Yeah, the twins.

JULIUS
Mine is Nicky the freshman. Have your kids been telling you about the stuff that's been happening?

RICEE
Yeah, they have. I've seen the videos and pics, but like I told them, the schools over here are like that, they need to be tough and focus on they education, they not here to make friends.

JULIUS
It's more than that, Ricee. If a school is predominantly white, they have the right to be racist and raggedy to our kids?

RICEE
Basically.

JULIUS
Ricee, it's 2022, we got to nip this shit in the bud, sis.

RICEE
Not your sis.

TAYLOR
We moved over to this area so our daughter can have a better education, not a traumatizing experience.

MELISSA
Well, what are we supposed to do about it?

JULIUS
I say we do what our kids did.

TAYLOR
But look what happened to them, Julius. They all suspended for two weeks, and then in-school suspension following that. My daughter gone be bussing tables at the restaurant for two weeks. My husband does not play that.

JULIUS
Who gone suspend us, Mrs. Taylor? And that's the thing, the best solution to all this is to send our kids home and not be in class? Where they will get behind for two straight weeks with 8 classes on their schedules. Some of y'all got 'em in AP classes…

TAYLOR
That's right. But what can we do?

JULIUS
Like I said: follow our kids' example.

MELISSA
And who are we going to get to participate?

RICEE
And who got time for all that, because I'm a full-time student and work a full-time CNA job at night, one that I actually got to head to in a few minutes.

JULIUS
Look, we ain't got to figure everything out tonight, we just got to do something simple. I do this. I organize, and I know I just moved to the school district, but I don't care if I've been here one day or none. If my child doesn't feel safe, I'm gone do something about it. Ladies, y'all pay taxes here, we elect the school board, we are the decision makers, and trust me, with a little strategy, I bet you our kids won't just be a set of monkeys to these folks no more.

MELISSA
So how does all this start?

JULIUS
Look, Melissa, I say let's all have a meeting. Let's invite all the parents of black students. We can have a strategy session, then we push, agitate, organize until our needs are met.

RICEE
What are our needs?

JULIUS
For my kid to be safe, but everyone has their own self-interest in this fight, we all have our own, but the same ultimate goal.

MELISSA
So, you're saying invite all parents of black children. You think they will really come to the meeting?

TAYLOR
How are we supposed to recruit black parents? Ain't that many black students in the school district.

JULIUS
We got to use our connections, be creative. We got to be willing to meet new parents, we can make flyers and have our children hand them out to black students to give to their parents, there's many ways.

MELISSA
I'm part of the PTA. I can access the list of parents and maybe make a few calls.

JULIUS
There you go, Melissa, that's what I'm talking about. Shoot, I may come pick my kid up and look for all the black parents to invite.

RICEE
So, what, are you the president of the black parent union?

JULIUS
Nah, but I'm digging the name.

TAYLOR
Well, if we do, I would love it if we could potentially meet on the weekend. I can bring my husband along, Y'all would be better at explaining all this to him than me.

MELISSA
I can tell y'all now my husband will not be making his way to this group, and I got to think of a way to persuade him to not discipline our daughter for being part of this protest.

JULIUS
Why would he do that?

MELISSA
Because she just got suspended

JULIUS
But for a racial incident that she stood up for herself on. I'm not trying to butt in…

RICEE
But you are.

MELISSA
My husband is a complicated man, and our daughter is in the college application stage of high school. A suspension in his eyes will be as if she dropped out of high school.

TAYLOR
I bet my husband will have the same attitude, but I'm gone bring him to this meeting.

MELISSA
I'll try but I know he won't have time, nor would he care for anything like this, so I'll be part of it on our behalf.

JULIUS
How about this Saturday?

MELISSA
That is very quick, only four days away.

JULIUS
It's that urgent! Especially when our children are losing educational time for addressing what is wrong!

RICEE
Oh, the speeches.

JULIUS
Excuse m- Never mind, look, I will call the Lee library for the multipurpose room and reserve it. I'm going to organize this meeting, regardless of who wants to be involved or not. However, I would love to have all of you *(looks at all three of them)* and your leadership as a part of this.

TAYLOR
I'll bring my husband, and I'll make a few calls to see what I can do.

MELISSA
I'll get that list as soon as I get home.

RICEE
And I'm going to work.

RICEE walks toward the end of the stage where she is met by CAMERON the reporter with a mic and a spotlight.

CAMERON
Hi, I'm Cameron Woods with KCHB 12. Are you one of the parents of the students disciplined?

RICEE
Two of the students.

CAMERON
Quick interview?

RICEE
(with attitude and sassy)
Nah, I am not ready for TV, but you might want to interview Julius Brown, the organizer that y'all always put on TV.

CAMERON
He lives in the Johnson Hill public school district?

RICEE
That's what I said.

She walks off the stage and lights comes on full stage.

MELISSA
How do you know Ricee?

TAYLOR
Right, because I felt some heat there.

JULIUS
Did you?

TAYLOR
I sure did. What you do to her, Julius?

JULIUS
Okay, Mrs. Mother, I've literally never met her until today. I've never felt that much tension, and I have messed with some big angry people.

TAYLOR
There's got to be some history there.

MELISSA
Agreed, you all think she's going to come back?

JULIUS
I wouldn't know, but I hope she does.

MELISSA
I've seen you on the news before.

TAYLOR
You do the protest.

JULIUS
Yeah, usually when the news showcases the shitty side of the city. They somehow get me on TV speaking out against them. I guess that's just part of the work.

MELISSA
What is it that you do, like your job title and stuff?

JULIUS
I'm an organizer for a Metro Faith for Justice, just organizing people of color and faith communities around race issues.

JULIUS (CONT'D)
So, we do more than just protest but we do a lot to ensure our voices are heard. That's why I'm always on TV. But since y'all asking me questions, what you young ladies do?

TAYLOR
Look at him tryna be nice, Melissa. Me and my HUSBAND, young man, own a soul food restaurant called Papa Tori that was once owned by my grandparents since the 70's - over the river.

JULIUS
Aw yes, I love that place. Y'all's smothered pork chops are so good, and that banana pudding at the end of the meal is always on spot. I've definitely seen you before, Taylor. That restaurant is a staple in that area, and the only place - maybe last place - that's still cooking chitlins on Friday.

MELISSA
Eww, no.

TAYLOR
She doesn't know what she is missing. I'm the one that cleans 'em and gets them right, so I know they are delicious. Next time you come, ask for that pork chop meal PapaTori style and I promise that you won't regret it.

JULIUS
I been needing a free meal.

TAYLOR
Oh no, not free, baby.

JULIUS laughs.

JULIUS
No, I'm just giving you a hard time. What about you, Melissa?

MELISSA
I used to be a preschool teacher, but once I had kids I stayed home. My husband owns a construction company, so I've been in this career as a stay-at-home mom for around 20 something years.

TAYLOR
I wish I could do that.

MELISSA
And I wish I was a business owner.

TAYLOR
Well, come on then, I'll sell you Papa Tori, don't play.

CEDRIC the school janitor walks in fiddling with the keys. He looks up and recognizes the group of parents still speaking.

CEDRIC
Hey folks, we about to shut this place down in a few minutes.

JULIUS
Alright now, we'll get out y'all way. *(looks back at the women)* Okay ladies, here is my business card, feel free to send me y'all information through email or my cell, and I'll start working on at least something tonight.

MELISSA
Okay, I'm really looking forward to this. To the change we are going to make.

TAYLOR
We will see.

JULIUS
Have some faith, Mrs. Taylor, please. Trust me a little bit, it'll take time, but you'll see the change.

CEDRIC
That didn't mean stand and continue talking. I gotta clean this place and I can't with y'all in here.

They all walk off stage, TAYLOR and MELISSA first. JULIUS stops and looks at CEDRIC.

JULIUS
Brother, we gone make some changes up here. You ain't gone have to deal with all that racist shit.

CEDRIC
Man, I work at night, ain't nobody studying you, nigga.

JULIUS
You don't care about the racism in these schools?

CEDRIC
I get paid, my kid gets to go here, and I got a daughter in college now who graduated from here. I've been treated good.

JULIUS
You should join our group. We about to organize parents to make changes out here.

CEDRIC
Man, you just up here to stir up some trouble. Just like y'all kids who left a damn mess in the gym that I gotta clean up. And here y'all are making more of it. I know about you, I should've known one of your kids was involved, but I ain't know you were here with the rich folks.

JULIUS
Are you that mad that we were talking about tryna make some change?

CEDRIC
No, my problem is I clean this building at night, and when they have their parent meetings, I ain't ever seen one of you black parents in those meetings making some type of change you talking about. Now y'all out here tryna do the most to make it tougher for these kids. At this point, we need to make sure our kids benefit from the education, so they can go to college for free like my daughter, and no more parents' meetings so I ain't got another damn classroom in this building.

JULIUS
Our meeting will be at the Lee Library multipurpose room, for your information. Meet us up there on Saturdays *(JULIUS extends his hand for a shake, but CEDRIC leaves him hanging.)* and what I ain't gone do is argue with another brother in a white school district. Have a good night.

JULIUS walks towards the other side of the stage. He is met with a spotlight and CAMERON the reporter, with a mic in his hand. They go live.

CAMERON
We are here with Julius Brown, who is a parent of one of the students who organized the protest. Julius, we have spoken to you in other capacities, but now here at the Johnson Hill School district - who would have imagined.

JULIUS
I know right, who would've imagined... Was sup?

CAMERON
Well, can you share with us what were the disciplinary actions against your child and the rest of the students?

JULIUS
Our children were suspended for two weeks, with a one week in-school suspension when they return. Let me remind you, this is all because they acted on their faith and values to stand up against racism, racism that has and is being ignored by the district. That's the real issue at hand.

CAMERON
I'm assuming your child will not be disciplined by you for any of this.

JULIUS
For what? I'm proud of my kid, and the district is going to have to answer a lot of questions about the racist culture created by

JULIUS (CONT'D)
the admin, teachers, and students. We not gone let them off hang on this one.

CAMERON
Are you saying you will be bringing your organizing skills to the Johnson Hill school district?

JULIUS
What I'm saying is we gone make some changes. Now I gotta leave. I got some strategizing to do.

JULIUS exits offstage.

CAMERON
You heard it here, I believe it is safe to say that Julius Brown, organizer in Kansas City who has a child in the Johnson Hill school district, will be organizing some type of action as we have seen in previous years with policing, immigration, and business development through the Kansas City metro. We have seen him win there. Drastic changes - some would say for the better. Will he be able to do the same in a suburb that just happens to be majority white? Stay tuned for more coverage on this story. Cameron Woods with KCHB 12.

Light dims up. CAMERON looks at audience as if they were a cameraman.

CAMERON
Yeah, I think we got a story on us. Were the shots good?

CEDRIC
I wish y'all would leave so I can clean this god damn building.

CAMERON rushes off stage. Lights out.

SCENE TWO

That Saturday, JULIUS is alone in the room. He has a backpack and sheets of paper that he sets in one of the chairs. He rearranges the chairs at the tables to sit in a semicircle. MELISSA walks in - without her husband.

MELISSA
Sorry, I couldn't persuade my husband.

JULIUS
You ain't gotta apologize, at least you're here! That's how it be sometimes. He didn't take it well?

MELISSA
No, he was upset and lashed out at my daughter before I let him know how I felt. He didn't understand but said as long as she don't fall behind.

JULIUS
That's not so bad, Melissa. We just got to make sure she doesn't fall behind.

MELISSA
I know my baby won't. She is too smart for all of that. I already contacted all her teachers to send over the assignments she'll be missing out on.

JULIUS
Maybe I can persuade your husband. Usually me and the brothas can sit down for a drink and talk it out. One good one-on-one with me and you'll feel invested.

Melissa laughs.

JULIUS
You don't think it will work?

MELISSA
Well, my husband isn't a brotha as you said.

JULIUS
He's white?

MELISSA
Yes, he is.

JULIUS
Oh.

MELISSA
Oh?

JULIUS
No, I'm sorry I just…

MELISSA
Didn't expect me to be married with a white man?

JULIUS
In all honesty, no. I don't know why I thought you was married to some Barack Obama looking nigga, but there's nothing like a Joe Biden.

MELISSA
Absolutely not! My husband looks more like an older Beto O'Rourke with a full beard.

JULIUS
How is that for you, if you don't mind me asking?

MELISSA
I love my husband, not his family, but I love him. We have been together since I met him when I was a teacher and he dropped off his niece at my school. He liked what he saw, but he had a lot of learning if he was planning on it.

JULIUS
How does your family take it?

MELISSA
My parents didn't care because I was marrying into money, isn't that crazy? That's actually why he is the favorite in-law. My siblings, on the other hand, thought I was a sellout, anti-black as you say, but they came around, especially when my daughter got older. But I'll say this, Julius: at the end of the day it was our decision, and we still support it, even when it's not easy, but therapy helps a lot.

JULIUS
Me or my wife should probably do that.

MELISSA
How about you tell me about your wife?

JULIUS
My wife picked up our son from school, so she already knew. She was pissed about the consequences - I had to hold her back from getting white and shooting the school up.

MELISSA
Oh.

JULIUS
I'm sorry, that was inappropriate. With your husband being white and shit. Here we are trying to get the kids in trouble who do stuff like that, and here I am doing the same. I'm sorry. That wasn't cool.

MELISSA
It's fine.

JULIUS
Okay, so anyways, wife was pretty upset, but she the breadwinner in the family. She's the dean of student services up at the juco, so her timing is tight, plus me and her can't work together on organizing, so she knows I got us.

MELISSA
Is that right?

JULIUS
Ha yes, in our younger days we were both organizers.

MELISSA
She was too? Oh, I'd like to hear this.

JULIUS
And now she's a Dean. Can you imagine that? I stuck with it though. We organized and eventually won a fight to modify a liquor license ordinance that was essentially prohibiting jobs for people who were formerly incarcerated when we were younger. Me and her organized, fought, loved, and fought so much more. Finally after a few years, she determined that she's done organizing, and she's definitely done

JULIUS (CONT'D)
organizing with me. We struggled with our public and private relationship in this work, which could have ruined our relationship. I mean, I agree I'm a pretty mean organizer. Good boyfriend, but she held them work grudges all the way home.

MELISSA
But was marriage easier?

JULIUS
Soulmates easy, colleagues trash.

TAYLOR and her husband BRODERICK walk in.

TAYLOR
Hey, y'all.

MELISSA
Hi, Taylor.

JULIUS
Y'all made it!

TAYLOR
This is my husband Broderick, and Broderick, this is Julius and Melissa. both of their children were suspended for the protest as well.

BRODERICK
Nice meeting both of y'all. you know y'all gone have to explain all of this too me. I ain't getting it yet.

JULIUS
Any way we can help, Mr. Broderick.

BRODERICK
You can call me Broderick, but what is the purpose of all this? Our kids were suspended. What are we supposed to do about it? By the time we make any changes our kids gone be back in school, maybe even graduated by then.

JULIUS
You know, I don't know what the group will decide to do, but regardless, our kids were disciplined for their actions, but no one was disciplined for the racist anything that caused the protest. If we don't do nothing, all this will continue to happen. I know it's a stretch but…

BRODERICK
You think a few parents, black parents, who ain't even half of the school district gone be able to create some change? And if so, what is it?

JULIUS
I think we can. I think if we put pressure and strategize, we can get something done. I'm not sure what that looks like—that's why I need parents to be involved in this collectively. We plan it together.

BRODERICK
I don't know, I'm here because my wife said, but I am not confident the leaders of this district will do anything about anything. They never have.

JULIUS
You ain't confident in the leaders, then what you gonna do?

BRODERICK
Oh, I don't know.

JULIUS
So you continue letting them be shitty?

TAYLOR
No.

JULIUS
So what you gonna do, Mrs. Taylor? You gonna push on them? You gonna meet with the superintendent? You gonna speak at the board meeting? You gonna run for one of those school board positions?

TAYLOR
School board?

JULIUS
You ain't ever thought of running?

TAYLOR
They ain't gone vote me in. I ain't white.

MELISSA
Could break the glass ceiling.

TAYLOR
I don't know about all that, but I'm gonna be part of the group, and help out here.

JULIUS
That's what I'm talking about. They have never had a group of black parents letting them know what the deal is.

TAYLOR
Alright now.

MELISSA
They never have, I'm sure.

ELIZABETH, a white mother, walks in and everybody stares at her with an awkward pause which she eventually breaks.

ELIZABETH
Hi, I'm Elizabeth. My son Quinton is a junior at the school, and he gave me this flyer to attend.

BRODERICK
Black parents, huh.

JULIUS
Yeah, yeah, hi, welcome, come in. Uh, we haven't started yet, just waiting for a few more parents.

ELIZABETH
I know I'm white, I see it in everyone's face. My child is black, I thought I should probably be here.

BRODERICK
You adopted?

TAYLOR
Broderick! Forgive him.

ELIZABETH
No worries, I'm used to it, my boyfriend in college was black. I'm pretty open about it because I'm used to getting asked.

MELISSA
Thank you for taking the time to come.

TAYLOR
I didn't even come to think of parents of bi-racial children, or white parents of black children.

BRODERICK
I wouldn't have thought they would come anyways.

TAYLOR
Broderick, act like you in public.

ELIZABETH
I know how white parents are, but I'm trying. My son comes home to me about things. I have no clue about anything, but I'm trying. I hope this gets me somewhere.

JULIUS
And friend, that is what we call a co-conspirator.

ELIZABETH
A what?

JULIUS
A co-conspirator, someone with us trying to get shit done.

ELIZABETH
So, an ally.

JULIUS
Kinda. An ally is like a white person that supports but really just takes up space, do it when its trendy. A co-conspirator gets shit done. Is that what you here for?

ELIZABETH
I'm here to learn.

JULIUS
Elizabeth, this group isn't a school. We are here to get things done, do it all together. If you just here to learn, you taking up space. We need people to work with us, be in the fight with us.

RICEE walks in.

RICEE
Y'all did all that organizing and only got two new people in here.

JULIUS
Who did you bring with you?

RICEE
No one.

JULIUS
Right, so thank you for joining our meeting. Look, I know it may not be a lot of us, and who knows who will make their way in here, but it's never been about the quantity of people but the quality of work we can get done. I organized a bill to ban out-of-school suspension in a school district with three parents and four co-conspirators. With a lot of work and commitment, we got something done. It does not matter how many people are here as long as we have a common goal of getting shit done.

MELISSA
Can we go ahead and start? I have to pick up my mother in-law to go grocery shopping in the next hour or so.

JULIUS
Let's do it then. We can have a seat, I printed off a few agendas. *(passes them out)* Feel free to let me know if we need to add anything, but I made it simple so that we can get straight to the point.

RICEE
Oh, you gone be the leader of this meeting?

JULIUS
I mean-

RICEE
Cause you already got yourself on the news.

JULIUS
I mean, I don't care. Does anyone want to be the leader of this group?

Pause for a second. No one says anything.

JULIUS
So-

RICEE
I think Melissa should be the leader of this group. She did kind of call it to order.

JULIUS
Well, Melissa?

MELISSA
Oh, I don't know.

JULIUS
Take a shot at it, just follow the agenda, and trust your gut.

TAYLOR
Go ahead and try, Melissa.

BRODERICK
If the lady doesn't want to, what y'all pressuring her for?

JULIUS
Well, Ricee nominated her so-

MELISSA
No, it's fine, I can do it.

MELISSA stands up and JULIUS sits down.

MELISSA
Well, let's go ahead and start with the first thing on the agenda, it says introductions. Maybe let's say the name, grade of our child, and what you want to get out of this? I guess I should go first. I'm Melissa, my daughter is a junior, and two boys - one freshman, one middle, and another son who is currently in the service. You know, after yesterday I feel like I want to be able to support my daughter in this decision she strongly feels about. I saw her passion, and last night, you all helped me understand that I needed to do more, and I think I can do that with this group. Taylor?

TAYLOR
Yes, I'm Taylor. We also have a daughter. She is a sophomore, and I in no way support my daughter getting in trouble, but I also heard what you were saying, Julius. It's 2022, and here we are dealing with the same stuff our parents and we went through. Something got to change. Go ahead, baby.

BRODERICK
I'm Broderick. As my wife said, we got a 16-year-old daughter, and I'm here because she brought me.

RICEE
I'll go next. I'm Ricee, and I got two twins that were involved in this. They were my sisters' boys, but when she passed, I adopted them at 21 when they were both nine. I also have a daughter in kindergarten that's in the district. And I honestly don't know why I am here, but I wanted to see what was going to happen. Mrs. Lady, go ahead.

ELIZABETH
I'm Elizabeth. I have a sophomore in high school. My son was showing me all the things that were happening, and you know I sent an email and called the administration, but no one seemed to care, which I thought was odd. So, when my son gave me this flier you all made, I figured this is where I'm supposed to be.

JULIUS
I am Julius. I have a freshman and two elementary-age kids. You know, we just moved here, but I was thinking about all the changes we've done in the neighboring communities, and it was clear that we could be doing the same here. Yeah, most of these people don't look like us, but that doesn't mean shit cause I'm not scared to organize against them.

MELISSA
Thank you, Julius. Got intros done. Next is, what is the real problem?

BRODERICK
That my daughter is about to be behind in school for getting suspended.

JULIUS
We got to look at the root of it. Let's dig deeper and lean into the actual problem.

TAYLOR
Yeah, baby, if all these racist incidents wasn't happening, our daughter and the rest of the kids wouldn't have showed out like they did.

ELIZABETH
So, the root of the problem is the unaddressed racist behavior created by the students, teachers, admin, with no solutions.

RICEE
Okay, white girl, I like you. You ain't like the rest of these white mothers.

TAYLOR
I will say, these white suburban mothers do have something, a stank I just don't like about them.

BRODERICK
Oh lord don't go telling them the stor–

TAYLOR
The worst decision that I ever made was to invite a few of my child's classmates' parents over to our restaurant so that they could come and try out some real down to earth soul food. These stanky bitches came with their family, and lord Jesus, every time I came around, they smiled in my face, said the food was good, but was treating our staff

TAYLOR (CONT'D)
like trash, complained about everything and the worst-

BRODERICK
Here she go-

TAYLOR
These bitches left us horrible Yelp reviews. I ain't know what Yelp was and was never on it until these fake Ugg-wearing plastic mannequin bitches started sharing their unnecessary opinions of my restaurant, a restaurant that's been here forever.

BRODERICK
She been talking about this for months now.

RICEE
What made you think it was smart to invite the-

TAYLOR
I'm a business owner, I'm always selling my business so people can come, and we can grow our base.

RICEE
Well, you don't know your audience.

BRODERICK
Young lady, ain't no audience, we have a business, and we need to branch across to everyone because they all need to taste our food.

RICEE
And now you got bad Yelp reviews. That's the problem, you got a staple in the

RICEE (CONT'D)
community over there, made a pillar because of the Black community, and here you are inviting white folks that don't appreciate good soul food! Fuck 'em, you don't need them, Papas Tori's gone survive without them, always has and always will.

It is quiet for a second. BRODERICK and TAYLOR look at each other.

MELISSA
Maybe we should get back on the agenda. I think we left off with Elizabeth stating the root. Next on the agenda is what is the solution and strategy. Any ideas?

ELIZABETH
I'll just say now that emails and phone calls don't work. I have also had meetings with them, and it has not gone well, but for other issues, like abortion rights, they might get you in...

JULIUS
So, if a white lady didn't have a decent meeting with admin, we definitely ain't. They met about technology, school lunches and Michelle Obama, but not on some racist shit.

They all sit silent for a moment thinking.

MELISSA
Let me put my teacher cap on. Let's step back for a moment. What is the solution we want to reach y'all? We all know "Stop racial things at Johnson Hill High," hell, the whole district, but what are the, the, the-

JULIUS
The demands.

MELISSA
Yes, thank you.

RICEE
I know- I got to do this for my job, a diversity, equity, inclusion training.

JULIUS
And an organizational audit, with an emphasis on its DEI culture.

MELISSA
Okay good, I'm sure our district doesn't have a director of diversity, equity, and inclusion, so maybe hiring someone for that.

JULIUS
All they gone do is add a top nigga in charge of that department, they gone tell 'em how shitty they are, then they're going to leave. We need more people of color in other leadership positions. And if they won't-

TAYLOR
Then we gonna have to add some Black leadership. Yeah, I like that. We need to find someone.

BRODERICK
I'm thinking about what my daughter would want me to think, and that is that the principals and them need to listen to 'em, and that anyone involved in the racism be disciplined, and more than my daughter, since she is out here missing two weeks of school.

RICEE
But how we gonna get that to them if they ain't gonna meet with us?

JULIUS
I got an idea, but I don't know how y'all will feel about it.

MELISSA
Well, what is it?

JULIUS
Look, we write a letter to the district and the high school admin and request a meeting with them on our terms, our location. Let them know about the demands we would like them to accept and tell them that if the demands are not met, there will be consequences - such as potentially organizing. All the black parents, or parents of black students, will move their students from the district - the school will lose students and money and could close down a school or two.

RICEE
That is a crazy idea.

BRODERICK
I have to agree with her on that one.

ELIZABETH
It would be a hard strategy, but really, it's just a threat to get a meeting, right?

JULIUS
Yeah, sure.

TAYLOR
You are not playing. You really want to do this, don't you?

JULIUS
Look, y'all, for now it's just a letter, and we do a press release, send it out to the media, give them Melissa's information so she can do the interviews and let them know we are real about this. Hell, we can get a petition going and do a campaign to get people across the region to send admin an email. If we don't meet with them by two weeks, then maybe we need to act and get our students out of there, cause clearly, they don't want them.

BRODERICK
I don't know, man.

TAYLOR
It would be hard to persuade parents to move their children. I mean, we moved over here cause the schools had a great teacher rating, high A.C.T. scores, and many of them go on to college.

JULIUS
But at what cost, y'all? have good grades and trauma? Look, we can come up with some type of system. We have charter schools nearby. I know, I haven't been the biggest fan of them, but some are authentic. We got private schools for those that can afford it, and hell, some of us got families who live over the river - use their address. Oh yeah, and there are some online schools. We can create an accountability program for the students to ensure that they are on track.

RICEE
That's easy for you to say, Julius.

TAYLOR
Here they go.

JULIUS
Ricee, what is your problem? Did you just come to attack everything I say and not come up with any type of a solution, or are you here to give business advice to people that have been running a restaurant that has been here for 50-something years? I've literally never met you until the past week and all you have done is challenge everything I say and I'm quite tired of it.

RICEE
This is my problem. You're an organizer, you literally make money off the deaths of each one of these black folks who get killed by the police, by just being on tv protesting any type of shitty situation that has to do with our city. You're there organizing, talking about being there for the poor, about the people, but look at you, get to come home in your suburban neighborhood while the rest of us still got to sleep in this - yeah I just admitted I don't live in this district. I use my auntie's address. But my twin's mama was killed near the very high school they were supposed to attend. I'm not having it. I don't get to just leave, but my twins do, and that is what this school does. Okay, they get a nigga here and nigger there, but they ain't got shot, haven't gotten anyone pregnant, and good sports programs. The opportunities are larger out here.

JULIUS
Ricee, that shit's deep, and I understand, but you don't know me. You ain't once asked me why I live here. I protested, organized, and agitated so many leaders and cops in that community that it was no longer safe for my family or me. We didn't run from the hood, we ran from the cops that were making the hood unsafe for us, that is why we bounced. I'm an organizer. If there's something wrong in my city, I got to be there, because if we are not out there fighting the fight, decisions will be made under our nose. I know you may not like how I move, but trust me, I care about more than just my kids, but for your twins, your daughters, everybody's kids in this room, our babies shouldn't be going through this.

RICEE
We gone see what you about.

JULIUS
I'm gone prove you right.

MELISSA
Well, I'm in.

TAYLOR
Me too.

BRODERICK
Hell, let's do it then.

ELIZABETH
I can help in any way you need.

They all look at RICEE.

RICEE
Okay. But if it gets to the point we need to move our children's schools, y'all gone hear from me.

JULIUS
We got you.

The stage turns dark with a spotlight on CAMERON as MELISSA steps into the spotlight. They are live.

CAMERON
The parents of the students suspended at Johnson Hill High School have organized a group of parents who are demanding a meeting with the district and high school administration. With me we have Melissa Davis, a leader of the Black Parent Union here. Mrs. Davis, what are the plans of your group?

MELISSA
We have sent a letter to the administration of the district and the high school to discuss the recent racial incidents that have happened around our children. We have mentioned some demands to include a diversity, equity, and inclusion director, training, and audit. We have demanded that the administration listen to the students and discipline those involved in the racial incident. While these are not all the solutions, these are the steps that we believe will open the door.

CAMERON
What happens if you all don't meet?

MELISSA
All I'll say is if our children made it back to school after being suspended and we still have not had a meeting, then there will be some drastic changes in the school district.

CAMERON
You heard it here, folks, on KCHB 12. Parents will act against the district if they have not met to discuss their demands. Stay tuned as we continue to bring more about this story in the coming days. This is Cameron Woods.

Lights out.

SCENE THREE

Three weeks later TAYLOR, BRODERICK, and RICEE sit near each other in conversation. BRODERICK'S leg is shaking, and RICEE is clearly upset. TAYLOR puts her hand on BRODERICK's leg to stop him.

BRODERICK
I still don't know how I feel about all of this. I'm still trying to figure out where we gone put our daughter so late in high school.

TAYLOR
I'm sure we can figure something out; they presented a lot of options.

RICEE
Our kids went back today, and because of this strategy, all the students are treating them like shit.

TAYLOR
Our daughter said the same. It's almost like we have no other choice but to remove our daughter from the district. It's too toxic.

RICEE
I just can't put my boys back in our actual school district. I'm not sure, and I definitely don't want them doing online work so they can stay home and act a fool. I knew this wasn't a good idea.

BRODERICK
We will see what Julius has planned for us.

RICEE
Melissa has planned for us. She's the leader of this group.

BRODERICK
She doesn't do it alone.

ELIZABETH walks in.

ELIZABETH
Hi, everyone.

She walks to sit and puts her purse down.

TAYLOR
Hi, Elizabeth.

RICEE
Hey, girl.

ELIZABETH
How did your children take their first day back?

BRODERICK
They got them in in-school suspension, walking them through the halls like prisoners, everyone treating them bad.

ELIZABETH
That's what I thought. Look - my son sent me a photo from an email the principal sent. It says, "Dear Students, we look forward to ending the year on a good note. Therefore, to do so, any student who interacts with the students responsible for the protest will be disciplined. Prom could potentially be on the line for a few of you. I ask you to make wise

ELIZABETH (CONT'D)
decisions and let's continue to be the Bald Eagles that we are!" Sent this to all students except ours.

BRODERICK
Isn't that some bullshit?

RICEE
Let me see the phone.

ELIZABETH stands up and hands it to her.

RICEE
Wow, that ain't right, look!

Passes the phone to TAYLOR.

ELIZABETH
My son said they couldn't talk to them because they were in in-school suspension, but even after school, on the bus, or any time or place, people either didn't talk to them or talked about them.

TAYLOR
Our daughter said not even the teachers made eye contact with them.

MELISSA and JULIUS walk in with a stack of paper, multiple pamphlets, and boxes of palm cards.

JULIUS
Hey, y'all.

RICEE
Have you heard about everything going on with the students?

MELISSA
What happened?

TAYLOR
They sent an email to the students to not interact with our kids or they will be disciplined.

ELIZABETH grabs the phone from TAYLOR who then hands it to MELISSA. JULIUS looks over her shoulder.

JULIUS
I figured something like this was going to happen.

MELISSA
Thank god we started working on some stuff.

RICEE
Oh, so y'all meeting without us now, making decisions?

MELISSA
No, we just pre-met before this meeting so that-

RICEE
-Y'all can already persuade us into a decision.

JULIUS
Chill, Ricee, we ain't do nothing we haven't already discussed as a group. We already decided what we were going to do when we sent out the email, letters, and press release. Now we got to act.

RICEE
I just feel like we need to be involved.

JULIUS
You're a full-time student and work at nights at a full-time job, Taylor and Broderick own a whole restaurant, Elizabeth is a lawyer—none of y'all would have had time. Me and Melissa met to set the agenda for this meeting and bring to you all some information that we got.

He sets the box down and passes out folder packets for each of them.

MELISSA
So, in the packet that Julius gave you all are business cards, palm cards, and flyers to persuade or get parents of black kids to move their children out of the school district.

TAYLOR
The whole district, not just the high school?

JULIUS
Yes.

BRODERICK
Oh, you two den lost y'all mind.

JULIUS
We can't make an impact with just the high school students leaving, they are only 10 percent, we got to be bold. The lower you get in grade, there's an increase in black students - altogether about 40 percent of the district, which would be a huge student population that they would lose. We need all the black students to leave so the district sees the drastic change and impact.

RICEE
We couldn't even get parents to this meeting, and you think we gonna persuade them to move their students out of the school district.

MELISSA
I said the same thing, Ricee, but listen, that's why we have the business cards, palm cards, and flyers that give out points on why it needs to happen and what the results will be. We have a website as well. The petitions and the email campaign collected many numbers and emails of parents who support our decision in the district. We may even have what Julius calls co-conspirators in there that will do the same.

ELIZABETH
I know a few liberal white parents that will support this, hell, even throw in some money.

JULIUS
Ha, organizing money is a good segway. We could probably tap into other minority groups.

BRODERICK
I did see more and more Mexicans-

TAYLOR
Hispanics.

JULIUS
Latinx.

RICEE
Spanish.

BRODERICK
Well, it's more of them, and y'all know what happens when black and brown connect.

JULIUS
We sho do. I spoke to the leaders of my org who are all on board with switching our focus. Lend a hand. We also have access to a voter database that will closely pinpoint all the parents in the district for text or phone banks.

BRODERICK
Phone bank?

JULIUS
Yes. We will call all the parents of black students in the district and discuss this issue and get them to understand the severity of this issue.

TAYLOR
Hold on, I want to finish this discussion about these school options and programs. Please explain.

MELISSA
Julius is excited. Go ahead explain the options.

JULIUS
Okay sorry. So, the flier has our recommended options to move our children out of these schools. We provide 1. an online option and be home schooled. 2 Those who don't live in the school district go back… I'll explain in a bit why it'll work. Ricee, give me a minute. 3. Melissa knows Reverend Marcus, whose church has a charter school, the more students, the more funding.

JULIUS (CONT'D)
However, all the teachers in that district are black. They only have a pre-k through 8. Then for those that can afford it, we provided some diverse private schools in the district. Some of these schools are going through a social justice phase because of all the murders, so there are many scholarships out there. I know this is an ambitious plan, but it can work if we do the work I just talked about.

BRODERICK
What is the work because I got a restaurant to run?

MELISSA
First, we get these flyers and things to our kids to hand to black students.

TAYLOR
But nobody's talking to them.

ELIZABETH
Look, I'll get them to my son to hand out to all the black students. I'll tell him to find a leader from each grade and hand them a set.

JULIUS
Good thinking.

MELISSA
I can get the list of numbers of black parents I got so we can do a phone and text bank and contact them.

TAYLOR
We can do it on a Monday when our restaurant is closed. We can provide food.

BRODERICK
Aw, it's just "we" like that.

TAYLOR
Yeah, WE.

JULIUS
He gone learn about we.

BRODERICK
What, are you messing with my wife?

TAYLOR
Broderick! Julius has just been in my ear about running for school board, but it just isn't right, we ain't really from here.

JULIUS
But you live here now, your child attends the district, don't make me give you another list.

TAYLOR
While I appreciate it, we got a business to run.

BRODRICK
I run the business so don't use that as an excuse.

TAYLOR
Hush on up, I need an excuse so he leaves me alone about it.

ELIZABETH
I think you would be a great addition to the board. You'd also be the first black school board member, and I think the first black elected official in this county.

TAYLOR
Now I definitely don't want to run, and it isn't a paid position, so why would I do all that to sit with a whole bunch of white men and one devil white lady?

MELISSA
We could do a phone bank for your campaign when we contact these parents, we persuade them, then we help them with the process, and follow-up with them again to make sure that they did it and go out and vote.

RICEE
You sound like Julius.

MELISSA
He's taught me a lot.

RICEE
Great. Well, let's see if you can tell us what he taught you about this sending our kids back to their own school district, because everyone is excited now except for me.

MELISSA
Ricee, we will be here to support you in all of this. I'll announce it here.

BRODERICK
Look, babe, she gonna run for office and break barriers since you wanted to wait.

TAYLOR death stares BRODERICK.

MELISSA
I have been inspired by the work that we have done and the many connections I have made since we went public about this, so I

MELISSA (CONT'D)
thought we should start a non-profit for black suburban students who have experienced racial trauma in the suburbs, catered to our students.

RICEE
Making money like Julius-

MELISSA
Do not try it. Please let me finish. This will be a hub to provide tutoring and mentorship services as they begin to adjust to their new educational environments.

JULIUS
And this is also another opportunity for them to stay connected as they transition elsewhere while it seems like a lot. High schools lead elementary age kids, gaining leadership and management experience, and we work with middle school kids - along with some volunteers and interns.

ELIZABETH
How do you plan on doing that?

JULIUS
We will start the nonprofit, file all the paperwork and charter with the state to become a 501c3. I think we ask Melissa to serve as the Executive Director since she is clearly passionate and has the most time out of all of us.

MELLISSA
I haven't worked in years, but I really think we could do something here.

JULIUS
All of us will serve on the board and guide the nonprofit. We will provide tutoring, extra educational opportunities, and fellowship activities. Let's make it fun to make sure that our students do not fall behind in their education regardless of district. Every student should be at the same reading, math, or anything level like these white kids regardless of where or how they go to school. This could really fill the gap we've been worried about.

RICEE
So, no matter online or the old school district, you are gone make sure my boys graduate and are prepared for college!

MELISSA
The real world, college, workforce, the service, whatever they choose. Look, it's going to take some work, but we found some funding-

JULIUS
Yes, y'all, the money to fund this program is all there. Tell 'em.

MELISSA
So, I got a few calls from some people who wanted to help the cause, so I let them know of the idea, and as of now, we have enough to hire me and at least three full-times and maybe a few part-times, stipend for student leaders. I really plan on making uh, uh-

JULIUS
A strong volunteer-based system.

MELISSA
Yes, volunteer based. The community has heard these students, so let's get them to participate. I can budge my husband to invest as well.

RICEE
Yeah, girl, you better get your reparations.

MELISSA
Inappropriate…but yes.

ELIZABETH
I think I can help with a building. I know the perfect person to contact with this.

JULIUS
How much would it be?

ELIZABETH
Let me work my magic, and maybe nothing.

BRODERICK
Now that is nice.

JULIUS
You see, Ricee? We good.

RICEE
I guess.

BRODERICK
So now what?

ELIZABETH
It's already out there. I think we need to act on this fast.

RICEE
What do you mean?

JULIUS
People already know that we plan.

TAYLOR
I thought only we know.

MELISSA
Well, we were on the news when we shared that we would be taking action if our demands weren't met. I also spoke to a few communities' leaders, but now looking back that probably wasn't a good idea.

BRODERICK
So, what do we do now?

JULIUS
It's time for us to be brave. We got to do some work. None of this was secret.

CEDRIC the janitor of the school dressed in regular clothes walks in.

JULIUS
Hey, you work for the district, you coming to make a mess with us here?

CEDRIC charges at JULIUS, grabbing a handful of his shirt while pushing him against the wall. Everyone stands up shocked.

RICEE
Oh my gosh, what are you doing?!

CEDRIC
You really going through with yo plan, you really tryna get my kids' education and opportunities out of their hands like that?

TAYLOR
Babe, get 'em.

BRODERICK goes to separate the two, as JULIUS was tryna get let go.

JULIUS
(shook)
I told you I ain't messing with you, nigga. I'm not finna fight another black man. What you heard is right. You gone be mad and kick my ass, or you gone join us?

JULIUS steps up to him as CEDRIC steps forward, but BRODERICK moves JULIUS back to get in between.

BRODERICK
What the hell is this, what's going on? Somebody please, cause I'll get my hands ready.

CEDRIC
I make a living cleaning that damn school and that's the only way my children have gotten to go to school there. My daughter now attends Nae College, one of the most beautiful black colleges in the country. I drove her up there three summers ago. Now my boys are top ball players for the school, college recruiters looking at them, and now you tryna take this opportunity away like the rest of 'em.

JULIUS
Have you ever asked her why she chose a black college?

CEDRIC
Cause it was a full ride.

JULIUS
You should ask her.

CEDRIC raises his voice and steps towards JULIUS, but Broderick is still in the middle to ensure no fight happens.

CEDRIC
What are you tryna say?

JULIUS
I just wonder why she chose a black college.

CEDRIC
Nigga it-

BRODERICK
Alright now, come on, y'all.

JULIUS
I just said ask her.

CEDRIC
Boy, I just-

TAYLOR
Broderick, you need to get him out of here.

BRODERICK kind of steps forward, hesitant. The LIBRARIAN steps-in.

LIBRARIAN
Is everything okay here?

ELIZABETH
Yes, we are fine.

LIBRARIAN
Can you all keep it down, please?

MELISSA
Absolutely, we are sorry.

LIBRARIAN
Thank you.

The LIBRARIAN walks out, and BRODERICK moves closer to CEDRIC.

BRODERICK
I'm not sure what's going on. But I ain't tryna put my hands on anybody. Who is this man?

CEDRIC is calming down but still breathing hard a bit as JULIUS moves away.

JULIUS
This is the night maintenance man at our children school.

MELISSA
I remember him. You work at the school—what is the fighting all for?

RICEE
I bet he was sent from the school to start some black-on-black stuff.

CEDRIC
No, my son attends that school.

RICEE
Then why you come up to him like that?

CEDRIC
What y'all doing is wrong. Y'all gone mess up these kids' lives. If y'all move all the black kids out of the district, they gone lose that good education, the college opportunities, being around things they ain't ever had to have something to dream for. What are they supposed to do now? I saw what y'all said on the news, and now I learned the talk from the admin at the school about it.

MELISSA
We have a plan for other opportunities. We could really make this work.

CEDRIC
(raises voice)
You not.

BRODERICK
Come on, brother, don't raise your voice at her.

CEDRIC
My boys are good. The older one got college recruits looking for both basketball and baseball, the younger only care about basketball. If y'all move all the black kids, they gone lose the season, and if I follow y'all, ain't no recruits gone follow us to no other schools. I want my boys to go far. I don't want them out homeless on drugs just like their older brother, so spaced out I can't even help.

The group is silent.

BRODERICK
Aye brotha, I'm Broderick.

CEDRIC
Cedric.

BRODERICK extends his hands, and CEDRIC looks then shakes his hand.

BRODERICK
I'm gone be honest with you, I wasn't too sure about this whole idea, and even about this young cat over there, but one thing I am sure about is my daughter, and my wife's decision to support her. I moved to this school district for my child to also get a good education, but like these folks said, at what cost? I don't need my child having racial troubles when I as a parent can do more for her to ensure her education is right. At some other school districts, she ain't got to deal with anything like that.

TAYLOR steps in to grab BRODERICK'S arm.

CEDRIC
But man, my boys is smart. If I move them districts, they gone fall behind, I just know it.

MELISSA
Cedric, we will make sure that that doesn't happen to your sons. All of us, look around, Ricee, Taylor, Elizabeth, Julius, we gone make sure all of our kids are successful. At the end of the day, that's why we are all here. You never know what happens, but we want to be there for each other.

Everyone's phone rings. They all receive a text alert of a video.

ELIZABETH
Oh my god.

They are all staring at a video of a black kid being choked until he passes out by a district school resource officer. Only the noises of the video are heard (rowdy students yelling "Stop," young kids, "I can't breathe," "Stop resisting."). Everyone's face is filled with hurt, disgust, and pain. This moment is intense with physical acting. TAYLOR cries and hugs BRODERICK at the end of the video. CEDRIC puts his head down with hand on head. MELISSA falls back in her chair while covering her mouth, eyes wide open, and ELIZABETH leans her head against a wall to cry. Shocked for a moment, RICEE throws her phone against the floor extremely hard, it breaks, and she bursts out a yell of hurt. JULIUS runs over and catches her before she falls, and they fall together. He holds her. The whole room is tense and emotional for a few seconds. TAYLOR, in BRODERICK'S hands, keeps weeping or crying out loud, "I'm gone do something about this" The lights dim. A spotlight appears center stage. MELISSA walks center stage to the spotlight and meets with CAMERON the reporter.

CAMERON
I can imagine how your group is feeling.

MELISSA
We are hurt, and more, I am hurt that as a parent, I have allowed my children to attend this racist school district. I am calling on all parents of black children, children of color,

MELISSA (CONT'D)
and supporters to remove them from the Johnson Hill School District. It is not safe for our children, and if you love your kids, you will do so. We need to act before one of our own children is killed, now!

She walks off.

CAMERON
A call to action has been made to parents of black children to remove their kids from the school district after a black student was choked to unconsciousness by school resource officers after a confrontation with a teacher. KCHB 12, this is Cameron Woods.

Lights out.

ACT TWO

SCENE ONE

Two weeks later. The spotlight is centered on MELISSA who is giving a speech at a protest. All the parents are behind her. JULIUS directly behind her, TAYLOR and BRODERICK holding hands.

MELISSA
Our children don't deserve to be treated like animals anywhere! For some of us, we made the decision to move into these neighborhoods for our children, our families, and ourselves to have a better life, but parents, we need to reevaluate what is truly best for our children. We pay taxes in this community, fund these schools, and they treat our children with the utmost disrespect. I'm tired of seeing videos of kids in black face and the school takes no actions. I'm tired of seeing our children be told to drop the locks and stop listening to nigger music. I'm tired of the racist tactics and culture ingrained in the school district. "I'm sick and tired of being sick and tired," as the once Fannie Lou Hamer said. Parents, our children deserve better, and the school district is not meeting the expectations our children deserve. We have demanded that the district meet with parents to discuss the very changes that need to happen. However, they have chosen to ignore us as if nothing has happened. This past week, we saw in the most disturbing manner sophomore Jamal Hendricks thrown on the ground, breaking three front teeth, then adding two more officers, all holding him down causing the poor child to lose his breath, go unconscious.

MELISSA (CONT'D)
They ought to thank God he didn't die because if he did, I promise this district would suffer more than they are about to. Parents, I ask you to take your children out of the school district immediately. We have leaders passing out information about how to do so. If that video didn't anger you then I don't know what will, because I'm mad as hell.

Applause from the crowd and parents.

JULIUS
Continue the energy, y'all. This is real, the feelings are real, and I feel it throughout the audience. Almost two months ago, my daughter, along with four other brave students led a protest in the gym of their high school. It was one of my proudest moments, but something that came out of that was a group of parents concerned for the safety of their black children, advocating to ensure their children are respected in a school district they believed in. But there was one parent I met, a mother of a sophomore daughter, and business owner of Papa Tori, a soul food restaurant over the river. She worked hard to grow a family business along with her husband, and now living in the Johnson Hill school district for over 10 years, with the hopes that their daughter would get a better education. I saw something in her, and I hope you all do too. We can't just be upset, but we have to take action and ensure our school district has leaders that understand a population of the school district has been underserved, unheard, and mistreated. I know

someone who can: Taylor Crawford. Please help me welcome her.

Another round of applause.

TAYLOR
(Nervous) Hi. My name is Taylor. Taylor Crawford. A proud wife to my husband, Broderick. A business owner. A member of this community. But most importantly I am a mother of a beautiful daughter. She was suspended with a group of students because they could no longer take every crude racist bit of culture created in that school district. Having racism is one thing, allowing it is another, and I had to learn the hard way after my daughter could no longer take it and act. But I find myself inspired by all those students and thank you to my fellow leaders from the Black Parent Union for helping me come to this decision. So, *(She looks at Broderick, who smiles and nods his head. She looks back at the crowd.)* I am here to announce that I am running for the Johnson Hill School Board District. I am running to ensure that my daughter, their children, and yours have a leader who is listening to their concerns and ensuring that something is done. It's time to work, and I'm going to work. Please join me, because I need your help, our children do. Let's get to work for them!

End scene.

SCENE TWO

Six months later. BRODERICK, TAYLOR, and CEDRIC are sitting down in the multipurpose room. The rest of the parents are off-stage.

TAYLOR
Cedric, how is everything going with your son's new school?

CEDRIC
The boy loves it. Most of the other kids from the ole school are going there as well. I don't know how I feel about it yet.

BRODERICK
We put our girl in the all-girls private school down the street from us. She wasn't feeling it, but the after-school program got me feeling better. You put your sons in it, right?

CEDRIC
That's the only thing that's making me not regret this decision. Ricee picked them from school and took them in the program in the buses.

BRODERICK
These children are spoiled, nice buses. I had a look at it.

TAYLOR
I'm happy they got Ricee on board to work with Melissa on this.

RICEE enters.

RICEE
What are you saying my name for? What I do? *(jokingly)*

TAYLOR
Girl, no, I was saying I'm happy you are working with the kids.

RICEE
I'm happy I ain't got to work a CNA job all night. This works perfectly with my school schedule.

TAYLOR
How's it been going?

RICEE
You know, it was a bit messy the first few days, but the kids didn't notice. They were all just so happy to be with each other. With all this change, I think they thought they wouldn't see each other. Which is weird because kids be on they phone the whole day. You should've seen them, they all just sat as if they were in a lunchroom and talked about their new schools, classes, and their excitement about not having to worry about some racist shit happening.

CEDRIC
How are my boys doing?

RICEE
One of your boys is an attention getter, in all the good ways of course. I have him doing something to keep him busy cause he has a lot of energy. And the other one, yeah, he likes the girls, and the girls like him, but he thinks he's slick and can talk to me like I'm one of them lil girls, he tried it today and I

RICEE (CONT'D)
checked him. Told him he needa stop acting like he was the world.

CEDRIC
Oh lord, them my boys. Let me know if I got to go up there and set 'em straight.

BRODERICK
Yeah, my girl too.

TAYLOR
You only saying that cause that the only place she gone be around boys now.

BRODERICK
Exactly.

RICEE
Either way, all y'all kids are doing great and the program is on fire. We got some good stuff planned. Melissa is on her shit.

ELIZABETH walks in.

ELIZABETH
Hey everyone! Ricee!

RICEE
Elizabeth!

ELIZABETH
My friend said you did a great job with the tour of the building.

RICEE
I'm happy he let us have the building and do whatever with it. The kids had fun decorating the rooms. Where did you meet him?

ELIZABETH
I served on his board. He is the Executive Director of a housing nonprofit that buys houses and builds houses to then sell to low-income residents. But the building you all are in was given to them by a group of nuns who no longer occupied the space. It was empty for years, and they tried years ago to rent it out, but it didn't work out.

BRODERICK
Well, thank God it didn't.

RICEE
Right, cause now we get it.

JULIUS and MELISSA walk in, and everyone stands up to give them a round of applause. JULIUS joins the applause.

MELISSA
Aww, y'all are too nice.

TAYLOR
No, you ought to be proud girl. You have done something amazing, both of you.

BRODERICK
Yes, both of you.

MELISSA
Now come on now. Taylor is running for school board, and they are scared! If you win you will be the first black school member, first black elected in the county. You are about to be history.

BRODERICK
Yeah, my baby is.

TAYLOR
It's been a lot of work, but my daughter and her friend been helping with making calls.

ELIZABETH
How is that going?

TAYLOR
Julius.

JULIUS
The girls have gotten some mean answers on the phone, but I told them not to worry about it cause it's not like we know them. Told them to act like they are acting. We gotta get through the bad to get the good ones to vote.

TAYLOR
They are working on it. And the Johnson Hill League of Women Voters are going to help knock on some doors, so the white ladies got us face-to-face in the community. An up-hill battle, but we got it.

JULIUS walks up to CEDRIC, who stands up.

CEDRIC
Thank you, and I'm sorry, man. I know I was rough on you, but you were right.

JULIUS daps him up and nods his head.

JULIUS
It's all good, brotha. We gone get you to run for office one day.

CEDRIC
Yeah, we might have to fight on that one.

They both laugh.

MELISSA
So, everyone, I want to make an announcement. *I* was told by my friend who works in the district office that 67 percent of black students in the district have officially transferred out. We still haven't received an official number of other students of color or white students that may have also transferred.

They all celebrate. JULIUS jumps with excitement with his hands in a fist.

CEDRIC
Wow.

TAYLOR
Now that is something there!

BRODERICK
What them other kids waiting for?

JULIUS
We aren't sure, but I bet it's the students who were adopted, live with a white parent, or parents just don't care.

TAYLOR
Well, how do we get to 100 percent?

RICEE
It's ambitious.

MELISSA
Well, we made it to 67 percent and that was ambitious. I think we got us a win.

CEDRIC
They worried. I'll tell y'all that.

BRODERICK
Well of course, they were surprised we were able to connect with other parents of color- Mexican, Asian. Shit, they were not playing about that video.

CEDRIC
I hear a bit of them conversations. This is working.

RICEE
You got to tell us more, Cedric.

CEDRIC
Last night, the principal, the superintendent, the chair of the board, and maybe a lawyer came out of the meeting room, and it was not a happy look. The white men left that meeting red. I wasn't sure what they talked about, but I knew it had something to do with the kids cause once they seen my black ass, they all shut it up.

JULIUS
Ain't you friends with the principal?

CEDRIC
That was before I transferred my boys out. They don't even acknowledge me unless they are talking about us. You shoulda seen their face turned ghost when they all walked out that room and saw me cleaning the hallway.

ELIZABETH
If the lawyer was involved, I'm assuming this has something to do with the state trying to butt in.

JULIUS
Aww shit. We need to capitalize on this immediately.

ELIZABETH
Are we on the same page?

JULIUS
You are a lawyer.

RICEE
Aww y'all are trying to sue the district.

JULIUS
We are not trying to.

ELIZABETH
We are going to. All we need is a good 25 plaintiffs in a class action lawsuit.

RICEE
What parents are gone do that?

ELIZABETH
We don't use the parents, we use the children. Let's get a few students from each class, each one of our kids, and we talk to some parents.

BRODERICK
How much is this gone cost?

ELIZABETH
Close to nothing. I'll file the suit and do the work pro-bono. It impacts my kids, so this is free, we just need parents to sign on.

MELISSA
Me and Ricee can write something up to send with the students tomorrow to give to their parents.

RICEE
I like how now that you're my boss, you just say instead of asking. I ain't mad at you though.

MELISSA
Here you go.

CEDRIC
I'm not trying to lose my job now. I feel like this group moves too quickly out of emotion, no consideration. I then agreed with you all this far, but now my money is really gone be messed with and I'm already on thin ice, folks.

ELIZABETH
You won't be. We are only using your child's name, last name.

JULIUS
And we need to act quick.

CEDRIC
They gone know, they gone let me go. You all are always making decisions that impact me more than y'all. This been my job for some years. Ain't no way I can let it go.

BRODERICK
Come on, brother. All these decisions we make impact all of us. You can't be selfish on this one.

CEDRIC
With all due respect, potna, you a rich guy living in the suburbs making money off of us hungry folks in the hood.

TAYLOR
Now, hold on, don't do that. We have a restaurant that was inherited from our family that is a staple. What, you thought we was supposed to live in the same neighborhood?

CEDRIC
Yo restaurant is still there.

JULIUS
Y'all, this ain't productive.

BRODERICK
Don't yo black ass come to my restaurant no mo.

BRODERICK stands up and walks up to CEDRIC. CEDRIC stands up.

JULIUS
Broderick.

JULIUS grabs BRODERICK by the arm, redirecting him.

CEDRIC
Dry ass chicken.

CEDRIC sits back down.

JULIUS
Cedric, brothers, come on.

TAYLOR stands up and walk towards CEDRIC.

TAYLOR
And I cook the chicken, by the way.

JULIUS redirects her back to her seat.

ELIZABETH
It is good chicken.

CEDRIC
You white.

ELIZABETH now stands up and walks toward CEDRIC.

ELIZABETH
That doesn't matter cause that chicken has been doing something to me.

RICEE
That chicken been getting you thick, white girl. Let 'em know.

JULIUS
All whi- Alright now, we need to stop! We have-

MELISSA
You are raising your voice, Julius. Let me take this one.

JULIUS sits down as MELISSA is up.

MELISSA
Listen, we have seen a lot of improvements already. I get that the next steps that we make aren't going to be easy, I know we move fast, but as I said many times before, and I'll continue to say, we can't wait. Cedric, this movement that we are creating is bringing in a lot of money from grassroots levels to corporations because they believe in this fight against racism in our children's schools. If need be, we will find something for you.

CEDRIC
You gone find me another maintenance job when I leave?

MELISSA
No. You deserve better. Director of Operations. Hell, if you want to leave that field, let's hear what you want to do.

RICEE
You know Melissa is real because your girl doesn't ever cuss and she just said "hell," so hell yeah… Cedric, come on.

MELISSA
Hell yeah!

RICEE
Okay, that's enough.

CEDRIC
I just want to make sure my family is fed and my kids gone be successful and educated. That's all my mama wanted for me, so I'm gone make sure my kids reach what I couldn't.

BRODERICK
Man, that's what we all here for.

CEDRIC looks over at TAYLOR and BRODERICK.

CEDRIC
I'm sorry, y'all. I really am. This just been a lot, being around y'all smart folks, and y'all just move so fast, but you all can do that. It's just different for me.

TAYLOR
Good, cause my chicken ain't dry.

TAYLOR reaches over BRODERICK to squeeze CEDRIC'S hand, and Broderick daps him up.

ELIZABETH
So, are we good to go on the lawsuit?

They all look at CEDRIC.

CEDRIC
What is this anyway? Explain it to me.

ELIZABETH
It's a class action lawsuit where an individual can sue on behalf of a group of people who have a similar claim. We'll probably add somebody's last name with the best reputation, so we will vet everyone, then add everyone's name in the suit. It won't just be us; we can add more students. But I have a team of law students who are currently working with me, who I know would love to volunteer some time on this, plus they get some good experience.

ELIZABETH (CONT'D)
I will guide them to work on this project. I would think we have a really good case, Cedric.

CEDRIC
CEDRIC!

ELIZABETH
Sorry, Cedric, but I think with you working in the district, it would add more emphasis to the case if your child were in it.

Silence as CEDRIC thinks about it, but answers are bothered.

CEDRIC
Gone head. But y'all gone get me a job when they let me go. Matter of fact, I want my job before they let me go.

ELIZABETH
This is perfect. I have a friend who's done a case similar to this who I'm going to call after this. We have a lot of potential to win, but mind you, once we add you all to the case and go public, there's a high chance of a lot of media.

JULIUS
Yeah, a lot of media.

RICEE
Here you go.

JULIUS
No, this is just a good opportunity to expose all the problems in the district, and if we-

A car burning its tires is heard. Everyone pauses to look toward the window. Then a brick is thrown through the window. They all duck and react, except ELIZABETH. She just reacts and doesn't duck—she ain't got the street smarts.

          CAR DRIVER *(optional)*
Bye, niggers.

They all look at each other, shook after they all ducked. JULIUS picks up the brick and looks at them. Lights out.

SCENE THREE

A week before election day. Seven chairs are on stage in the multipurpose room, four in the front and three behind which are high tops, a bit larger or sitting on a platform so that you can see all the parents in their first TV interview. BRODERICK, TAYLOR, MELISSA, and CEDRIC are all in the room. They are clearly nervous for their first interview. They are all dressed well in business casual. No one is basic or extra thus far.

CEDRIC
Where are the young folks at?

MELISSA
Julius said he was on his way, and I just seen Ricee at the office, but she said she was going home to get ready for the interview.

BRODERICK
She gone do a lot.

TAYLOR
How you gonna assume, Brod?

BRODERICK
She about to be on the TV set. You know how this young girl is.

ELIZABETH
Well, I think we all look good so far.

CEDRIC
Yeah, I had to pull this shirt from the bottom of the pile. Took me damn near forty minutes to iron it.

BRODERICK
That's why I get my wife to iron my stuff.

TAYLOR
You told me because you needed to fix something in the car so you couldn't.

BRODERICK
Didn't you notice the car smelled good when you got in it?

TAYLOR
All you did was add a damn tree in the car?!

BRODERICK
Baby, don't do all this now.

CEDRIC
My wife ain't gone do none of that. We just started talking again.

ELIZABETH
Are you and your wife separated?

CEDRIC
Nah, but our work schedule for the last 11 years has been off. She works days, I work nights, and now that I'm here, this takes up some of the time.

MELISSA
But you guys get weekends and stuff, don't ya?

CEDRIC
Back in the day, but she joined her little church group activities, and I'm here with you all or doing overtime.

ELIZABETH
You should bring her.

CEDRIC
Ha, she blames y'all for the reason we don't get along, so I'm not about to bring another hardheaded person y'all got to persuade. Y'all already had to deal with me.

BRODERICK
And that was not easy one bit.

They all laugh.

CEDRIC
Y'all sho did. But working with Melissa and Ricee at the building is nice. I got to see my wife and have a nice family dinner on a weekday. I can do this some more.

TAYLOR
Amen to that.

RICEE walks into the room, looking extremely beautiful and a bit extra for a TV interview with her tight, short, sexy red dress with accessories and high heels.

BRODERICK
(Struck)
Look. At. Her… What I tell y'all?

RICEE
Don't hate, Broderick. Mrs. Taylor don't look like this.

BRODERICK
I ain't hatin.

TAYLOR
Ugh, uh baby, Mrs. Taylor look just a bad as you mamas. The only thing is I ain't going to do all that you are doing.

MELISSA
You weren't playing when you said get ready, huh?

RICEE
No, you like it.

MELISSA
We ain't got no other choice.

MELISSA looks at CEDRIC, who is clearly getting a good look at RICEE. RICEE, whose back is turned toward CEDRIC, can feel him looking.

RICEE
Don't stare too long now, Cedric.

CEDRIC makes a full circle and looks at the window to ignore that whole situation.

ELIZABETH
Well, if I was young and sexy as you, Ricee, I might've worn something like that?

RICEE
Girl, you should've. Age ain't got nothing to do with it, and for a white girl, you do got a little something going on back there.

ELIZABETH
Do I?

RICEE
Yes! We gone go shopping. I'm gonna get you right.

MELISSA
Me too.

BRODERICK
Her too.

TAYLOR death stares BRODERICK, who then joins CEDRIC at the window of shame. They all watch him.

TAYLOR
Me too, for me though.

RICEE
Yay! We are about to have a girls night, and we are doing it my style! So, we gone have to cancel one of these little meetings and do brunch, mimosas, and shop.

ELIZABETH
We love mimosas.

MELISSA
What if we get drunk?

TAYLOR
I think that is her point.

RICEE
You got it. When you are drunk, you don't care what you spend money on, and when you buy clothes like that, you step out of your comfort zone to pure sexiness. I'm gonna have all of y'all looking NOICE!

JULIUS walks in with a box of shirts; he is wearing a hoodie that says "black parents united" with a fist under it. He is dressed very casually.

JULIUS
Was sup, y'all! I just got a call from the reporter. He will be here in a few minutes. He ain't got his cameraman with him today, so he had to go pick up the equipment.

MELISSA
What you got in the boxes?

He sets them down on the table, opens the box, and pulls out a shirt with the same design as his black hoodie.

JULIUS
Shirts so we all match in the interview.

TAYLOR
Absolutely not.

JULIUS
What you mean?

RICEE
You ain't noticed how good I look?

JULIUS
(Flirty)
Yeah, I noticed-

Gets hit by MELISSA.

RICEE
I'm not going from this to matching with you all, no offense.

MELISSA
The shirts are nice, y'all.

RICEE
They are, and I'll wear it at work, but not for this interview. We are about to be on TV.

BRODRICK
You worried about the message we leave or how we look?

RICEE
Both. Y'all can wear y'all lil' shirts, but I'm not.

JULIUS
I literally texted y'all for shirt sizes for this.

CEDRIC
Well, I'll take their shirts if they don't want 'em.

JULIUS
Uhh, we only got one that's yo size.

CEDRIC
Aww, okay.

He grabs his shirt from Julius.

CEDRIC
I spent forty minutes ironing this one though.

MELISSA
How about those that want to wear the shirt do, and those that don't, don't?

JULIUS
Sounds good with me.

JULIUS looks around, and only ELIZABETH grabs a shirt.

ELIZABETH
I'll go put mine on.

She walks out the room to go change.

CEDRIC
Well, at least you and the white girl gone match.

JULIUS
I guess so.

He picks up the box and sets them up against the wall.

JULIUS
Well, they're over here if y'all need them.

BRODERICK
You sad?

JULIUS
Over a shirt?

BRODERICK
Yeah.

JULIUS
No, not at all. We are good. This ain't our biggest battle.

MELISSA
What do you mean?

JULIUS
This reporter we are meeting with can over-analyze things.

MELISSA
I've never experienced that with him.

JULIUS
He's good with on-the-spot interviews, but a sit-down interview he will play devil's advocate quite dirty.

While some people are in their small talks, MELISSA gathers everyone.

MELISSA
Hey, everyone, I think we should all listen to Julius. He has a few tips before we meet with Cameron, the reporter.

They all gather around.

JULIUS
Check me out, y'all. This reporter has done good thus far in sharing our story, but a lot of it is because he lacks research, knowledge, and is trying to get anything now. This is going to be a bit different. At this point he has done research on all of us, on our group, on the district, and if he is dirty, our children, but I doubt that. He will seem sweet in the beginning 'till he hits you with unexpected low-key shady questions. Be patient, it's okay not to have the answer immediately. I'd prefer if you all take the time to think of your answer before you just answer, and don't frustrate yourself. Remember this is just like a regular conversation at the reunion. Or at least try to make it like that.

RICEE
If I don't make a fool out of myself, then I am good.

TAYLOR
Amen to that.

ELIZABETH walks back in with her shirt under her blazer. She lays her blouse on the table.

MELISSA
You made the shirt look cute.

JULIUS
Oh, I didn't?

MELISSA
Not like her. Elizabeth got it looking NOICE as Ricee says.

RICEE
Okay, Melissa, with the language.

ELIZABETH
Thank you, Melissa.

CAMERON peeps his head through the door.

CAMERON
Knock, knock, knock! Hello, everyone. I'm Cameron from KCHB 12. How are you all?

Everyone greets him.

JULIUS
Hey, what's up, Cameron? We got all the parent leaders here. You just let us know how you want to go about this.

CAMERON
Hi, everyone. Can I get you, you, you, and you on the bottom row, and the rest of you on the top row? I'll set the camera up as you all sit.

Bottom row: JULIUS, MELISSA, RICEE, and CEDRIC. Top row: ELIZABETH, TAYLOR, and BRODERICK. ELIZABETH stops JULIUS before they sit.

ELIZABETH
Hey, I had a question.

JULIUS
Wassup?

ELIZABETH
Do you think that I need to be in this interview?

JULIUS
What are you talking about?

ELIZABETH
You know… I'm white.

JULIUS
What, don't you want to be on TV with a bunch of black folks?

ELIZABETH
Julius, no! What I'm saying is, do I need to be in the interview? Would I be taking up too much space?

JULIUS
Elizabeth, this is not the time to start with this white guilt shit.

ELIZABETH
Okay.

ELIZABETH walks toward the door, but JULIUS stops her.

JULIUS
Liz, look. How long have you been in this fight with us?

ELIZABETH
For almost a year now.

JULIUS
Right. And why?

ELIZABETH
My son.

JULIUS
Your black son.

ELIZABETH
My black son.

JULIUS
This was not about you in the beginning. You did it because you have a black son. Period. So don't make this about you now. Not now. We need you to be here. You got all the info and insight on this legal shit because you got us. If you not here, that's fucked up. You're are part of the team, okay?

ELIZABETH
Thanks, Julius.

JULIUS
Plus, you are the only one that decided to wear the shirt. I can't be in that fight all the way by myself.

They chuckle and part ways.

CAMERON
I think we can start on this interview.

They all sit in their seats and get comfortable. CAMERON sets up the camera. Once he is done, he sits down, take out his notepad from his bag, and his water bottle, which he takes a sip from before he starts.

CAMERON
Okay, so some of you look nervous. Please don't—just relax. We are going to chat about all the work you all have done and really get deep into it. So, I'll throw maybe some generic questions open to everyone, and also some specific questions, and I'll just name that person for the question.

MELISSA
Sounds good.

CAMERON
Okay, let's get to it.

Starts camera.

CAMERON (CONT'D)
One of you please tell me how this group started.

MELISSA
A few months ago, almost a year ago actually, a few of our children protested by doing a sit-in at the gym of the school as a reaction of racial incidents that no one had been held accountable for. Our children were then disciplined, and after a discussion with each other in the hallway of the school that night, we decided to do something about it, with a call to action to parents of black students. We continued to add parents who also needed to be here.

CAMERON
So, is this fight just about racial incidents or about your kids being disciplined?

JULIUS
Both. Our schools failed our children, especially our black children by allowing kids to get away with racist social media posts, teachers saying "nigga," coaches creating anti-black environments, and our children feeling unsafe. When our children protested, they knew the consequences, however who would've known that they would've gotten disciplined when no one else did for their other actions.

CAMERON
Julius, what do you say to people who say you just like being attached to any social or racial drama? I mean, you were in the city organizing. Some of us would've thought you lived in those communities, only to find out you live in the big house in the suburbs while you are somehow attached to the racial issues here.

JULIUS
My organizing works across the whole metro. I lived in that very community, and I have family that still does, that's why it's in my self-interest. However, two things. One, because of my organizing and activism, it hasn't been too safe for me to live in the very community I love. And second, I have a hard-working wife who bought the house with her money, not mine. My only purpose is to support the decision she wants to make, and if that is what attaches me to social drama, then it is what it is, but this wasn't my fight in the beginning. This was my child's fight. When she asked me to help because of my experience, I needed to because I couldn't stand to see my daughter face racism in the eyes every day just because of the decisions we made as parents to move here.

CAMERON
I noticed that a lot of you have moved here. Why did you all decide to move here considering the majority is white and actually predominantly? Mrs. Taylor and Mr. Broderick?

They look at each other.

CAMERON
You both own a restaurant over the river in a predominantly black neighborhood. Why did you come this way, away from your own restaurant?

BRODERICK
My wife and I moved over to this neighborhood because we worked hard to grow our restaurant. Hell, even opened a

BRODERICK (CONT'D)
second one so that we can better our family, our situation, our lifestyle, and our daughters' education. This district was supposed to be the number one in the state and in the metropolitan, which was true, but not for my baby. They didn't and don't care about my daughter.

CAMERON
So, what do you say to those that would say you are making money off the "hood" to live in the suburbs?

TAYLOR
Absolutely wrong. We are not making money off our HOOD. We are as invested in that community regardless of where we live. I was born and raised there, just as my husband, just as my daughter for the first few years of her life, and if our restaurant left that neighborhood, then it would really be a food desert. We've had chances to move our location, but we haven't because that's home. But where we lay our heads at night is different because we did it so that our baby girl can get a good education, and that is still our goal. It doesn't matter where we live, they know where our heart is and they know the love we have, ask anyone down there.

CAMERON
So now you live in the district?

TAYLOR
Excuse me, we have lived in the school district since my daughter was in the 3rd grade, and we have lived in this district before I inherited the restaurant from my

TAYLOR (CONT'D)
parents. My husband bought this house with his money. So let's get that straight.

CAMERON
Well, what makes you qualified to be on the school board?

TAYLOR
I am a resident, which is the only qualification needed. But most importantly, I am a mother of a child who was neglected by leadership. I'm running to ensure no other child feels like that.

CAMERON
Well, the election is a week away. There's talk that it could be tough for you to win as a woman of color in this district.

TAYLOR
I'm not sure what the outcome will be, but I trust that we worked and continue to work hard to get support from voters.

CAMERON
Unfortunately, neither Ricee nor Cedric can vote for you.

RICEE
What do you mean?

CAMERON
Well, Cedric was custodial service, so his child was only allowed to attend on the basis that he works for the district, and you, well, you use someone else's address, because your registration to vote is actually a few blocks from the Crawford's restaurant.

JULIUS
What are you trying to get at, Cameron?

CAMERON
What I'm saying is you all are a peculiar group of people to really be fighting for this issue. I give you all props for being diverse, but half of you don't live in the district so you kinda don't need to deal with these problems, while the other half of you is rich.

MELISSA
What does that have to do with it?

CAMERON
How does it not? Melissa, your white privileged husband has a million-dollar company. Elizabeth, you have your own law firm and adjunct at the college. You both just mentioned you're basically starting a franchise. How can you privileged parents talk about racism?

MELISSA
Because racism sees no money, finance, education—all it sees is color. My daughter may be going to college for free compared to some of these kids in the district, yes; however, that doesn't excuse the fact that she has dealt with issues because of the color of her skin. Her hair was torn from her because it wasn't real. Bullied because of her full lips, wide nose, and beautiful black skin, but money didn't save her from any of those comments. All that has nothing to do with my white husband. My daughter is still black, cause no one at that school sees her white side. If they did, we wouldn't be here right now.

CAMERON
Would any of you like to add?

RICEE
I am not ashamed of the decisions I made because I wanted my boys to get a good education. What I am ashamed about was my blindness and not acting sooner. My boys should've gotten better, so yeah, maybe I was wrong for using the wrong address to give them something better, but I'm going to make sure no one else goes through that ever. Period.

JULIUS gives RICEE some dap.

CAMERON
Cedric, you no longer work for the district so even if you all do win, what are you trying to win that your child can't go back to, use another address?

CEDRIC
And that's fine.

CAMERON
Anything else?

CEDRIC
Nope.

CAMERON
So, what about this lawsuit?

ELIZABETH
Yes, we have filed a suit against the Johnson Hill School District, superintendent, school board, and principal on the count of emotional damages to our children for the many racial incidents that had been ignored.

CAMERON
What makes you think that this will go anywhere?

ELIZABETH
The historic Brown v. Board of Education.

RICEE
Come on, girl.

JULIUS
She finna blow.

CAMERON
Oh, come on.

ELIZABETH
The language in the historic suit states that "Education is perhaps the most important function of state and local governments. Compulsory school attendance laws and the great expenditures for education both demonstrate our recognition of the importance of education to our democratic society. It is required in performance of our most basic public responsibilities, even service in the armed forces. It is the very foundation of good citizenship. Today, it is a principal instrument in awakening the child to cultural values, in preparing him and her for later professional training, and in helping him and her incorporate normality to their environment. These days it is doubtful that any child may be reasonably expected to succeed in life if he is denied the opportunity of an education. Such an opportunity where the state has undertaken to provide it, is a right which must be made available. On. Equal. Terms." So, all students must be protected from harm, especially when our

children feel threatened by the current environment.

TAYLOR
Come on, girl.

CAMERON
So, you don't see this as performative, maybe even on you as a parent. You're a white lady, you got a shirt that says Black Parents United, which you aren't, and now you're sharing Brown v. Board of Education case points.

RICEE
Hold up. Yeah, she's white, white as hell, actually. But none of this is performative. We are all here because our children have faced real issues that should not be faced by our children. She may be a white parent, but she has a black child. She deserves to be at this table, and thank God she is because we needed her just as much as she needed us.

CAMERON
What else other than powerful words are you going to have?

MELISSA
Evidence.

CAMERON
Speak more on that.

MELISSA
We have evidence that will destroy this district, from social media, teachers' accounts, video, even dug into the racist policies within student handbooks and code of conduct. We even have interviews from black and brown staff members who have had enough.

JULIUS
But also, our movement. We as a group made a call to action for all parents of black children to move them districts. For online schooling, private to those who could afford, we had some charter school investments, and even some of us in the suburbs had to use family members in the hood to move our kids' district. Now look, our district looks so pale, you barely see any students of color.

CAMERON
So how are you all feeling about the news today that the district may have to close two elementary schools, one middle school, and cut a lot of staff from the high schools?

MELISSA
What?

CAMERON
Yes, today the school board had a special meeting where they discussed this. Due to the decrease of students, they will not receive as much funding from the state as usual; therefore, they need to make some drastic changes. You all were able to organize more parents, not just black parents but most minority groups, and even a slight white population have shaved off. The school is holding special meetings in an hour.

They are all shocked as their faces turn to smiles.

BRODERICK

Hell yeah!

JULIUS

Awe shit.

TAYLOR

I need to get down there, y'all. Did you all hear what he said?!

MELISSA

Girl, yes!

RICEE

Oh yes!

They all begin to clap, cheer, and celebrate. Spotlight on stage, and Cameron walks to it.

CAMERON

It's clear from the celebration behind me that the parents are proud and consider this a win. With all their hard work, they are finally seeing results. From their children feeling safe in their new schools to their old school facing challenges to stay open because of the many black students now gone. The district has made no comment on the suit or the closing of schools. They do, however, have a special session meeting scheduled in an hour. Continue to follow KCHB 12 for more coverage on this year-long fight for justice in the Johnson Hill School district later on at 6pm tonight. This is Cameron Woods.

Lights out.

SCENE FOUR

A long table is center stage with seven chairs on one side and one chair on the other. The superintendent's back is to the crowd. He only faces the parents.

SUPERINTENDENT
I wasn't expecting to meet with you all. But I want to thank Board Member Crawford for setting up this meeting.

MELISSA
Well, we've been asking for a meeting with you since we started this group. You declined each one of our requests, superintendent.

JULIUS
And now that we have won the lawsuit, you want to meet.

SUPERINTENDENT
None of this has been easy.

RICEE
Ugh, uh, don't you start with them white tears.

SUPERINTENDENT
Excuse me?

RICEE
Don't try being apologetic now because that wasn't the same energy you had at court.

SUPERINTENDENT
I just didn't know. I wasn't there.

TAYLOR
Sir. You didn't know because you didn't try. You listened to the principals, teachers, hell, even the white kids, but never met with ours or us. You excluded us from anything and everything, and you knew they were treating our kids wrong after they were disciplined, because, as we found out in the suit, it came from your suggestion, which means you actually did know.

SUPERINTENDENT
I am a white man.

ALL PARENTS
We know.

SUPERINTENDENT
Let me finish. As a white man, all those issues didn't seem as extreme as they happened to be, but now I know. And I'm sorry.

CEDRIC
For what?

SUPERINTENDENT
For racism.

BRODERICK
That's not what you are supposed to apologize for.

SUPERINTENDENT
For all the racist incidents that occurred under my leadership.

RICEE
Nope, he tryna get something out of this. I know trifling men when I see them.

SUPERINTENDENT
I'm not trying to get nothing; I just get nervous.

MELISSA
Is that right.

SUPERINTENDENT
Yes.

CEDRIC
He is nervous, I don't blame him, but he wants something.

JULIUS
It makes sense. What, you want us to get your ass out of some shit?

SUPERINTENDENT
You all won the lawsuit!

ELIZABETH
Yes, we did.

SUPERINTENDENT
Look, the school board is on my ass now. You all won the lawsuit, closed some of our schools, and now our student population looks like a milk jug. If I don't fix this, I will be without a job.

JULIUS
Where do we come in?

SUPERINTENDENT
I need to fix our district. I need you all back. What do I need to do? Make every day Black History Day? Want soul food for lunch? Should every Friday be Black Friday where we share a civil rights fact? Do I need to wear a dishiki-

BRODERICK
Boy, I want to whoop yo ass.

TAYLOR
Superintendent!

SUPERINTENDENT
Sorry, sorry, sorry.

ELIZABETH
Well, sir?

SUPERINTENDENT
I don't know what I'm doing, especially with this issue. I just don't get it, but I'm begging you all. We got a mess back there; we look like the days when we didn't like each other.

JULIUS
What, a couple days ago?

RICEE
Minutes.

SUPERINTENDENT
Look. You all won the lawsuit. You have closed two elementary schools, one middle, and our poor high school is being run by subs.

SUPERINTENDENT (CONT'D)
because we can't afford teachers because the state no longer gives us money for your children. And now these idiots are asking for a 15-dollar minimum wage a fucking hour. For what? And let me not start on our athletic program. Now that your kids are gone, we have been dropped out of the ranking because we are so bad. So, all of you, I'm begging. *(He gets on one knee.)* I am begging you: return, come back, we accept the demands, but our district is now being closely watched by the state. And we will give you your job back, we will.

TAYLOR
Superintendent, sir, get up, have some respect for you self.

CEDRIC
You are acting like I got fi-

CEDRIC stands up and so does JULIUS.

JULIUS
Give us a minute, can you step out so we can talk?

SUPERINTENDENT
(Stutters)
Take all the time you need.

SUPERINTENDENT leaves the room.

MELISSA
You all are wrong for that.

They all burst out laughing, dapping each other up.

JULIUS
He told people he didn't want to meet with us cause we were ghetto and scary, so that's exactly what we gave him.

BRODERICK
That man is crazy.

RICEE
He got on his knees. Ain't nobody told him to do that.

MELISSA
Anyways.

RICEE
What are you doing? Are we really thinking about this?

JULIUS
No, we are just wasting his time, so he thinks we are actually discussing this because I know we all gone say no. I had to get 'em out of here before he meets the Cedric that *we* know.

They all chuckle. They all look around in agreement.

MELISSA
Are we certain? Just making sure.

JULIUS
I mean, y'all, look at us. A year and a half ago some of us were in a hallway arguing about disciplining our children and doing something about this.

JULIUS (CONT'D)
And now, because of each one of you, the same man that didn't pay us any attention is begging us to help him fix the district.

TAYLOR
So, we really ain't gone help?

JULIUS
We did. We helped when we sent those recommendations and even added it to the suit, which he is now required to do.

MELISSA
Kind of feeling like we destroyed that district.

JULIUS
Hold up, leaders, don't start feeling guilty. You all need to be proud. Ask your children how they are feeling now that they are in different schools. Check their grades and look at the improvements. Look at the nonprofit you all have created. We have won a suit and closed schools. The suit says they must accept all the recommendations we made. It's their turn to do the work, cause I'm not doing it for them anymore. We aren't those types of people. And lastly—then I'll get off my soapbox—the relationships that we have built with each other are deep and strong. It's their time to take the baton, do the work, and fix those problems. There are no permanent enemies or friends. But right now, we are doing good and so are our kids.

BRODERICK
I'm with you, brotha. This y'all decision.

CEDRIC
Me too.

TAYLOR
Now hold the hell on, y'all didn't get me elected to this fucking school board for nothing!

RICEE
You said that right.

MELISSA
It just doesn't feel right.

JULIUS
You know what, you're officially an organizer, you want next steps. Well, what are our new demands?

Everyone begins to think.

RICEE
Well, Taylor is on the school board now…

JULIUS
What if we ask him to make her the board chair?

TAYLOR
They not gone do it, they won't vote for me, they still ain't even congratulate me and I serve with them now.

MELISSA
But we can get him to persuade the board to make the decision.

CEDRIC
If they need our help, they better.

TAYLOR
I do love this group; I appreciate you all thinking that I can really do that. Back in the day, all I did was work and be with my man, but it's nice to have a group of friends, if I can call y'all that.

They all shake their heads yes.

TAYLOR (CONT'D)
And my baby girl is just glowing. I've never seen her be so proud of her blackness. Something changed her and she's out in college doing her thing. Imagine that we started when she was a senior, and now she's in college. But I still care for y'all kids. I'm invested in this.

MELISSA
And don't forget you made history! We also grew a new organization; we are thriving financially. Students' leaders across the board, and Ricee has made this one of the most fun experiences not only for these kids but for me.

CEDRIC
I got a new job and my boy still getting letters regardless of where he's from.

ELIZABETH
Y'all have taught me how to be a better mother to my black son, and I went a few pant sizes up, Taylor and Broderick.

BRODERICK
You keep coming?

TAYLOR
I wasn't going to say nothing, but baby that cornbread looks good on you.

RICEE
Y'all gon make me cry, cause I really ain't like y'all and now I do.

JULIUS
Then, all, I don't know about y'all, but I think we maybe we should tell 'em our demands. Make Taylor board chair, then we will help the school district. Sincerely, the Black Parent Union.

JULIUS raises his fist, the group follows, and then ELIZABETH does. They all laugh together, including her, and hug each other. Lights out.

END.

MIRRORS FOREWORD

Mirrors by Kaitlin Gould takes us on a journey into the complex and often surreal world of eating disorders. Alice's mind is a powerful thing. Diagnosed with bulimia, she embarks on a journey of healing and reflection. As she falls down the rabbit hole of her illness, the more absurd her reality becomes. Her only comfort comes from an unconventional therapy group that challenges her to confront her deepest fears and insecurities, but also help each other on the road to recovery. Written with honesty and sensitivity, *Mirrors* is a reflection on the absurd, humorous, and tragic realities of living with eating disorders.

Mirrors was first presented in 2016 as a 15-minute short for the Edinburgh Fringe Festival and was workshopped by Bodhi Theatre in September 2018. *Mirrors* had its premiere production in February 2020 with Kansas City Public Theatre. The play was produced in a small-scale format for a two-night run at Charlotte Street Foundation's Capsule studio. This original production was directed by Nathan Bowman with the following cast:

ALICE/RED QUEEN: Kaitlin Gould
DR. CATHERINE/MOM/NARRATOR: Dawn Youngs
DEE: Liz Kerlin
MISSIE/SISTER/OTHERS: Melissa Trierweiler
ZARA/OTHERS: Tehreem Chaudhry
MARYN/OTHERS: Janetta Leigh
HARRY/DAD/OTHERS: Terraye Watson

The Kansas City Public Theatre production was followed by a workshop performance in the summer of 2022 at Teatro LATEA in New York City, directed by Courtney Seyl with the following cast:

ALICE/RED QUEEN: Kaitlin Gould
DR. CATHERINE/MOM/NARRATOR: Javana Mundy
DEE: Madeline Burton
MISSIE/SISTER/OTHERS: Anna Russell
HARRY/DAD/OTHERS: Dhane Ross
MARYN/OTHERS Kristin Sgarro
ZARA/OTHERS: Petrina Ampeire

MIRRORS

A Play

By: Kaitlin Gould

Mirrors Cast, or GROUP:

- Alice/Red Queen – Femme presenting. An artist, bohemian, anxious, depressed, and in denial. Privileged, but unaware of it. Diagnosed with Bulimia Nervosa. The Red Queen, as described, is loud, belligerent, controlling, and bossy; she is Alice's neurotic alter ego through which her eating disorder is manifested.
- Dr. Catherine/Mom/Narrator – Femme presenting. Grounded, professional, and deeply cares for others. She leads the Group Therapy sessions of her own accord to try and do some good in the world. She has seen a lot. Mom is sensitive, wails a lot, and only likes to talk of happy things.
- Dee – Femme presenting. Depressed, hurt, rough on the edges and cynical. She does not trust easily or often. As sarcastic, if not more, than Alice. She has been anorexic for over a decade and in and out of various therapies and treatments. It's unlikely she willingly sought out treatment to begin with.
- Missie/Sister/Others – Femme presenting. Shy until she's comfortable, but not afraid to stand up for herself. Optimistic. Diagnosed with binge eating disorder; however, it is more likely that she has OSFED and has likely been misdiagnosed, causing her to do a lot of research and work on her own. Sister is very pregnant the entire show, and she is matter of fact, dominant, and headstrong in her opinions. Like Alice, she believes she is right.
- Zara/Others – Muslim. Femme presenting. Self-aware, welcoming, and speaks her mind freely. She very much wants to recover from her eating disorder. It's likely she too has been misdiagnosed, leaving her to do a lot of research and work on her own. Diagnosed with Bulimia Nervosa.
- Maryn/Others – Trans or non-binary. Anxious. Humor as a defense mechanism. They feel safe in Group and seek to provide that same space for others. Self-aware, and likely realized they had a problem on their own, without any outside influence or resources. Diagnosed with OSFED and fluctuates between restrictive eating and binge/purge behaviors.
- Harry/Dad/Others – Male presenting person of color. Very much "Big Brother" energy. He feels at home with Group and is comfortable expressing himself. He likely sought out treatment on his own. Dad is almost a stereotype: he does not show emotion well and says very little.

A Note on Language:

- Eating disorder terms and facts are constantly changing as we continue to study, learn, and understand more about them. As such, some facts and names might be outdated. Please research the correct terms accordingly, so that the appropriate language is being used. This is a triggering, difficult

subject to navigate, and it is vital that the language used to describe it is used correctly.
- This does not apply to contexts in which people are intentionally misusing correct language (i.e., the Pills, Supermodel, or Friends scenes).
- Please ensure content warnings are issued when casting and producing this play and avoid triggering or harmful research. Providing helpful resources is encouraged.

A Note on Casting:

Age, race, gender, and body type do not matter when casting this production. However, there are some rules that must be followed:
- In terms of age: they are all adults. Dr. Catherine is likely older than most of them, but not necessarily.
- Maryn must be non-binary, trans, or gender fluid.
- Harry must be a male identifying person of color.
- Zara must be Muslim. It is up to the actor playing Zara to decide how religious she is and what she wears.
- Alice is privileged. That does not inherently mean white.
- Sister, played by Missie, must be very pregnant the entire show.
- Dee, who is severely anorexic, should not be type cast based on her body type.
- Many folks experience eating disorders and will never get treatment because of how their bodies are perceived. This is a sensitive topic and must be considered when casting this show.

A Note on The World:

- Movement should be used when necessary to enhance the storytelling.
- Actors, especially during monologues or stylized scenes, should feel free to include the audience as much as possible.
- / indicates lines where characters speak together or over each other.
- A blank space indicates the actor is allowed to improvise.
- Lines between parentheses indicate the actor has the freedom to speak or act that line.
- Ensemble lines between quotations should be divided up amongst the actors accordingly.
- "Eat Bitch" and "Drink Bitch" can be said by the audience, fellow actors, voiceover, whomever, depending on the vision of the team.
- Group Scenes should be almost chaotic. Actors should feel free to let their characters shine through: talk over each other and ad lib as often as possible without distracting from the scene.

Pre-show: ALICE is on stage, curled up beneath a pile of trash.

Scene 1: The Beginning.

*Lights. The stage is covered in trash. As the play progresses, actors should leave trash all over the stage.
In the center there is a red bucket—Alice's bucket.
Suddenly, a loud, obnoxious alarm starts ringing, which Alice ignores.*

VOICE OVER:
TIME TO… WAKE UP.

*Eventually, she acknowledges the alarm and attempts to stand, but feels numb and heavy. Once she stands, she looks out at the audience, unaware of them at first.
She stares at herself, poking and prodding at various body parts.*

Alice:
There's something about mirrors… Our reflections. It's just me, and me, face to face…

A cupcake appears.

VOICE:
EAT, BITCH!

Alice throws the bucket on her head, becoming Red Queen.

Red Queen:
EAT, BITCH!

*Beat.
She is now aware of the audience.*

She plays with the bucket during the monologue:

Alice:
I'm not staring at myself out of vanity. My reflection is everywhere. You don't want to see yourself? Good luck. What else should I do? My brain could be playing tricks, it could change perspective, OR it could be telling me the truth—why shouldn't I believe my brain? Reality is a relative term. Ah, the great existential crises. Who am I? Where am I? Who are you? How did I get here?

A drink appears.

VOICE:
DRINK, BITCH!

Red Queen:
DRINK, BITCH!

Lights.

Scene 2: A Very Merry Un-Birthday

Alice:
How did I get here? I guess I'll start from the beginning and go until I've reached the end. Then stop. … I woke up feeling heavier than normal. Then I heard something, no, someone… a voice… *Her.* Loud. Belligerent. And the only way I could pacify her was to do what she commanded of me. And the *relief* I felt. Until my family found out—

*HARRY, DR. CATHERINE, and MISSIE enter as Alice's family.
They have a trash cake (this can be edible or not).
They sing a very sped up, almost chaotic version of 'Happy Birthday.'*

Dad/Mom/Sister:
Happy birthday to you! Happy birthday to you! Happy birthday, dear ALICE. Happy birthday to you!

Alice:
Oh, uh—

Mom:
Happy birthday, baby!

Alice:
Thanks—

Dad:
Now just LOOK at that cake!

Sister:
Thanks, Dad.

Mom:
You must have spent hours on it.

Sister:
I did.

Beat.

Alice:
Oh, yeah. Yummmmm. Looks great.

Sister:
Thank you, Alice. Now blow out the candles and /make a wish!

Dad/Mom:
Make a wish!

A ringing noise.
Alice hugs her bucket, looking at the trash cake.
Family eagerly awaits her wish and consumption of the cake.

Alice:
May I be excused?

Sister:
I worked myself to near death over a hot stove, for what? For what?!

Alice:
I just. Need to pee…

Mom:
Now, now. Don't you appreciate all the hard work your sister did for you?

Alice:
I do, but I—

Dad:
It's time for cake.

Alice:
I don't feel so good—

Mom/Dad/Sister:
Make a wish! Eat the cake! Make a wish! Eat the cake! Make a wish! Eat the cake! …

The ringing grows.
Alice's family's chants speed up and become more aggressive.
Alice hugs her bucket tightly.
She goes to take a bite.

Red Queen VO:
Oh Alice.

Alice's family shoves the trash cake in her face.
Lights. Alice throws the bucket on her head.

Red Queen:
EAT BITCH!

Beat.
Her family stares at her, confused.
Mom starts wailing.

Mom:
My baby has a problem! I've failed as a mother!

Sister:
Oh great, look what you've done!

Sister comforts Mom and they step aside. They whisper to each other and encourage Dad to say something. Dad stops beside Alice.

Dad:
You know, you really shouldn't smoke. And you shouldn't drink so much.

Alice:
…I know, Dad. I'm sorry. I can't help it.

Dad:
Well… Your sister. Your mom. They think maybe you need to see someone.

Alice:
What do you think?

Dad:
[Pause] Yep.

FAMILY exits.
Lights.

Scene 3: You Should See a Therapist

A waiting room.
"Rehab" by Amy Winehouse is playing quietly in the background.
A moment.

Alice:
Sooo, now I'm here. … Waiting.

Lights. DOCTOR enters.

Doctor and Dietician are fast talking for-profit American Healthcare workers. This should feel very Tweedle Dee/Tweedle Dumb.

Doctor:
Alice. *(Beat)* I hear you've been really sick. What's going on?

Alice:
Well, actually… It's not that I am *really* sick. It's more that I'm making myself sick? Or, maybe I am, and… I don't know what to do.

Doctor:
I'm glad you're here, you're doing a brave thing. I'll write up a list of people I recommend you call. Psychiatrists, psychologists, dieticians—

Ding.
Doctor carries on as DIETICIAN swoops in.

Dietician:
And here's some information to help rehabilitate your eating habits—

Doctor/Dietician:
That is going to be our biggest challenge.

Dietician:
I'll need to take your weight every time I see you—

Doctor:
We'll need to keep an eye on it—

Dietician:
It is imperative to your recovery—

Doctor:
And we want you to get better—

Dietician:
I'll have you face away from the scale when we weigh you—

Doctor:
Right now you're around—

Alice:
You want me to not know my weight?

Dietician:
During recovery, seeing your weight change is triggering and can cause relapse—

Doctor:
[Announces Alice's weight – it should be absurdly, unrealistically over or underweight].

Dietician:
I need to monitor how it's progressing.

Doctor/Dietician:
Now, as far as therapy goes—

Doctor:
I've written up a list of some therapists I can refer you too—

Alice:
Not rehab!

Amy Winehouse Reprise.

Dietician:
People that can help you.

Doctor:
I'll write up your referral—

Dietician:
And we'll see how it goes—

Doctor:
You can see if she's a good fit—

Dietician:
Everyone works differently with different therapists.

Doctor:
I'm also going to prescribe you a medication.

Alice:
Oh good, just drug me up, take my money, and send me on my way.

Doctor:
I can see you're hesitant.

Dietician:
There will be an adjustment period.

Doctor:
Different medications work differently for everyone—

Dietician:
There are several solutions we can try to help you.

Alice scoffs.

Doctor:
You know, I'm on this medication myself. I have depression, and it helped me start to feel like myself again.

Alice:
I don't know "myself." That's why I'm here.

Doctor:
Well. Let's give this a try, for now.

Dietician:
We'll get you scheduled in for once a with week your therapist,

Doctor:
Your dietician,

Dietician:
And your doctor.

Both:
We're here to help.

DIETICIAN and DOCTOR exit.
Alice is alone on stage, overwhelmed.
A generic fast-food logo appears, and trash is thrown at her as she takes in the smells.

VOICE:
"EAT BITCH!"

Alice throws the bucket on her head.

Red Queen:
EAT BITCH!

Lights.

Scene 4: Therapy Part 1

VOICE OVER:
TIME FOR…THERAPY!

Alice stands outside the door of the therapist office, staring.

Dr. Catherine:
Alice?

Alice:
… Here we go.

She sits.
Dr. Catherine is smiling.

There is a long, long, long, long, long pause.

As long as the actor feels comfortable to make the audience uncomfortable. And then even longer.

Dr. Catherine:
How are you today, Alice?

Alice:
Fine, thank you.

Dr. Catherine:
What brings you in?

Alice:
[Joking] Oh well, you know.

Dr. Catherine:
No, I'm afraid I don't know.

Alice:
I'm here because I have a problem.

Dr. Catherine:
And what would that problem be?

Alice:
I feel like you already know the answer to that question.

Dr. Catherine:
Alice, I can't help you unless you are honest with me about why you are here.

Silence.

Alice:
(Begrudgingly) I'm here…Because. I think. I have. An… *eating disorder*.

Dr. Catherine:
Very good! Admitting it is the first step.

Alice:
Yeah, no shit.

Dr. Catherine:
What was that?

Alice:
Yes, it is!

Dr. Catherine:
Care to share more about that?

Alice:
Not particularly.

Dr. Catherine:
Very well. There's no need to feel rushed. But I will say this: the more I know about you, the more I can help you get to the root of this problem.

Alice:
Great.

Dr. Catherine:
You don't seem too enthused about being here.

Alice:
Yeah.

Dr. Catherine:
I understand. This is hard, but it's a brave thing you're doing. Recovery is a long, challenging road. Relapses are common…

Lights.
The ringing returns.
Alice manically throws the bucket back onto her head.

Red Queen:
What's this lady going on about? We're fine! Only the bad ones die. She thinks you're a piece of shit, that your behavior is unacceptable. She wants to take this away from you! Like *hell* she is!

Alice removes the bucket.

Dr. Catherine:
Well… we're at time for today. I would encourage you to think of some topics you'd like to discuss for next week – it's your hour, after all.

Alice:
I thought the point of therapy was to make me feel better—

Dr. Catherine:
It isn't a miracle cure. You have to do the work. Addiction is a hard battle to fight. I am here to guide you through that fight, but only if you let me.

Dr. Catherine stands.

Dr. Catherine:
So. Same time next week?

Alice nods, stands.

Dr. Catherine:
In the meantime, if you need somewhere to go, I'd recommend coming to this group I run. It's not traditional therapy, per se, but I think you would benefit from being around others who understand what you're going through.

Alice:
Great, another medical bill—

Dr. Catherine:
It's free, actually. I wanted to help others feel less alone on this journey. The choice is yours—join if, and when, you feel ready.

Alice:
Why is it I'm only getting all help and attention now that people think there's something wrong with me?

Dr. Catherine:
You'd be surprised what happens when you change your perspective—

Alice:
I don't need people thinking I'm crazy.

Dr. Catherine:
[Smirks] Alice, everyone is crazy. In their own way.

Lights.

Scene 5: Fears We Face, or Group Therapy, Part 1.

VOICEOVER:
TIME FOR…GROUP!

Enter GROUP ready for the session. Alice stumbles in last Group feels like a family, and they tend to speak over each other. Actors should feel free to improvise and have audible reactions during Group scenes.

Dr. Catherine:
How are you all today?

GROUP mumbles various responses.

Dr. Catherine:
We have a new member joining us this week. Everyone, say hello to Alice—

Unenthusiastic cheers from GROUP.

Dr. Catherine:
Let's make her feel welcome—you all remember how scary it was your first time here. Now, let's get started. Our game this week is: How Would You Handle It?

Missie starts to raise her hand to speak.

Harry:
My brother tried to feed me a bag of chips the other day…

Dr. Catherine nods for him to continue.

Harry:
I mean… My family does this all the time. It's a way for them to feel a sense of control over the situation. But like. Come on, that's not helping.

Dr. Catherine:
How would you handle it?

Harry:
I'd… Snatch the bag, rip it open, throw the chips on the ground, tear the bag up, and then I'd stomp the chips into the carpet. And then I'm make him lick it up. "How do you like it, Dave?!"

Dee and Harry laugh at this. Missie eagerly raises her hand.

Dr. Catherine:
Yes, go ahead, Missie.

Missie:
My parents bought me a cookbook… It's called *Skinny on the Go: Cheap Meals to Help You Lose Weight Fast*.

Beat. Reactions from Group.

Dr. Catherine:
And how would you handle it?

Missie:
… I mean, it was a nice a gesture.

Dee clears her throat, encouraging Missie.

Missie:
I'd take it, smile, say thank you, and then… I start tearing each page out, one at a time, and I rip them up, until the whole thing is one big pile of tiny, ripped pieces of paper. And then I set it on fire! And, and laugh as it burns before her eyes!

Missie laughs, almost maniacally. Positive reactions from Group. Maryn raises their hand.

Maryn:
Mine isn't food related.

Dr. Catherine:
That's okay. Triggers aren't always food related.

Maryn:
I got a call from my ex while I was at work…

Dr. Catherine:
What happened?

Maryn:
I *absolutely* screened that shit. They avoided me for months, and now all of a sudden, they're calling me during office hours? I snapped! I ran out the back and made myself puke behind the dumpster. *(Beat)* I was doing so well.

Dr. Catherine:
You're still doing well. Some days are bad days, but they don't define you. And today you're here. You showed up. Celebrate your successes, big and small. Now, how would you handle it?

Maryn:
I would… answer it, let them say their piece, then I'd say mine... maybe throw in a casual "Fuck You."

Dee:
Pretty tame for you, Maryn.

Maryn:
I'm so tired of wasting my energy on shitty people. Plus, it's not like they're here, like I can't just shove their face in a toilet and give them a swirly or something. Although…

They share a smirk together. Dee approves of this.

Dr. Catherine:
Very good—who's next?

Zara raises her hand.

Dr. Catherine:
Yes, Zara—how was your family dinner this week?

Zara:
My mom was on bathroom watch. Again. They don't know what to do. They think, "Oh, just keep an eye on her, just feed her." Every time I got up to pee it was like, "Sound the alarm! There she goes!"

Dr. Catherine:
And?

Zara:
I kind of like Maryn's swirly idea... But. What I'd do is: I grab all the food on the table—I'm throwing it everywhere. At my brothers, my parents, my aunt and uncle. I throw everything out the window and smash the plates and flip the table! Now who's gonna stop me from peeing?

Harry:
No one, that's who!

Zara:
Damn straight.

Dr. Catherine:
Dee? Anything from you this week?

Dee:
(Beat) I mean, nothing new. The typical "why don't you just eat" bullshit. My dad ignoring me. My mom pretending I'm normal. Everyone uses this code around me to talk about me.

Dr. Catherine:
Anything in particular?

Dee:
Honestly? All of it. I mean, all the little comments, they add up. You start to boil over.

Dr. Catherine:
How would you handle it?

Dee:
I wish I could actually boil, like a tea pot. Steam blowing out of my ears, the whistling, all of it. Maybe I wouldn't release in other ways, I wouldn't hurt anybody, or myself.

Harry:
Deep.

Dee:
Why thank you. Maybe I'll write a book about it.

Dr. Catherine:
Joking aside, writing or journaling could be a good solution. It can help you decompress, let some of that steam out. Now, that just leaves Alice.

GROUP turns to look at her.

Alice:
Yes?

Dr. Catherine:
You've been quiet. Maybe something happened this week?

Alice:
Nope.

Dee:
Oh my god, come on!

Harry:
Let that steam out!

Missie:
It's fun, and it helps.

Alice:
Pretending to hit people and set books on fire isn't really what I'd call fun, so...

Zara:
Pretending you're okay is?

Alice:
That's not what I said—

Dee:
She's just another new, rich girl who's / gonna give up and go to some swanky rehab center in like two weeks—

Alice:
/ I'm sorry, what?

Maryn:
/ Dee—

Dr. Catherine:
Quiet, please. Alice, it is normal to be nervous or uncomfortable your first time here, but I do encourage you to participate. I can't stress the group aspect of group therapy enough.

Beat. GROUP is expectantly looking at Alice.

Alice:
Well. I guess, a friend said something shitty.

Groans from GROUP.

Alice:
I haven't seen her, or any of my friends, in a while. She has this brilliant idea to take me out to eat, which is a recipe for disaster, and what do you think happens. So, we're leaving, and she goes: "You know, I really thought you'd be better by now."

Dee:
Better get used to that.

Alice:
Excuse me?

Dee:
Guess how many friends I lost after six months of doing this? A year? Two years, five—people take until you have nothing left to give and then they bail.

Alice:
What's your problem?

Dee:
What's *your* problem?

Dr. Catherine:
Dee. Alice.

Missie:
What I think Dee means is, we've all lost a lot of friends because of this. It's hard, but we're here for you.

Maryn:
We have each other.

Alice:
I thought she'd be more understanding. If I was sick, actually sick / —

Dee:
/ *[To Harry]* This bitch!

Zara:
/ We are actually sick.

Alice:
Okay but, if I had cancer, nobody would be like: "Wow I know you've been doing chemo for a while, I really thought you'd beat cancer by now." It's ridiculous.

Harry:
People are ridiculous.

Dr. Catherine:
How would you handle it?

Alice:
I don't know...

Missie/Zara/Maryn/Harry:
"Go for it!" "You got this!" "It can be anything." "Just try."

Dee:
Come on, dude!

Dr. Catherine:
Alice, they won't let you leave without giving them an answer.

Alice:
I would, I don't know, I'd tell her off—

Dee:
Oh my *god*, you're killing me.

Alice:
No, I would. I'd punch her but what good is that going to do?

Dee:
Make you feel better.

Alice:
All these people hurt us with their words. If everyone was out here throwing food at each other, the world would be chaos.

Harry:
Feels pretty chaotic to me.

Alice:
Plus, if I can use my words against her, to make her understand how I feel, maybe she won't say things like that—

A final "over it" look from Group.

Alice:
And if not then, yeah, maybe I'd give her a swirly, or, whatever.

Group accepts this answer.

Dr. Catherine:
That's a good start, Alice. We'll work on it for next week.

Lights.

Scene 6: SMOKE BREAK.

GROUP disperses.
Dee crosses to smoke a cigarette.
Dr. Catherine exits.
Alice goes to smoke a cigarette, seeing Dee.

Alice:
Oh, uhm… See ya—

Alice starts to leave.

Dee:
Hey. Newbie. Where you going?

Alice:
…home?

Dee:
Need a light?

Alice, unsure, looks at Dee.

Dee:
Oh come on, take the god damn light.

Alice does, still unsure of Dee.

Alice:
I thought I was just another rich bitch who's going to—

Dee:
Look, you can't blame us for not trusting you.

Alice:
You don't know me—

Dee:
You don't know us. We have to protect each other. People come and go. A lot of them have used us, or hurt us—

Alice:
Why would I hurt you?

Dee:
Why do people do the things they do?

Alice:
Why, okay—whatever. I don't know what I'm doing. I don't want to be here, but I *know* something's wrong with me. And, my family, their disappointment—I have to try.

Dee:
Well, good luck to you. I've been doing this a long time. The disappointment doesn't go away. It only gets worse. You can only burden them for so long before it becomes easier to ignore you.

Laughter from GROUP as the rest of them come over to Alice and Dee.

Zara:
Hey! Alice! We're all going out. Wanna join?

Alice:
You all were kinda rude to me in there, and now you want me to hang out with you?

Dee:
We're rude to everyone. / It's part of our charm.

Missie:
/ I wasn't rude.

Harry:
/ You'll get used to it. We grow on you.

Alice:
Yeah, I don't know—

Zara:
Come on, it'll be fun!

Harry:
Weren't you just saying how shitty all your friends are?

Maryn:
Might as well hang out with us instead.

Missie:
Yeah, we're fun!

Alice:
Okay. Sure. Where are we going?

Lights.

Scene 7: The Drive Through

Lights on GROUP sitting in a car formation: Maryn is the driver, sitting next to Missie in the front. Harry and Dee sit next to each other in the middle. Alice and Zara in the back. *Note: the items Missie orders may change based on the current menu or be improvised, so long as they are the most absurd items.

Voice:
Hi and welcome to Jack in the Box. How may I help you?

Missie:
Hi, yes, could I um, please may I have one [Sriracha curly fry burger munchie meal], [one stacked grilled cheeseburger], and [one chick-n-tater melt munchies meal]? *[Beat]* Anyone else want anything?

Fast food bags are tossed at Missie as she wolfs down her food.

Alice:
Nobody sees the irony of a bunch of people with eating disorders going to a drive thru after therapy, do they?

Dee:
Quiet in the back!

Maryn:
Not all eating disorders are created equally.

Missie:
Did you know, actually—binge eating is the most common eating disorder but it's the most dismissed. People assume that I need to exercise, or that I don't have self-control—

Harry:
Which is partly true—

Dee:
Bitch, none of us have self-control.

Alice:
Soooo, we're enabling each other?

Zara:
Not exactly.

Voice:
Welcome to Taco Bell, my life is terrible, what do you want?

Missie:
Please could I have [one double decker], [one quesarito], one [crunchwrap supreme], and one naked chicken chalupa?

Voice:
We don't sell the naked chicken chalupa anymore, ma'am.

Harry:
Aww damn.

Missie:
Oh, uhhhhhm…then….one [cheesy gordita crunch], please? And a Baja Blast?

Zara:
Make that two!

Harry:
Three!

Maryn:
Four Baja Blasts, please.

Fast food bags are thrown once again.

Missie:
It's less suspicious if they think you're ordering for multiple people—

Maryn:
As the saying goes: if you can't beat 'em, join 'em.

Alice:
Wait—so you do this after every group therapy session?

Harry:
Yup.

Alice:
Isn't this counterproductive to our therapy—

Dee:
Jesus Christ buzz kill! Look, we're all still *going* to therapy so we're *obviously* not better.

Harry:
It's a lot less
isolating if we
do this
together.

Zara:
If Missie needs us to go with her on her drive through binges, then that's what we do. And if you need us to hold your hair back while you throw up your dinner, then that's what we do.

Missie throws some fast-food bags across/off stage.

Alice:
Now what are we doing?

Dee, over it, picks up a piece of trash and throws it in the back at Alice.

Voice:
Welcome to Arby's, we have the MEATS! But our food will destroy your insides. Please don't eat here.

Missie:
Please could I have one [Reuben], one [fire roasted Philly], and four large curly fries?

Maryn:
Make that five.

Harry:
Six!

Zara:
One for me too!

Missie:
Seven large curly fries.

Voice:
Any drinks?

Missie:
Oh, a Dr. Pepper. Diet.

Fast food bags are once again thrown at the group.

Alice:
I just—when I thought you said going out—

Dee:
What, did you think we meant a bar?

Alice:
Kind of, yeah.

Dee:
How is that any better than what we're doing?

Alice:
You go to a bar to drink.

Maryn:
That's still consumption. It's no different, whether its alcohol or food, we're all addicts.

Zara:
One damages your stomach, one destroys your liver.

Harry:
I don't know, the night's still young. Maybe there's time for both.

*Harry and Dee laugh.
Missie throws the remaining food bags off stage.*

Missie:
Alice—I used to do this by myself. I would go to a side street by an empty park and just eat, and eat, and eat, and then I'd start sobbing. Alone. I do things you wouldn't even think of. The diets my parents have forced me to be on, hiding food in my room, unsolicited diet tips from strangers, forcing myself to go days without eating—I got turned away at inpatient because they said I weighed too much. I know what I'm doing is

Missie (cont'd):
wrong and I hate that I feel this way, but. My problem doesn't look like your problem.

Dee:
That's why we do it.

Zara:
If it makes you uncomfortable, you don't have to come with us.

Missie:
It's okay—this isn't for everyone. Every day I battle this self-hate and disgust at what I'm doing, but at least I know I'm not alone this time.

Maryn:
Or the next time. And there's always a next time.

Harry:
No matter how many times you say you won't.

Zara:
We all end up doing it again, anyway.

Missie:
So we might as well do it together.

Lights.

Scene 8: The Hunt

DR. CATHERINE enters as Narrator, a real off-brand David Attenborough type.

*A ding: Missie enters first. Movements should be chaotic and animalistic.
Binger: Binge eating disorder.
Ana: short for anorexia.
Mia: short for bulimia.
E.D. short for eating disorder.*

ED can also be referred to as OSFED (Other Specified Feeding or Eating Disorder, formerly known as ENDOS).

Narrator:
Here, we see the Binger in her natural habitat. Though she is awake primarily during the day, it is in these late hours of the night that she feels most at ease hunting. She is not worried about competition or other predators lurking about. No, she is safe to binge as freely as she pleases.

A ding: Dee and Harry enter.

Narrator:
Ah, the Anas! They are less like the bingers. It is the absence of food that brings them joy. Perhaps they'll consume a fermented beverage, perhaps a smoke, perhaps nothing at all.

A ding: Zara enters, and Harry begins interacting with her.

Narrator:
The Mias are more like the Binger. They enjoy an omnivorous and restrictive diet. Starting with a lighter option, such as a single stick of plain celery, grants their mind permission for when they catch scent of something more…satisfying.

A ding: Maryn enters, eyeing Dee and Harry.

Narrator:
Sometimes, a Mia will go off the rails and decide to become an Ana. These are what we simply call E.D. They are very mysterious. They drift between various packs.

Maryn and Harry come together.

Narrator:
Back at the pantry, the Binger and Mias know there are bigger, more mouthwatering prizes to be won. They are cautious, they must be. The slightest noise could cause commotion from those sleeping nearby, disrupting any chance they have at their feast.

They attempt to be quiet.
Dee, Harry, Maryn exit.

Narrator:
So far, so good. Then…

VOICE:
EAT, BITCH!

BOOM! An eruption of eating, grabbing, consuming.

Narrator:
They POUNCE!! They have lost all thought to remain quiet, determined to go in for the kill. But they aren't done yet—

Zara drops any trash and rushes off stage.
Missie grabs bags of food to take off stage with her.

Narrator:
The Binger takes the remains of her prey back to where she knows it will be safe. With her. The cave in which she dwells remains isolated from the rest of the family. There, she will be able to enjoy her meal in peace, without any disturbances or being asked bothersome questions. She is free to feast until she pops.

Lights.

Scene 9: How Do You See Yourself? Or, Therapy Part 2.

VOICEOVER:
TIME FOR...THERAPY!

GROUP enters for their own individual therapy sessions.
Dee enters last.
This should feel very routine, and lines should flow one right after the other.

Dr. Catherine:
Today, we'll be doing some drawing. I want you to draw how you see yourself.

They begin drawing on pieces of paper.
Drawings should be grotesque and absurd.

Dr. Catherine:
What is your least favorite part about yourself?

Alice:
My stomach. Sometimes I wonder if I'm on that show where you don't realize you're pregnant.

Missie:
My face. If I had a prettier face: no double chin, or higher cheek bones, then maybe I wouldn't feel so bad about my weight.

Zara:
My thighs. I feel like a gelatinous balloon.

Maryn:
My arms… Sometimes, I'll stand in front of my mirror, flexing my arms like a

Superhero, wanting to be so buff that I bust out of my t-shirts.

Harry:
My chest. I'm supposed to be lean, but not too skinny. Muscular but not too bulky. A dad bod with abs. But instead, I'm *(searching)* this.

Maryn:
People are constantly projecting their perception of how they think I should look onto me.

Missie:
When people see me on the outside, *if* they see me at all, they just see the fat girl. They don't see that I'm shrinking on the inside with every pound I gain.

Zara:
When I decided to get help, my doctor misdiagnosed me. He thought I might be pregnant. Yeah. (Pregnant). They did bloodwork, tests, everything, but eventually they figured it out. And then my parents figured it out… A year into treatment, I decided to become vegan, because vegans aren't fat, right?

Alice:
My friends are always doing some fad diet. Like, I can prove my worthiness by controlling what I eat.

Maryn:
People romanticize this. It's irresistible to control your weight.

Dee:
Why not be in control of everything about yourself?

Harry:
Everyone just assumes it's about your looks, but it's deeper than that.

Zara:
There's a heaviness that you can't get rid of.

Alice:
I'm at war with myself every single day.

Maryn:
I'm longing to feel at home in my body, but I wake up the next day exhausted from the fight.

Dr. Catherine:
Has there ever been a time since your diagnosis that you've felt good about yourself?

Dee laughs.

Dee:
Absolutely not.

Zara:
The best I ever feel is when I'm with my grandparents. They don't judge me or try to control me, they just *love* me—and, if you even think about trying to be vegan around them, you better just accept that lamb is a vegetable.

Maryn:
Leaving my shitty job to pursue something I'm actually passionate about, *and* leaving my toxic ex. For the first time, I felt like I'd taken control of my life, like I was unstoppable.

Alice:
Music. Performing, creating, singing, any of it. Like, who I am when I'm performing is who I really am, but then the song ends and… then what?

Missie:
When I went on birthright. We went to the Dead Sea, and everyone floats. I didn't feel like the "big" girl. There was no jealousy, no competition, I was just me.

Dee:
Oh wait, I lied, I did Molly once and felt like a goddess. That was amazing. Until it wore off.

Harry:
Moving to a new city for school. I had a fresh start, a new environment, new friends, new me, but. Here I am. So.

Dr. Catherine:
So?

Harry:
It didn't last. Eventually, reality sinks in.

Maryn:
Money starts getting tight: therapy bills, medical bills, it starts to add up.

Alice:
Why bother.

Zara:
I'd love to spend the rest of my life traveling, on the move.

Missie:
Maybe it's an escape, but at least it's on your terms.

Dee:
Life's not like that.

Harry:
Your problems will always find you.

Dr. Catherine:
What problems found you this week?

Dee:
This is such a competitive thing. I don't look at them *[indicating to Group]* and say, "Oh (okay) you're a bitch because you're skinnier than me," but we're all jealous.

Missie:
I see someone skinnier than me walking down the street and I think:

All:
Wouldn't it be easier if I looked like them.

Harry:
Who am I supposed to talk to about this? "Bros don't get eating disorders, bro." But I've had one since my mom put me on Weight Watchers in the seventh grade.

They hold up their drawings.

Maryn:
Everyone has to comment on your looks.

Zara:
You're thick.

Alice:
You've got curves.

Missie:
You're big boned.

Maryn:
You're too bony.

Harry:
You're pudgy.

Dee:
You're fat.

Maryn:
You hear something enough times and you start to accept it as truth.

Alice:
I wish I could see myself how others do. Maybe I'd see what's missing when I look in the mirror.

Lights.

Scene 10: Life...On Pills

VOICEOVER:
TIME FOR...WEIGHT CHECKS.

*Enter DR. CATHERINE and ALICE.
Alice hops onto a "scale" –a ding.*

Dr. Catherine:
Your weight is up this week—

Alice:
Hooray.

Dr. Catherine:
Very good. Have you been taking your medication?

Alice looks out, a confession:

Alice:
I haven't been taking them. For a while, this was helping, a bit. But lately, I feel numb. Nothing excites me or enrages me anymore. And now all I hear is:

Dr. Catherine:
Remember to take your medication.

Alice:
And I am on the lighter end of the spectrum. I'm not bipolar, I'm not schizophrenic. I'm just a girl with anxiety, depression, and bulimia, and I don't need these pills. I refuse, I cannot, will not, absolutely no—

Dr. Catherine:
Take your fucking pills, Alice.

Alice:
Okay. Fine.

Lights.

Lights. 80s commercial music. Dr. Catherine exits as the rest of GROUP enters.

Zara:
Have you been feeling down in the dumps lately?

Harry:
Do you no longer find the joy or meaning in your day-to-day life?

Dee:
Do you wake up and wonder, "Why bother? What's the point?"

Maryn/Missie:
Then have WE got the thing for you!

Maryn and Missie throw pills. Woohoo!

Missie:
Try Prozac—

Maryn:
Lexapro—

Missie:
SSRI's!

Maryn:
MAOIs!

Maryn/Missie:
And MORE!

*Maryn and Missie start to pass out pills.
Alice and Dee avoid them.
Harry and Zara take them.
Zara has a good reaction, Harry does not.*

Zara:
WOW! I feel like me, but *better*!

Missie:
Now, antidepressants can be different for everybody.

Maryn:
Sometimes you gotta really fuck up your brain chemistry before you find the right one.

Zara:
Side effects may include:

Harry/Dee/Alice:
"Nausea and vomiting," "diarrhea or constipation," "dry mouth," "headache," "dizziness," "anxiety," "agitation," "insomnia," "sexual dysfunction,"—

Zara:
Weight *gain*!

A beat. The three look at each other.

Maryn:
And weight loss!

Ooooh's and ahhhh's.

Dee:
Because we can't possibly just use weed.

Alice:
The natural plant that came from the earth isn't natural, so here!

Dee:
Take these pills we made!

Missie:
It gives you the munchies, which is very unhelpful for a binger.

Harry/Zara:
"And an anorexic." "And a bulimic."

Dee:
Don't say we didn't warn you.

Lights shift as Alice takes her pill.
Movement: the moment of the commercial where we see the impact.
Maryn and Missie continue as happy salespeople.
Harry and Zara experience side effects and exit.
Dee, over it, exits.
Alice morphs into numbness, unable to move.

Alice:
Welcome to life on pills.

Lights.

Scene 11: Group Therapy Part 2

VOICEOVER:
TIME FOR…GROUP!

Lights. Dr. Catherine, GROUP enter. They are in the middle of a very heated debate, talking over each other. Actors can have side conversations/ad lib until Harry speaks.

Alice:
I'm telling you, Christmas is the worst!

Dee:
No way dude, Easter is worse!

Maryn:
Fourth of July. How am I supposed to have a beach body while eating barbecue?!

Missie:
We eat for eight nights—how does that help me not want to binge?

Zara:
You all don't know shit about Eid.

Harry:
You're all fucking nuts!

Pause.
Group turns to look at him.

Harry:
What's the one holiday where you're expected to consume an obscene amount of food?!

All:
Thanksgiving.

Dr. Catherine:
That's a good point. Thanksgiving is coming up, and maybe this is a good time to address any fears or concerns you all have?

Alice:
Being around family.

Maryn:
Trying to maintain control.

Missie:
My family commenting on how much I eat—

Zara:
Or don't eat.

Dee:
Someone always has a comment about my body or eating.

Harry:
Last year my mom tried to spoon feed me yams. Yams! "They're yams!" she said, "they're good for you!" I know she's trying, but after all the progress I've made this year—if she starts again, it will awaken the Beast.

Alice:
Beast?

Harry:
Him.

Alice:
Wait. You hear someone too?

Harry:
More like some *thing*. This beast that festers in my mind.

Alice:
(No way.) Do the rest of you hear someone?

Missie:
I do. It's like there's a devil on my shoulder.

Zara:
Mine's more of an image, like a loud shadow monster.

Dee:
I imagine mine to be an ugly, disgusting loser. It's the only way I can make him shut up.

Beat.
Everyone turns to Maryn.

Maryn:
Don't laugh!

Maryn awaits reassurance from the group before continuing.

Maryn:
I imagine mine to be more like… a dragon.
Some people laugh.

Missie:
[Very serious] Like Smaug?

Maryn:
I don't know what a smog is, it's just what I see!

Alice:
I can't believe it! I thought I was losing my mind.

Dr. Catherine:
Mine was a woman, too. A very mean, angry woman. It was like seeing red. She finally went away for good about two years ago.

Alice:
[Mind blown] You had one too?

Dr. Catherine:
That's why I started this group. We haven't always had the awareness and resources that we do now. Plus, it's easy to hide behind the façade of diet and fitness culture. The more I talked to other people, the more I realized how common this is.

Alice:
I can't believe it—this whole time I thought something was wrong with me—

Zara:
Something is wrong with you. With all of us.

Alice:
I know, but I mean like—I have this monster living in my head. She yells and screams, and some days it feels like I just want to rip off my head.

Maryn:
I'm certain we all feel that way.

Dee:
Damn, when do I not want to rip off my head?

Dr. Catherine:
We've all got a monster inside of us, but how do you act when that monster appears? You aren't alone, Alice. This illness is immensely isolating, but that's the beauty of coming to Group. You can reflect on what's going on inside of you without fear of judgment or shame. That's a good note to end on, everybody. I'll see you next week.

Group disperses.

Missie:
We have each other—even if that's all we have, at least it's something.

Red Queen (VO):
Oh, Alice.

A ding: Alice looks at her phone.

Alice:
Oh my fucking God!

Lights.

Scene 12: Have You Heard About Alice?

VOICEOVER:
TIME TO… HANG OUT WITH YOUR OLD, SHITTY FRIENDS!

Maryn and Zara enter, the scene picks up mid-conversation.
Harry and Missie enter one-by-one as the scene progresses.
Lines should be split accordingly.

Friend:
"So like, I've been doing this new diet."

Alice:
Oh yeah?

Friend:
"Yeah. I've lost a soooo much weight—I'm skinnier than you now!"

Alice:
Cool.

Friend:
"Ugh. I am *SO* bloated, I just started my period. I feel so fat."

Alice:
…Yeah.

Friend:
"I hear you're going to rehab."

Alice:
Well, actually, no I—

Friend:
"You know, that's a really brave thing you're doing."

Alice:
…Thanks?

Friend:
"I've definitely struggled with an eating disorder before."

Alice:
Oh, really? That's—

Ensemble:
"Yeah, I just have this really weird relationship with food." "Like, I forget to eat sometimes." "Or I just feel really gross in my clothes." "Like, nothing really fits me right anymore."

Alice:
Oh. Yeah, that's totally the same thing—

Friend:
"So do you like see a shrink and everything?"

Alice:
Um. Yeah, I started seeing her a few months ago and there's this group I go to—

Friend:
"Oh, wow. That's crazy."

Alice:
… Sure.

Friend:
"So like, you've been bulimic for how long now?"

Alice:
Umm, a few years now, maybe?

Friend:
"Oh wow, and you only just started seeing someone?"

Alice:
That's what I just said—

Friend:
"Wow, okay rude—" "I still can't believe you're not better by now."

Alice:
Yeah, well. It takes time. So.

Friend:
"Why don't you just eat something?"

Alice:
I'll work on that.

Friend:
"Oh my goddd. Did you see Sarah's post from the other day?" "She looks so grossssss."

Alice:
I mean, I don't think she—

Ensemble:
"She went on a diet and then gained all the weight back," "Ugh. I need to go back on my diet." "I'm trying this cleanse actually—" "I prefer to drink my calories." "Have you heard about Alice?"

Freeze.
Everyone turns to look at Alice.

Ensemble:
"I really wanna lose five pounds." "How do I make my thighs smaller?" "I read a Buzzfeed article about how to get a sixpack in a week!" "It's so much easier for guys to lose weight," "—she's been lifting, she's so bulky now." "Have you heard about Alice?"

Freeze.
Everyone turns to look at Alice.

Ensemble:
"I totally forgot to eat yesterday." "How do you forget to eat?" "I'm like, sooo anorexic now." "Have you heard about Alice?"

Freeze.

Everyone turns to look at Alice.

Lines should feel like a broken record. Alice begins to feel more and more isolated and eventually hides beneath her bucket.

Ensemble:
"Bulimic bitch." "I prefer rolls to ribs." "Nothing tastes better than skinny." "I'm so bloated and fat." "Just eat something." "You're so not fat." "You have like the perfect body." "You're too skinny."

"Fat" "Ugly" "Dumb" "Anorexic" "Ew!"
"Fat" "Gross" "Stupid" "Bulimic" "Ew!"
"Fat" "Disgusting" "Worthless" "Crazy Bitch" "Ew!"

Friend:
"Have you heard about Alice?"

Everyone turns to look at Alice. Ew.
A drink appears.

VOICE:
"DRINK BITCH!"

Alice/Red Queen:
DRINK BITCH!

Friends disperse.
Lights.

Scene 13: Do You Wanna Be a Super Model?

Music, Lights.
HARRY, MARYN, ZARA, and MISSIE enter.
ALICE, fully relapsed, has her bucket on her head.
Big smiles: it's a grotesque high fashion QVC sales pitch.

Lines should be split up accordingly.

VOICE OVER:
TIME TO... PARTY!

Red Queen:
Do you want to be adored?

Ensemble:
Oh yeah.

Red Queen:
Do you want to be admired?

Ensemble:
Oh. Yeah.

Red Queen:
Do you want to be the envy of the world?

All:
Oh (fucking) yeah!

Movement: The stage is their runway.
Note: The weight can be changed as needed.

Ensemble:
"120?" "Oh, no, no, no. That won't do." "113?" "We're getting warmer!" "110, look out world!" "112?!"

Record Scratch/Music Stops.

Alice:
We'll just have to work that much harder!

They all run in place. Beat.

Ensemble:
"108?" "Almost there!" "105!" "Finally!"

Celebration. Beat.

Alice:
But I think we can do even better!

Ensemble:
"101...100...98!"

Alice:
We've brought those triple digits down to double digits!

Applause and cheering. Ensemble mirrors Alice.

Alice:
Oh thank you, thank you! Oh stop, you're too kind. I really couldn't have done it without the help of my mentor. She's shown me the way. Girls have started complimenting my perfect body. Guys started noticing it too—my last date said:

Ensemble:
"Wow, I've never seen a girl eat an entire pizza—and hot wings—in one sitting!"

Alice:
Now, I know what you're thinking:

Ensemble:
"Alice, HOW did you do it?!"

Alice:
Well, it's all thanks to what I like to call the "Mia Diet." At first, you do it once or twice a week, then a few times more, then once a day, several times a day. You'll do it:

Ensemble:
"At home." "At work." "A party." "A restaurant."

Alice:
After Thanksgiving at your grandma's, and before you know it, you're eating one, single, itty bitty, teeny tiny bite, and you'll

hear her, loud as ever: *[as Red Queen]* WHAT HAVE YOU DONE, HEIFFER?! PIG! OUT WITH IT! So you obey. And the *relief* you feel!

Ensemble:
"Of course, there are other ways to shed off those pesky, extra, unwanted calories."

Alice:
Skipping meals and diet pills are obvious. Laxatives are good, but risky—take them on your day off. Smoke, drink 'til you puke. Have lots of sex—it's cardio, dummies.

Ensemble:
"Think of it as a cleanse."

Alice:
You purge, and never have to worry about counting a single calorie ever again. And at the end of the day, your best friend is there for you! Of course, these are my suggestions.

Ensemble:
"If you're looking for more tips, then look no further than your nearest Pro-Mia or Pro-Ana website!" "They've got all the recommended tips for a proper binge and purge, including:" "What foods to eat." "What foods to avoid." "Post-purge tooth care." "Proper form." "And when to weigh yourself."

Alice:
Set goals for yourself: you had 200 calories yesterday?

Ensemble:
"You can do even better today!"

Alice:
My latest tip I've discovered involves taking a bite of food, then throwing some in the trash.

Ensemble:
"Then taking a bite of food, then throwing a bite in the trash."

Alice:
That way you can still convince your loved ones you've eaten your lunch!

Ensemble:
"The sandwich may taste good—"

Alice:
But *nothing* tastes as good as skinny feels.

Wink. Smile.

Alice:
Want to restrict your eating but can't think of a way to cover it up?

Ensemble:
"Oh, I'm doing intermittent fasting." "I only eat what cavemen ate." "Oh, I'm keto now." "I don't eat anything with a soul."

Alice:
If you're looking for inspiration, look no further. We've got:

All:
Thinspiration!

Alice:
And remember, most importantly, it is all about *control*.

Lights.

Scene 13: Alice and Dee

HARRY becomes BARTENDER.
DEE sits at one end of the bar, back to the audience.
ALICE enters, bucket on her head, not noticing Dee.

VOICE:
DRINK, BITCH!

Red Queen:
DRINK, BITCH!

Bartender:
On the rocks or neat?

Alice:
On the rocks, please.

Bartender:
One rock bottom bitch drink coming right up.

Alice takes off her bucket, as Dee slides over.

Dee:
BOO!

Alice:
AHH! What the fu—

Dee:
Nice to see you too, pumpkin.

Alice:
What are you doing here?!

Dee:
I could ask you the same thing.

Alice:
I'm meeting some friends.

Dee:
Oh?

They look around at the very empty bar.

Alice:
I'm really early…

Dee:
Look, what you do on your own time is none of my business.

Alice:
Okay.

Bartender:
One rock bottom bitch.

Dee:
Oh, I'll have one, neat!

Alice stares at Dee.

Dee:
Don't you want the company?

Alice:
Don't you want to be alone?

Dee:
It's been so long since we've seen you in Group.

Alice:
I've been busy.

Dee:
Yeah? With what.

Alice:
Life. Stuff. Things.

Dee:
Whoa there, don't talk my ear off.

Alice:
Seriously, I'm fine. I needed some time to myself. I'll be at Group next week.

Dee:
Yeah. I've tried that one before.

Alice:
I'm not trying anything.

Dee:
So you pretending to meet up with your friends, alone at a bar, on a Tuesday….

Alice:
You've been here longer than me!

Dee:
My point exactly! You don't think I know what you're dealing with?

Alice:
No, I really don't think you do.

Dee:
You and I are a lot more alike than you seem to realize.

Alice:
In that we both have eating disorders and bad attitudes?

Dee:
We may both be sarcastic, anxious bitches, but I can help you.

Alice:
I'm not anxious, I'm depressed, so….

Dee gives her a look.

Bartender:
One neat bitch.

Dee:
…..

Alice:
…..

Dee:
…..

Alice:
What do you want?!

Dee:
To be your friend! To help you! To love you! Open up, bitch!

Alice:
Oh my god.

Dee pulls out a cigarette, offers one to Alice. She accepts. They smoke.

Dee:
Why haven't you been coming to group?

Alice:
I…

Dee:
Relapse?

Alice nods.

Alice:
And with Thanksgiving coming up, seeing my family… I'm terrified.

Dee:
You know we have these things called phones, right?

Alice gives Dee a look.

Dee:
Seriously, though. I get it, I really do. Your first big family meal during treatment *suuuuucks*. Eating in front of everyone, all the comments, it's triggering. A few years ago, I turned the oven up all the way and burnt all the pies so bad the oven caught on fire.

Alice:
You did not—

Dee:
I did! My dad cried about it on the phone to the fire department.

Alice:
Dads, am I right?

Dee:
Yeah dude. *(Beat)* You don't have to go through this alone.

Alice:
I feel like I'm drowning and no matter how close to the surface I get, she pulls me right back down, telling me I'm a failure, a burden… I can't escape her.

Dee:
Tell that mean bitch in your head she needs to shut up.

Alice:
It's not just her, though. It's everyone. My family, my friends—

Dee:
We don't think that about you.

Alice:
My other friends.

Dee:
You have other friends?!

Alice gives Dee a look.

Dee:
Oh fuck them.

Alice:
They're my friends.

Dee:
Not if they make you feel so shitty about yourself that you relapse.

Alice:
Why do you always act like there's an easy solution to everything?

Dee:
Easy isn't the same thing as simple. You know the biggest problem in my life? The reason it's so much harder than it needs to be? Me. Once I realized that, life got a lot simpler.

Alice:
I'm so tired of feeling this way.

Dee:
Well, then drink your bitch juice and do something about it!

Alice:
You're the bitch, not me—

Dee:
We're both bitches.

Dee offers Alice her hand. They stand and begin walking.

Dee:
And you aren't alone, okay?

Alice:
I don't know how I'm going to make it through this–

Dee:
We'll do it together.

A moment, they look at each other.
A nod.
Lights shift suddenly...

Scene 14: The Mad Thanksgiving, Or: Learning to Eat.

Ding.

Alice:
It's today. The Superbowl of Eating and the worst day of the year for someone like us.

Dee:
Birthdays, Labor Day, Halloween, Christmas, Valentine's Day, Easter, Memorial Day, Fourth of July. There's a National Food Day for every day of the month!

Alice:
October 8: National Fluffernutter Day.

Dee:
July 21: National *Junk* Food Day.

Alice:
April 11: National Cheese Fondue Day.

Dee:
February 18: National Crab Stuffed Flounder Day.

Beat.

Alice:
But Thanksgiving really takes the cake.

Dee:
Last year, I got banned from six different drug stores for buying laxatives. Bet you didn't think they could do that, did you? But they did. To me.

Alice:
Last year, I threw up fourteen times. I think. I lost count after seven or eight, but I know it was double digits. This year, I'll have to be clever. I didn't even make it to my sister's house before I barfed up my breakfast.

A breath. They look at each other.

Alice:
Here we go…

Doorbell. Lights.
DR. CATHERINE, HARRY, and MISSIE enter as Mom, Dad, and Sister.
Dee sits off in her corner, isolated from her family, as Alice feels consumed by hers.

All:
Happy Thanksgiving!

Ding: A feeling of tunnel vision.

Mom:
Who's hungry?

Dad/Sister:
I am! I am!

Beat. They look at Alice.

Alice:
Yeah. Totally. (Me too.)

The following lines move like rapid fire.

Sister:
We've got:

Dad:
Mashed potatoes—

Mom:
Sweet potatoes—

Sister:
Stuffing—

Dad:
Turkey!—

Sister:
Mac and cheese—

Dad:
Green bean casserole—

Mom:
Don't forget the gravy!

A beat. They forgot the gravy.
Change places.
Alice is dragged along for the ride.

Dad:
What about dessert?

Sister:
I made the apple pie—

Mom:
And here's a pecan pie!

Dad:
What about the pumpkin pie?

Sister:
We made that too—

Dad:
Cool Whip?

Sister:
We've got plenty!

Change places.

Mom:
Who'd like to say grace?

Sister:
How about you, Alice?

Red Queen:
For Fuck's Sake—

Sister:
What was that?

Alice:
[As fast as she can] ... God is good, God is great, thank you for this food. Amen.

VOICEOVER:
TIME TO... EAT!

Another ding. Change places.
Alice is desperate for her bucket but tries to fight it.
Dee continues to observe.

Mom:
Time for a family photo!

Alice throws the bucket on her head.

Red Queen:
Oh, Jesus Christ—

Dad:
C'mon everyone, gather around the table.

Sister:
Where do you think you're going?

Red Queen:
May I be excused?

Sister:
We're about to take a photo. It can wait.

The ringing noise returns.

Red Queen/Alice:
I just, I need a moment—

Mom:
We're taking the photo.

Dad:
Do what your mother says.

Red Queen:
I don't want to take a picture right now—

Mom:
It's Thanksgiving—

Sister:
Get over yourself and take the photo.

Red Queen:
I will but I need to go to the bathroom.

Sister:
You're not using the bathroom right now.

Red Queen:
You're not the boss of me.

Mom:
Stop acting so ugly, today's supposed to be a nice day—

Red Queen:
A holiday dedicated to feasting with your bulimic daughter is supposed to be a nice day?

Dad:
We could have taken the photo by now.

Red Queen:
I'm not taking the fucking photo!

Alice starts to exit.
Mom begins to wail, upset.

Sister:
Oh, great. Look what you did. Are you happy now?

Red Queen:
No. I'm not. I'm not happy, I'm never fucking happy.

Mom:
Stop using that language!

Red Queen:
You have no idea what it's like—

Sister:
I'm a doctor, I know what it's like.

Red Queen:
I NEED TO GO TO THE GOD DAMN BATHROOM, NOW!

Mom:
Our holiday's been ruuuuuined!!

Dad:
If you're so unhappy in this family, then you can leave.

Sister:
You're being so dramatic—

Alice:
I'm so sick of this shit! If you took like two minutes to talk to me, maybe I'd tell you how much progress I've made, that I'm getting better. But you don't ask—you can't even acknowledge the problem. *[Beat]* I can't do this anymore.

Dad/Mom/Sister:
"Stop overreacting," "Get ahold of your emotions," "Just eat!"

Alice, defeated, crosses to Dee out of desperation.

Dee:
Fuck it.

Alice and Dee have a grand outburst, destroying the feast.
FAMILY filters off stage, and Alice rages off leaving Dee.
Lights.

Scene 15: Dee's Monologue

DEE sits alone on the stage. She has her drawing from Group.

Dee:
I don't have a problem. I don't. I work my ass off at some dead-end job I hate because it helps pay the bills. I finally get home and what's there to eat? I don't want to cook, I'm exhausted. Sometimes I skip meals because I don't have time to eat, or I forget to eat. I'll make a drink and I'll tell that voice in my head, "HEY YOU! I AM HAVING THIS GOD DAMN DRINK AND YOU'RE NOT GONNA MAKE ME FEEL SHITTY ABOUT IT!" But…he does.

Voice:
It's not my ass that's getting fat, fat ass.

Dee:
All I'm trying to do is maintain. I'm treading water here, so who cares if I lose a few pounds? *[She holds up her picture from therapy with magazine cutouts she's added to it]* This is gonna be me someday. … We live in a world where the fat ones are berated for eating anything at all, but the skinny bitches are condemned if they don't. It's okay to skip meals if you're on a diet, but how dare you count calories if you're anorexic. Bunch of self-righteous jackasses. Everyone thinks it's about being thin. No matter what you say, that's all they will ever hear.

Voice:
"Here, eat this bag of Doritos." "No, no, you finish the dessert. You can get away with it."

Dee:
Like eating a slice of cake is somehow cheating at something—but what they don't know is you're cheating and winning. (*Beat. A hopeless confession.*) I've tried everything: cognitive behavioral therapy, inpatient treatment, art therapy, exercises, rehab! I am thousands of dollars in medical debt because insurance runs out after about three months—you're on a constant timeline to "get better." I see the pro-Ana sites, magazines, Instagram, Facebook, the fucking filters, the "Do This Not That" diets and workouts, my own reflection. I can't escape it! … This path has led me to a life of loneliness. My family gave up after about the seventh relapse… That was five years ago. I've been doing this for ten. It's easier to pretend your daughter is normal if you don't acknowledge her.

Pause. Lights shift.
A teacup appears.
She is desperately drawn towards it.

Dee:
When you're convinced that you are damaged and unworthy, all you want are the simplest of life's joys: like a family. A happy family. It's all I've ever dreamed of. I meet the love of my life, we settle down, have a couple kids. The white picket fence. How naïve, how stupid.

She picks up the teacup.

Dee:
If, and that's a big if, but *if* I'm not infertile because of *this*, well either way, I can't have kids, because they'll make me fat. You laugh, but my monster has convinced me it's true. He's what I'm married to. Every day I try to divorce him, and every day he wins. He took away my voice, my body, my mind—so what else is there? What's left?

She looks out at the audience expectantly, waiting for an answer she does not get.

VOICEOVER:
Time to…

Beat. Defeated. She takes a sip of the tea. She looks out one last time, her farewell. DEE exits, leaving her drawing behind. Lights.

Scene 16: Death of the Group

Enter Dr. CATHERINE.
She picks up Dee's drawing that has been left behind.
She looks out to the audience.
A breath.

Dr. Catherine:
Often times, my patients express frustration around friends and family, people who are supposed to understand. What makes me especially good at my job is that I know. I lived it. Everyone's journey does not look the same, and it shouldn't. I want you all to understand that. … I was bad, I mean hooked up to an IV bad. Lucky for me, the websites weren't an issue yet; but we still had television, magazines, advertisements plastered everywhere. If you can control someone's body, you've successfully taken their mind. That's why eating disorders are especially tricky: you think you're in control. So you start seeing these ads, prints, etc., and it's so easy to think, "If I eat right, and workout, I'll look like that too," not realizing that your body type and their body type aren't the same.

She takes in the drawing.

Dr Catherine:
I was told I wasn't sick enough, *thin* enough, to be treated. I almost died. Eventually, somehow, miraculously, I got to a point where I decided enough was enough. I wanted to go to school for fashion and ended up becoming a psychologist—thank God I did, because here we all are. Sometimes your dreams, your purpose changes. I see a lot of people, and I've helped a lot of people. But sometimes…

A moment. This is hard for her.

Dr. Catherine:
Only when you see the hospital beds and IVs, the feeding tubes. The body bags. The notes they left behind. Only then do you realize that it will never be enough.

Dr. Catherine exits.
Lights.

Scene 17: Relapse.

Lights. Music.
Alice stumbles in with her bucket.
A flask appears.
Lines should move rhythmically.

Voice:
DRINK, BITCH!

Alice:
I'm going out.

GROUP enters.

Harry:
Life is short!

Maryn:
And I am gonna live it!

Zara:
I am gonna have fun!

Missie:
And no one can stop me!

Alice:
I drink. Again. And another. I puke.

Harry:
Cigarette?

Missie:
Drink.

Zara:
Dance.

Maryn:
Another.

Red Queen:
OUT WITH IT!

Group:
Puke.

Harry:
Cigarette?

She hears a song she likes.

Alice:
AHH SHIT, THIS IS MY JAM!

Voice:
Ma'am, could you please keep your feet on the ground?

Alice:
Fuck you, I'm not a ma'am!

Missie:
Drink!

Zara:
Dance.

Maryn:
Another.

Red Queen:
OUT WITH IT!

Group:
Puke.

Harry:
Cigarette?

Voice:
Miss, I think you've had enough.

Alice:
FUCK OFF!

Missie:
Drink.

                    Zara:
Dance.

                    Maryn:
Another.

                    Red Queen:
OUT WITH IT, PIG!

                    Group:
Puke!

                    Missie:
Drink.

                    Zara:
Dance.

                    Maryn:
Another.

                    Red Queen:
Pig.

                    Missie:
Drink.

                    Zara:
Dance.

                    Maryn:
Another.

                    Missie:
Drink.

                    Zara:
Dance.

                    Maryn:
Another.

                    Missie:
Drink.

                    Zara:
Dance.

                    Maryn:
Another.

Beat. They stop moving.

                    Harry:
Cigarette?

                    Zara:
Uhm, should you be driving?

                    Alice:
I'm fine!

Flashing lights, the sound of a siren.

                    All:
(General, elongated expletives)

GROUP disintegrates off the stage, leaving Alice, who collapses onto the floor.
Lights.

Scene 18: Sisterly Love.

MISSIE enters as Sister. She pokes and prods Alice until she wakes up.
Alice groans.

                    Sister:
Happy with yourself?

                    Alice:
Not particularly.

                    Sister:
Don't be a smart ass. Come on.

Alice:
How did I get here?

Sister:
You called me. At 4am. To come get you and your weird, drunk friends because a cop pulled you over while you were driving around a parking lot.

Alice:
… Is everyone okay?

Sister:
They were loud. They slept on my floor. And they didn't look much better than you do right now, but they're all fine. Now. Come on. We're getting lunch. I'm hungry, and I'm pregnant.

Alice:
She's due any day now and she doesn't let any of us forget it.

HARRY enters as Waiter.

Waiter:
Chips and salsa?

Sister:
Yes!

Waiter:
Any drinks?

Sister:
Coke. No, diet coke. No. A coke. No. Diet. No. Coke.

Waiter:
We carry Pepsi products, ma'am.

Sister:
Iced tea.

Alice:
Can I get a margarita…on the rocks…the big one. Please

Waiter nods and exits.
Sister looks judgingly at her.

Alice:
We are at a Mexican restaurant. And I need a hair of the dog.

Beat.

Alice:
We order. Most the meal is spent discussing the baby. I do *not* want to talk about last night, but she occasionally makes some sort of remark—

Sister:
And I would never let my daughter in the same car as someone—

Alice:
That I ignore as I pick at my all you can eat chips, trying not to eat too much.

Waiter returns with trash, throws it at them.

Waiter:
Here you are—

He exits.
The ringing starts, and a cacophony of noise infiltrates Alice's mind.

VOICE:
"EAT, BITCH!" "DRINK, BITCH!"

Voiceover:
TIME TO… GO TO THE BATHROOM!

Alice, overwhelmed, puts the bucket on her head.

She stands and starts to exit.

Sister:
For fuck's sake, Alice!

Pause.
Alice, dumbfounded, takes off her bucket and sits back down.

Sister:
I don't care about the drinking. Or the smoking, even though it's disgusting. I don't care that you made a stupid mistake that could have ended terribly last night.

Alice:
You're not going to tell / mom and dad are you?

Sister:
/ Oh my god! Sometimes, Alice, you're so immature. I know you aren't okay. I know you're sick. And we have tried to help you, but we don't know how. I don't know how to help you.

Alice:
I told you, I'm fine—

Sister:
No. No you're not. Look at you. You're going to wither away.

Alice:
You don't know what it's like—

Sister:
I know what it's like, Alice—

Alice:
You took me to a Mexican restaurant.

Beat.
Waiter enters.

Waiter:
More drinks ladies?

Sister:
[Upset, near tears
Jeeeesus, guy, read a fucking room!

The waiter exits.
It is uncomfortable.
They sit, unsure.

Sister:
How? How can I help you? Help me to understand.

Alice goes to speak, but she has nothing to counter with, nothing to say.

Sister:
I want you to be around when my baby is born. I want her to grow up with you in her life. But if you keep living like this, you aren't going to be alive much longer.

Lights.

Scene 19: The Trial of Alice

Alice:
My sister doesn't tell my parents, but she insists I go back to therapy and start taking my medication again. Not wanting to deal with any more lunches, I obey.

VOICEOVER:
TIME FOR… THERAPY!

Enter DR. CATHERINE.
Alice crosses and sits, silent.

Dr. Catherine:
How are you today Alice? … How was the week? … Things have been hard for you lately, haven't they?

The ringing returns.

> **Dr. Catherine:**
> What's wrong?

> **Alice:**
> Nothing.

> **Dr. Catherine:**
> You seem upset today. Distracted, maybe?

> **Alice:**
> … It's too much.

> **Dr. Catherine:**
> What is?

> **Alice:**
> Dee. … This. My life.
> Everything.

> **Dr. Catherine:**
> Let's start with one thing at a time.

> **Alice:**
> I just… I can't believe it. I thought she'd say something, you know? And I keep thinking: that could have been me, or any of us.

> **Dr. Catherine:**
> It's hard to lose someone close to you, especially when you're recovering from similar illnesses.

> **Alice:**
> Can we stop saying that please?

> **Dr. Catherine:**
> What?

> **Alice:**
> It's not an "illness" I'm not "sick." I don't have "triggers."

> **Dr. Catherine:**
> How would you describe it?

> **Alice:**
> I don't know.

> **Dr. Catherine:**
> Can you try?

Alice shakes her head.

> **Dr. Catherine:**
> Let's talk about the other night then.

> **Alice:**
> I was having fun.

> **Dr. Catherine:**
> You've been doing that a lot lately.

> **Alice:**
> My social life and this life have nothing to do with each other.

> **Dr. Catherine:**
> They're one and the same.

> **Alice:**
> I can't do anything. I can't eat how I want, I can't go out, I can't talk to my friends. I can't be around my family.

> **Dr. Catherine:**
> You can't do anything if you don't try.

Beat.

> **Dr. Catherine:**
> Alice. I'm concerned about how you are coping with all of this. I can't tell you what you should or shouldn't do, but it is my job to interject when I believe your safety is as risk, and I'm worried—

> **Alice:**
> I'm *fine*. My weight went up. I'm getting better.

Dr. Catherine:
Your weight is maintaining. That's not an indication that you're getting better.

Lights.
Alice is in full Red Queen mode.

Alice:
What do you want me to say? Everyone can go on a diet and it's fine, but I want thigh gap and I have a problem. So what if I die? At least I'll die thin.

Dr. Catherine:
That's quite a statement to make, Alice.

Alice:
Everyone keeps saying it's not enough. I'm not eating enough, not enough this, or that, or the right foods. I eat. I eat cakes. Chips. Snacks. High calories in small doses to later hurl back into a toilet. Have you ever tried to puke after a Chinese buffet?

Dr. Catherine looks at Alice, pausing like in their first meeting.

Alice:
Are you on my side or not?

Dr. Catherine:
The trouble with eating disorders, the trouble with any addiction, is that you have to want to change. So many people come through this office, and I have helped a good number of them. But I have seen too many cases end tragically. I've had people stop coming. I've had people who want to keep coming and can't afford it. I've had people who were told they weren't sick enough—thin enough—to be treated. And I've had patients like Dee—

Alice:
Dee didn't really want to get better.

Dr. Catherine:
Dee tried. She tried her hardest for a long time, but at the end of the day, her monster consumed her. Alice, I know you're in there. I don't want you to lose this battle, too. You can come and lie to me all you want, but I can't help you if you don't let me in.

Beat.
Alice finally opens up.

Alice:
I mean, is this it? For the rest of my life, having my family panic every time I go to the toilet. Constantly in debt. Never being able to enjoy a fucking slice of pizza. That my worth is based solely on how small I can make my body. And she's there, nestled in my brain and always telling me, "Not yet!" Until my teeth begin to rot, and my heart begins to palpitate, and it makes me want to rip off my own head!

Dr. Catherine:
Alice. Breathe.

A moment of breath.

Alice:
Every night I go to bed praying I will wake up, and every morning I wake up wishing I hadn't. … When will it be enough?

Dr. Catherine:
When you wither away to nothing, maybe. But as long as you're here, living and breathing on this earth, it won't ever be enough.

Lights as GROUP enters.

Dr. Catherine:
You're not alone, Alice.

Zara:
You have so many roads that can take you so many places, but it's your choice which one you take.

Harry:
The world is chaotic, but imagine how liberating it could be to embrace that chaos. To give into *not* being in control.

Maryn:
You stay enroute, and continue to wither and waste away, or you can forgive yourself, and you can grow.

Missie:
You're going to fail. Constantly. But if you need us to hold your hair back or if you need us to go to a drive through, then that's what we'll do.

Dr. Catherine:
And when you find you've lost yourself, remember to breathe. It takes time. One day you'll look in the mirror and see yourself for who you truly are, and all this will have felt like a bad dream. But. The choice is yours.

Beat.

Alice:
I don't want to be like this anymore.

Lights.

Scene 20: Reflections.

Alice looks out at the audience, taking them in like she did at the beginning.
She turns to her bucket.
As she speaks, she sets it up in front of her, looking at it.

Alice:
There's something about mirrors… Our reflections, facing ourselves. Our inner monsters.

Alice stares at her bucket.
Cupcake appears.

VOICE:
"EAT BITCH."

Cupcake disappears.
Alice is still staring at her bucket.
A moment between it and her.
Lights.

End of play.

FAMILY SPOUSES (A CHRISTMAS STORY) FOREWORD

In *Family Spouses (A Christmas Story)* by Prisca Jebet Kendagor, we are invited to step into the chaotic and heartwarming world of a large, extended family as they navigate the highs and lows of the holiday season. When Prisca set out to write this play, she did so with the intent of writing a "by-the-book," feel good, family Christmas story, but through the lens of her unique experience as someone who is from a family of African immigrants. *Family Spouses* celebrates the bonds that hold us together, even when we feel like we are falling apart.

KCPublic worked extensively with Prisca Jebet Kendagor in its first five years as a company. Prisca was KCPublic's inaugural Playwright-in-Residence where, over the course of two years (prolonged due to the COVID-19 pandemic), she developed her play *The Holy Trinity* that had its premiere production in March 2022 at Charlotte Street Foundation. *Family Spouses (A Christmas Story)* was performed as a staged reading in December 2019 at Charlotte Street's former Capsule studio space.

FAMILY SPOUSES: A CHRISTMAS STORY

A Play

By: Prisca Jebet Kendagor

CAST OF CHARACTERS

The Spouses

PAUL- White male, mid to late thirties, doctor. Been married into the family for a while now and has the most experience maneuvering the ins and outs. Very laid back and likes it when everybody else is. His goal is to make sure all the spouses feel the same, even if that job seems impossible.

JACOB- Male, early to mid-thirties, actor. This is his first Christmas with Tamera's cousins, and he's heard all about them. His goal is to be liked and make a good impression specifically with these members. Yes, he cares about her parents and all that, but really, he knows that this is Tamera's chosen family. That is why this gathering is so important to him, especially if he wants to be a part of it.

AMY- White female, full figured, female, mid-twenties to early thirties. Much like Jacob, she is one of the newer spouses in this gathering, but this is not her first rodeo. Out of all, she is the one who is most desperate for acceptance, especially from Julia.

CHARLES- Non-black man of color, early to mid-thirties, salesman. Dating Ruth for a while and now engaged, this is a man who finally feels just as accepted by the cousins as Paul is, and he is very happy about that. He tells the truth as it is—much like Ruth.

NIKKI- Non-black woman of color *[playwright sees her as Asian American, but this can be played with.]* who has just returned from traveling with her husband. Since they eloped in Thailand, she doesn't have as deep of a connection to the family as others but is still quickly accepted. Her goal is just to make it through this Christmas holiday.

The Siblings/Cousins (aka, *The Five*)

TAMERA- Black woman, mid-thirties, playright and screenwriter. She is the last of the five to find a serious partner, so regardless of what she says, this Christmas dinner is important to her...and she kind of hates that fact. She simply wants everybody to love Jacob the same way she loves Jacob.

JULIA- Black woman, mid to late thirties. Out of The Five, she is definitely the matriarch of the group. Kind, loving, and slightly neurotic, she simply wants what's best for her brothers and sisters (this includes her cousin). Often trying to fight against the stereotype of her African family as a matriarch, she has habits she can't help but exert, no matter how hard she tries.

RUTH- Black woman, late twenties to early thirties, event planner. Extremely confident and doesn't really care about your hurt feelings. Not in a bad way, but simply in a way that means she gets things done. She comes off as walled off at first, but once you make your way into those walls, you're part of the family. Period. Does a lot of observing.

JOSH- Black male, mid to late thirties. Bartender manager who has been clean and sober for six years. Yes, he is Julia's twin brother, but he is also the exact opposite of Julia. He's aware that his sisters may have an issue with his partner Amy, but that doesn't really bother him that much. He loves her, and she loves him. That's all that should matter.

MARK- Black male, mid to late thirties, travels the world for a living. The oldest out of The Five, he has the same goal as his old friend Paul: make sure everybody has a wonderful time this holiday. Slightly protective of Tamera since she's the last of the group to find somebody, he enters this gathering with an open mind, trusting his baby cousin's judgement...a little.

ACT I

[Scene opens on PAUL sitting in the living room watching TV and drinking a beer. JULIA can be heard off stage.]

JULIA
Paul!

PAUL
Yeah!

JULIA
Has anybody showed up yet?

PAUL
I would've told you if they had!

JULIA
Not necessarily!

PAUL
Nobody's here, Jules!

JULIA
Ok! *[She ENTERS from the kitchen.]* Turkey is ready and prepped.

PAUL
You said you trusted Tamera.

JULIA
Yes, and I do.

PAUL
So why are you preparing the turkey?

JULIA
They take like seven hours.

PAUL
She said she knew how to do it in 90 minutes.

JULIA
It's just thawed and marinated, I'm only helping.

PAUL
[Just looks at her.]

JULIA
I'm getting wine. *[She EXITS.]*

PAUL
[Continues watching TV.] We've been doing this holiday dinner for about ten years now, and every year she still manages to have at least one panic attack. *[Turns to audience.]* It's ok, we'll get through it like we always do.

Believe it or not, this is one of our favorite holiday traditions. Julia and I have been married for about seven years, but we've been together much longer. Ten years ago, her cousin Tamera texted us on Thanksgiving evening saying she didn't want to go to Topeka again and of course just like any other time Tamera comes calling, Julia said-
[Points stage left. Spotlight on JULIA and TAMERA.]

JULIA
Come on over! How long will you be?

TAMERA
Oh I don't know, an hour?

JULIA
Can you get here in 45 minutes?

TAMERA
Girl, you know I can!

JULIA
Ok, see you soon!

TAMERS
Yay! *[Spotlight off.]*

PAUL
She lived two hours away from us. *[Rolls his eyes and just laughs.]* That's pretty much how all our hang outs go. Which by the way, I have no complaints here, I love the family I married into. That was the first year of Siblings Holiday Dinner. My brothers and sister-in-law all came over that night too, and well, we had such a good time that we decided to make it an annual thing. No parents, no aunts or uncles, just us. I mean we're in our 30's now, and Julia and me have a kid, so that shouldn't matter anymore right?

JULIA
I have six missed messages from mom!!

PAUL
[Just looks at audience.]

JULIA
Paul!!

PAUL
Yeah?!

JULIA
Tamera's at the door!!

PAUL
[Looks at his phone.] Oh they are here. *[EXITS to open the door. Can be heard offstage.]* Hey!

TAMERA

Cousin!!

PAUL

What's going on, guys?!

[TAMERA, JACOB, and PAUL all ENTER with groceries and luggage.]

How was the flight?

TAMERA

Quick and painless.

JACOB

All you can ask for.

PAUL

Well that's good.

[JULIA ENTERS with glasses and a bottle of wine.]

JULIA

Tamera!!!

TAMERA

Julia!!!

[They run and hug each other, super excited. Without missing a beat, JULIA pours wine into one of the glasses and hands it to TAMERA.]

JULIA

The trip was good?

TAMERA

As good as can be expected.

JULIA

I would say so. You're riding first class these days. Hi, Jacob.

JACOB

Hi.

JULIA

Oh come on, let's take those things to the kitchen. Paul, help them with their luggage.

PAUL

[Already holding luggage.] I, um-

JULIA

[Taking TAMERA to the kitchen with her.] Now I want to hear about everything you've been up to.

TAMERA

We've been talking about it.

JULIA

Yes, but it's not the same as hearing directly from you. Tell me about the Tony's!

TAMERA

Not until I see my nephew. *[They EXIT. JACOB and PAUL just stand there with luggage and look at each other.]*

PAUL

You'll get used to this.

JACOB

I hope so.

PAUL

[Taking his bag.] Hand me that I'll take it to your room. You're in the back here again.

JACOB

Great, thanks.

PAUL

Do you want anything? I have a good bourbon.

JACOB

You read my mind.

[PAUL EXITS with the bags for a moment. JACOB sits and awkwardly waits. He's a little nervous—this Christmas dinner is a huge step for him and TAMERA. PAUL re-ENTERS with two glasses of bourbon. He sees how nervous JACOB is and laughs.]

PAUL

Relax. *[Hands him a glass.]*

JACOB

That obvious?

PAUL

Yeah. This is no different than any other time you've been here.

JACOB

Paul. Come on. You know it is.

PAUL

It's not for me.

JACOB

Well yeah duh, it's not you I'm worried about.

PAUL

You guys keep mentioning that in the group text. Why are you all worried about Julia?

JACOB

She's really important to Tamera.

PAUL

So are you. You're with her more, that's the only thing that should matter. I keep telling you guys this.

JACOB
Yeah well, this is the first time I'm meeting everybody at once, so yes. I'm nervous. Tam's been talking about this dinner for years. It's the highlight of the holidays for her.

PAUL
It's the highlight for all of us. You know why?

JACOB
Why?

PAUL
Because nobody here gives a shit.

JACOB
Yes, they do.

PAUL
I don't and look how long I've been in this family.

JACOB
[Laughs.] Well, you'll have to advise me then.

PAUL
[His phone goes off.] Something tells me I'll have to advise all of you.

JULIA
Paul!!

PAUL
I know they're at the door, sweetheart! *[He gets up and goes to the door. Off stage.]* Hey guys!

JOSH
What's going on?

AMY
Hi!

[TAMERA and JULIA ENTER. JOSH, AMY and PAUL all ENTER.]

JULIA
You're late.

JOSH
[Going to hug TAMERA.] No, I'm not, this is African time. What's going on, cousin?

TAMERA
How are you, Josh?

JULIA
[Taking the bags from AMY still talking to JOSH.] You said you'd be here early.

TAMERA
So did everybody else.

JULIA
I know.

AMY
Hi, Julia.

JULIA
Did you guys bring the desert?

JOSH
You know we did. Also, I brought mint and ginger for something?

JACOB
Uh, yeah. That's for the mocktail drink I'm making.

JOSH
Oh great. *[Hands him the bag and just looks at him for a moment. Then TAMERA.]* This him?

TAMERA
[Smiles.] Yeah.

JOSH
[Extends his hand.] Jacob? Josh. I'm the twin.

JACOB
[Shakes his hand.] Good to meet you.

JOSH
This is my girlfriend, Amy.

JACOB
Yeah we've been texting. Good to finally meet you in person.

AMY
Thanks, you too.

JOSH
Who else is coming?

JULIA
Everybody.

TAMERA
Mark and Ruth are on their way with their people.

JULIA
I can't believe everybody's bringing somebody.

TAMERA
[Goes to JACOB.] Apparently. Wow, I haven't seen Mark since he got back from ...Brazil?

JOSH
China?

PAUL
Narnia!

JULIA
How do none of you know where Mark has been?

PAUL
He travels everywhere.

TAMERA
Can you tell us where he's coming from?

JULIA
Yes, he's…. he and Nikki are coming from … from... uh…

PAUL
Haha.

JULIA
Shut up!

JOSH
Where's my nephew?

TAMERA
Napping.

JOSH
[Gets up.] Sweet, I'm gonna go wake him up. *[EXITS.]*

JULIA
Josh, no!

TAMERA
Relax, I'll go with him. Jacob, you ok?

JACOB
Yeah. Go ahead.

PAUL
We're keeping him entertained.

TAMERA
Ok. *[She's about to EXIT. Gives a look to JACOB. He winks to reassure her. JULIA notices this interaction. TAMERA EXITS.]*

JULIA
Jacob, you want to come with me to the kitchen to fix your punch?

JACOB
What? Oh yeah sure. *[Looks at PAUL questioning.]*

PAUL
We'll be out here.

JULIA

Ok. *[Taking JACOB with her.]*

AMY

Do you need any help?

JULIA

[EXITING with JACOB in hand.] No, we got it. *[They EXIT.]*

AMY

[Just stands there.] She hates me.

PAUL

She doesn't hate you.

AMY

Don't lie to me. Yes, she does.

PAUL

You're just trying too hard.

AMY

And yet nothing is working—she doesn't talk to me. Hardly anybody in that family talks to me. Just you guys.

PAUL

Because you try too hard, just relax. Look, Amy, I promise they'll all warm up to you. Hey, look on the bright side—you're not the new one anymore.

AMY

She already likes him better than me. She's talking to him in the kitchen.

PAUL

That's not always a good thing.

[RUTH and CHARLES ENTER. RUTH immediately walks in owning the place, puts her bags down.]

RUTH

Where's Julia? I need to talk to her.

PAUL

In the kitchen.

AMY

Hi, Ruthie.

[TAMERA and JOSH ENTER.]

TAMERA

Ruth, hi!

RUTH

[Kisses her on the cheek and proceeds to take her to the kitchen.] How's it going? You're coming with me. *[To JOSH.]* I'm talking to you later. *[She and TAMERA EXIT.]*

JOSH
Seems about right.

CHARLES
Yep. *[Proceeds to greet everybody.]* Josh, my man, how are you?

JOSH
Good, good. I'm glad you two could make it. *[Looks at AMY.]* What's wrong?

AMY
Nothing, everything is great.

[JACOB ENTERS with a bottle of wine and a soda water.]

PAUL
You escaped!

JACOB
Yes, I did, and I bring gifts. *[Looks at AMY. He pours her a glass of wine.]*

AMY
I'm fine.

JACOB
Uh-huh. *[Hands JOSH the soda water.]*

PAUL
How was it in there?

JACOB
You know.

JOSH
Ha, my sister give you the third degree?

JACOB
Yeah.

CHARLES
You're lucky it's just us kids. If the parents were here, it'd be a different story.

AMY
It's true.

CHARLES
Charles, by the way. Ruth's fiancé. Good to finally meet you.

JACOB
[Shakes hand.] Thanks, you too.

CHARLES
[To PAUL and JOSH] So this is the one, huh?

JOSH
Apparently.

PAUL
We're going to take him before the council for judgment later.

[They all laugh. Still laughing, JACOB looks at AMY as if to ask, "But really, are they?" She shakes her head no.]

CHARLES
So, you're an actor, Jacob?

JACOB
And director, yeah.

PAUL
He's been on Netflix.

JOSH
Yeah, he has. I saw the show. It was great.

CHARLES
I can't believe Tam's a showrunner.

JOSH
Oh, I can. The women in this family are driven and focused. They make stuff happen.

PAUL
I know that's true.

AMY
I really liked your character this season. I'm actually a really big fan.

JACOB
Thank you.

CHARLES
So how hard did you have to work to get that part?

JACOB
[Laughs.] I know what you're getting at, and no, it wasn't anything like that. We were working together before we actually got together.

CHARLES
Alright then.

AMY
But I thought *US Weekly* said that you two were sleeping-

PAUL
More wine, Amy? *[Continues to pour into her glass.]* I wonder where the other two are.

JOSH
I told you, we run on African time.

CHARLES
Is that the same as CP time?

JOSH
It's later.

CHARLES
I wouldn't be too sure about that.

[They all laugh. TAMERA rushes in looking at her phone.]

TAMERA
Paul, hurry up and open the door.

PAUL
Are they here?

TAMERA
They're close.

JOSH
They're lost, aren't they?

TAMERA
Duh.

PAUL
I'll go wave them down. *[PAUL EXITS. TAMERA sits next to JACOB and AMY.]* You guys doing ok?

JOSH
My girlfriend's nervous.

AMY
Babe! Oh my god!

TAMERA
Why are you guys nervous? It's literally not a big deal.

JACOB
That is not what you have been saying.

JOSH
What have you been saying?

TAMERA
I haven't been saying anything.

CHARLES
You don't have to say anything. We just know.

JACOB
Yes. Exactly.

JOSH
Know what?

TAMERA
Yeah.

CHARLES
How important you all are to each other. We've been talking about it.

JOSH
So? Family's important.

CHARLES
I'm not hating on that, believe me, I understand. I just also happen to understand where these two are at. God, it feels good to have some seniority now.

TAMERA
Seniority?

JOSH
There is no seniority.

AMY
Yes, there is.

TAMERA
[Turns to JACOB to reassure him-]

CHARLES
Don't lie to him.

[PAUL ENTERS with MARK and NIKKI.]

PAUL
Look what I found!

MARK
Merry Christmas, family!

[JOSH and TAMERA get up immediately to greet him. CHARLES follows.]

TAMERA
Mark! *[Hugs him.]*

MARK
What's up, cousin! *[Hugs JOSH.]* Little brother!

JOSH
Big brother!

MARK
You guys remember Nikki?

NIKKI
Hi.

TAMERA
[Hugs her.] I remember. Hello. Welcome back to the states.

NIKKI
Thank you. Josh, how are you?

JOSH
[Hugs her.] I'm great.

MARK
[Looks at JACOB and AMY] We have some new people here.

CHARLES
We do, and they're terrified.

NIKKI

I know. We've been texting.

MARK

As terrified as you were?

CHARLES

I'm engaged to Ruth. You know full well she grilled me on any possible questions you guys had for me when we first met.

TAMERA

That's true.

[They all laugh.]

MARK

Where are my two sisters?

JULIA

[ENTERS looking at her phone. RUTH follows.] Paul, open the door, Mark and- *[Sees them.]*

TAMERA

I told them first.

[RUTH runs to MARK and hugs him. She also hugs NIKKI.]

JULIA

Why didn't you tell me they were here?

MARK

[Hugs her.] Oh relax, Jules. We're here now.

JULIA

[Looks at NIKKI.] Nicole, how are you?

NIKKI

I'm great.

JULIA

I haven't seen you since the wedding. You two got here ok? Rested and everything?

NIKKI

Oh yeah, everything's great.

JULIA

Good. *[Pause.]* Well, come over here. *[She goes and hugs NIKKI. CHARLES pours more wine for AMY.]* Well, come on, everybody's here, let's get the food started. Do you guys need anything?

RUTH

We should just go ahead and bring the cooler out here. Lord knows we're all gonna need it.

JOSH

Speak for yourself.

RUTH

We'll be back.

TAMERA

I'll just hang out-

JULIA

[Taking TAMERA with her.] You need to finish the turkey.

TAMERA

[Not happy.] You already started it.

JULIA

I know, but it's not finished.

TAMERA

Even though I told you I knew what I was doing.

JULIA

And you still do, come on, it's not finished. It's still not smashmocked.

TAMERA

Spatchcocked.

RUTH

[Laughs.] I told you she'd be mad.

JULIA

I'm sorry.

TAMERA

[Rolls eyes.] It's fine, I'm sure I can do something with it. Come on, ladies. *[The three ladies begin to EXIT to the kitchen.]*

JULIA

Nikki, you too. *[Everybody stops.]*

NIKKI

Oh. Ok.

AMY

Do you ladies want me to-

[Baby cries.]

JULIA

Oh no.

PAUL

I got him.

MARK

Nope, the uncles got him. I mean I should at least meet the little man, right?

JOSH

You ladies go ahead, we got him. *[He looks at TAMERA as if to say, "Take Amy with you."]*

TAMERA

Yeah, they got it. Uh, Amy, come to the kitchen with us.

JULIA

Oh I think we got-

TAMERA

[Dragging AMY.] Come to the kitchen with us Amy. *[The women all EXIT with RUTH left. She watches them EXIT. Looks at the boys.]*

RUTH

This is going to be fun. *[She EXITS. Baby KING cries a little more.]*

JOSH

Your uncles are coming, little man!

MARK

And we have presents! *[They EXIT to the nursery.]*

JACOB

Is this everybody or are we expecting another caravan?

PAUL

[Laughs.] Nope, this is it.

CHARLES

Hey, did we ever figure out what Julia's deal with Amy was? I'm pretty sure Ruth has an issue with her too. Has Tamera said anything?

JACOB

Why would I know?

CHARLES

They talk to her, she talks to you; thus, you'd know.

JACOB

Well, I don't know. *[Pause.]* I mean not really. *[Pause.]* She's new?

CHARLES

You're new.

PAUL

How many times do I have to say that doesn't matter-

CHARLES

It matters a little bit. You've just forgotten because you've been in the family for so long.

PAUL

Which means I know how things work here.

CHARLES
We all know this is an African family. The ladies all bond in the kitchen. Being asked to join is a big deal.

JACOB
I really don't know what to tell you.

CHARLES
Do they like her at all?

JACOB
[Nothing. He drinks his drink.]

PAUL
God damnit.

CHARLES
Ha! I told you! [Sits next to JACOB.] Tell us my friend, what do you know?

JACOB
I don't know anything. [Silence. CHARLES and PAUL just look at him.] Tam said Amy rubbed her the wrong way last time they were here.

CHARLES
Knew it. I told you.

PAUL
You didn't know.

CHARLES
I have a gift in observation. It's what I do. Tell us more.

JACOB
That's literally all I know. Honest.

MARK
[Heard from the kitchen.] Look who just woke up!

JULIA
[Talking to a baby.] Did you wake up for your family?! Yes, you did!!

RUTH
Give him here!

MARK
Wait your turn. I just met him!

[Everybody in the kitchen continues to react to BABY KING. After a moment AMY and NIKKI ENTER with a cooler.]

NIKKI
We come bringing refreshments.

PAUL
It's a Christmas miracle! [Laughter.] How's my son?

CHARLES
Being spoiled rotten?

NIKKI
Of course. *[She and AMY sit.]* I don't understand how you all keep each other straight. How many aunts and uncles does he have?

[PAUL and CHARLES sit and think. Silence.]

AMY
It can't be that many.

CHARLES
Shh. We're doing math.

PAUL
Divide by two, carry the three…

JACOB
[Laughs.] It's not that many.

PAUL
I don't know, I guess 20? Does that sound right?

CHARLES
Mmm, that seems low.

NIKKI
Low?!

TAMERA
[ENTERS.] Jake, King is walking now!

JACOB
[Gets up.] Oh, no kidding?

PAUL
Hey, Tam, how many aunts and uncles does your nephew have?

TAMERA
He's your son.

PAUL
I can't keep it straight.

AMY
Why does he say your nephew?

TAMERA
What?

AMY
I was just curious why he calls King your nephew.

TAMERA
Oh, because I'm his aunt.

AMY

[Genuinely confused. She doesn't mean any harm by this line of questioning.] Oh, I thought you were their cousin.

[JULIA and RUTH ENTER.]

TAMERA

I am.

AMY

Oh, so he's not really your nephew, he's just your cousin, right? Twice removed or whatever?
[Pause. Awkward.] Right?

TAMERA

No. He's my nephew.

AMY

I mean yeah, but like not really, right?

JULIA

Excuse me?

CHARLES

[Clears throat indicating for RUTH to intervene.]

RUTH

Uh-huh. Tamera, I think you need to check the turkey.

JULIA

You know full well she just put it in the oven.

TAMERA

[Pleasant.] She's right. I need to check on it. Anybody need anything?

CHARLES

Nope, we're good.

TAMERA

Ok. *[She looks at RUTH and JULIA. RUTH hands her a fresh glass of wine and they EXIT. TAMERA stops.]* Nikki, are you coming?

NIKKI

I'll be there in a minute.

TAMERA

Okay, great. *[As she turns, she switches from pleasant to annoyed. She takes a drink and EXITS. Silence. Everybody who is drinking drinks.]*

AMY

I think I made a mistake.

CHARLES

["Yeah no shit."] Yeah?

AMY
I'm sorry.

PAUL
It's fine, it'll pass, they'll get over it. Tamera's not mad.

JACOB
[Laughs and drinks.]

PAUL
Tamera's not that mad. It's fine. You guys are really thinking way too deep into this. There's no being accepted, that's the point of these dinners. Charlie, tell them.

CHARLES
Nope, I worked too hard to become a future brother-in-law. I'm not risking it.

PAUL
Risking what? There's nothing to risk. Nikki?

NIKKI
[Says nothing.]

PAUL
Oh my-... Okay, let's just change the subject.

AMY
Maybe I should just go.

PAUL
No, no. You're a part of this family.

CHARLES
[To himself.] Not yet.

PAUL
[Hears him but ignores him.] It will be fine. New topic. [Silence.]

AMY
So... none of us are black. That's interesting? [Immediately regrets it.]

JACOB
[Gets up.] Jesus Christ.

CHARLES
What is wrong with you?

AMY
I don't know I'm nervous.

NIKKI
It's okay, we talked about this remember?

CHARLES
We all agreed not to say stupid shit.

NIKKI
We agreed to help each other.

PAUL
That one. That's what we agreed to.

JACOB
[EXITING] I'm going to see King. Nikki, I'll tell them you're out here bonding. *[He EXITS.]*

CHARLES
Even he's allowed in there.

PAUL
Nobody is allowed or not allowed-

AMY
[Tears.] Shut up, Paul. Yes, they are! *[Pause.]* I'm sorry.

NIKKI
It's ok, it's ok. You're just nervous.

CHARLES
Hell yeah, she's nervous, as she should be. She's ruining this dinner!

PAUL
Nobody is ruining the dinner!

AMY
[Still upset.] Yes, I am!

PAUL
It hasn't even started yet!

NIKKI
Ok, Amy, calm down. Just breathe. *[Breathes with her. They breathe together. AMY calms down.]* You're thinking way too hard about this.

PAUL
I have been saying that since they got here.

NIKKI
It's different coming from a woman. *[To AMY]* Did you bring anything to contribute to the meal at all? Some sort of gift or-

PAUL
An offering?

CHARLES
Yeah, did you do that?

NIKKI
Anything will help.

PAUL
Um... I was joking about the offering.

AMY
I did bring some food.

NIKKI
Good. See, this can all be salvaged.

PAUL
There's nothing to salvage.

CHARLES
Wait. *[Everybody stops]* What did you bring?

AMY
[Looks at him, knowing once again she messed up.] Um-

[JACOB ENTERS.]

JACOB
You brought potato salad'?!

CHARLES
Knew it.

AMY
Josh helped me make it.

PAUL
We are not leaning into this stereotype.

NIKKI
Yeah, come on, guys.

CHARLES
[To Paul.] Can you make potato salad?

PAUL
For your information, my mother-

JACOB
No, she can't.

PAUL
Yes, she- *[There's no point in arguing, he's right.]* Dammit, you're right. She can't.

NIKKI
It's not whether or not it's good—it's the thought that counts. You came with something, that's what's important.

AMY
Is it though? Because it doesn't feel like it.

NIKKI
It is. Trust me.

[MARK ENTERS.]

MARK
How are we doing out here?

NIKKI
We're great.

MARK
Why does everybody look panicked?

CHARLES
Amy brought potato salad!

MARK
[Sits with NIKKI.] That's an interracial rookie mistake. Come on, Amy, this isn't your first rodeo.

AMY
You don't seem concerned.

MARK
I'm not.

PAUL
So everything's good in there?

MARK
[Laughs.] Oh no.

CHARLES
Told you.

MARK
But it doesn't matter.

PAUL
See?

NIKKI
It matters a little bit.

MARK
Says you. Julia could tell me today that she despises everything about you, and I'd marry you all over again. Is it nice to have our family's approval? Yes, but trust me. In the long run, it doesn't matter.

NIKKI
Yes, but... did she actually say that or?

MARK
No, she didn't say that.

NIKKI
[Relieved.] Okay, good.

MARK
[To PAUL.] This is what I've been missing out here?

PAUL
Merry Christmas. *[Takes a drink.]*

[JULIA ENTERS with the punch JACOB prepared. TAMERA and RUTH ENTER with appetizers.]

PAUL
Oh, thank god, food is here.

JULIA
It's just the appetizers.

RUTH
Lots of appetizers.

TAMERA
I told you we were going to overdo it.

JULIA
You can never have enough. *[To NIKKI.]* Nikki, everything ok?

NIKKI
Yeah, my dish can wait. You ladies had it under control.

RUTH
She and Paul are counseling everybody.

JULIA
Counseling everybody on what?

CHARLES
[Goes to RUTH.] She's joking. *[Kisses her and looks at her as if to say, "Please don't."]*

RUTH
Mm-hm.

JULIA
Oh guys, Jacob made a nonalcoholic drink and it's really good.

MARK
[Drinking from his cup.] Yeah, it is.

RUTH
Boy, we told you to wait!

JULIA
When did you get that?

MARK
He gave me and Josh some while we were back there. He wanted us to test it.

JACOB
That was a while ago.

MARK
Yeah, I know. I got more.

[JULIA indicates to RUTH to hit MARK. RUTH hits MARK. Laughter. TAMERA is proud of JACOB. JACOB notices.]

AMY

[Stands.] Where's Josh?

RUTH

Watching King out back.

AMY

[Upset and EXITING.] Excuse me. [She EXITS.]

JULIA

What happened?

NIKKI

[Following.] Nothing that can't be handled excuse me. [She EXITS.]

TAMERA

Why does this feel like regular Christmas?

JACOB

Now's not the time to debate when Jesus was actually born, babe.

TAMERA

[Hits him] That is not what I'm talking about, you know that! Drama's been happening. Why has drama been happening? This is literally why we have these holidays.

CHARLES

Tam, I assure you everything is fine. There was just a little misunderstanding here and there. It's actually kind of funny. You should write a show about it.

RUTH

Are you lying to your future sister-in-law?

CHARLES

What? No.

RUTH

Yes, you are. Everybody in this room can tell.

CHARLES

I am not lying- [Looks at JACOB. JACOB moves away from him.]

PAUL

Haha, you got caught.

CHARLES

I thought we were a united force.

JULIA

A united force? A united force against what?

[PAUL looks at JULIA. JACOB and CHARLES sheepishly look at TAMERA and RUTH. MARK sits there and laughs.]

MARK

[To JULIA.] You're mom now.

JULIA

What does that mean?

TAMERA

Why are you guys looking at us? We're not a part of this.

RUTH

I am. *[Unapologetically sips her wine.]*

CHARLES

I chose the honest one!

TAMERA

I am not a part of this. Whatever this is.

JULIA

I still don't know what's going on.

PAUL

You're being rude, Jules.

MARK

Yep.

JULIA

I'm being rude? How am I being rude?

PAUL

Jake, Charlie, tell your partners they're being rude.

RUTH

[Gives CHARLES a look.]

CHARLES

Nah, I'm good.

TAMERA

[Looks at JACOB.] Well?

JACOB

You guys are her family. You're important to her.

TAMERA

Wait a second. That wasn't a denial; it was a defense.

RUTH

Yes, it was.

MARK
Ruth.

RUTH
What? I'm the only honest one here right now. *[Pause. To CHARLES.]* Plus, I'm really enjoying this. It feels like home.

CHARLES
Anything for you, baby.

TAMERA
Why was that a defense? *[Silence.]* Am I being rude, Jacob? *[Silence.]*

JACOB
So you know how you say you're really bad at holding grudges?

TAMERA
Jacob!

JACOB
You have to promise me you won't hold a grudge when I tell you the truth.

TAMERA
I-

RUTH
Uh-uh. Don't make a promise we all know you won't keep.

TAMERA
[Looks at RUTH. Then back and JACOB.] I will try not to hold a grudge. Now please, just tell me. I won't get mad.

JACOB
[Pause.] You're being a little rude.

TAMERA
How the hell could you say that?!

JULIA
Don't call a member of my family rude! That's rude!

TAMERA
What have I done to get that judgment? I have been nothing but nice since the moment we got here! *[To JULIA]* Have I been nice?

JULIA
You've been wonderful! You have no idea what you're talking about, Jacob! And to think I was actually starting to like you!

JACOB
[Excited.] Really?

CHARLES
Congratulations, man.

PAUL

Not the point! Julia, stop yelling and let them settle this.

JULIA

He's calling my cousin rude!

PAUL

Because she's being rude!

RUTH

Oh snap!

TAMERA

What?

JULIA

Don't call your sister-in-law rude!

PAUL

She is being rude. All three of you are being rude! Jacob, if you're going to be a part of this family, you're going to need to learn to stand your ground.

CHARLES

Or you know, just agree with everything your partner says.

RUTH

[Smiles and kisses him.]

PAUL

You were making a point.

JACOB

[Silence.] But she likes me.

PAUL

Jacob!

JACOB

[Pause] You... you are kind of being mean to Amy. And I understand, she is a strange one, but... she's just trying to survive this dinner like the rest of us.

PAUL

[Takes a drink.] Which, by the way, hasn't even started yet.

JACOB

And I think she was depending on you to back her up.

TAMERA

Me?

JACOB

Yeah.

TAMERA

Why?

RUTH

Because you're the nice one out of the three of us.

CHARLES

[Shakes his head in agreement.]

TAMERA

Why does everybody think I'm so nice?

JACOB

[To himself.] It's because they haven't produced a show with you yet.

TAMERA

Excuse me?

JACOB

Not important. Look, I love you because you're understanding and empathetic. So just imagine what having three women not like you feels like. *[Silence.]*

TAMERA

[After a moment.] I think we should give Amy another chance.

RUTH

Nah, I'm good.

JULIA

What chance, and why?

PAUL

Julia.

JULIA

Why are we talking about this like this dinner is some sort of test or competition?

CHARLES

Because it is, and for a minute you were winning, man. Congratulations on getting Julia to like you.

MARK

And well earned. I like him, too.

JACOB

Oh really?!

RUTH

He's alright.

CHARLES

That's essentially as close to "I like him" as you're going to get from her.

JACOB

Oh wow! This is amazing, best Christmas ever!

PAUL

I really feel like we're straying away from the point here.

TAMERA

Sorry, yes. I'm going to go talk to Amy.

RUTH

You can't make us like her.

MARK

Nobody can make you do anything.

CHARLES

[To himself.] Ain't that the truth.

RUTH

[Looks at him.]

CHARLES

Nothing, baby.

JULIA

This is so silly.

PAUL

It's not silly. We created these dinners to avoid the drama and now there's drama. I want my peaceful dinner back.

[JOSH ENTERS.]

JULIA

Drama didn't start until Amy started showing up. Maybe it's not us that's the problem!

[Silence. Everybody stops and looks at JOSH. JULIA turns at looks at him.]

JOSH

What's up, sis?

JULIA

[Long pause.] I don't like Amy. None of us do. She's not good enough for you.

JOSH

Excuse me?

JULIA

I said what I said. Ruth and Tamera agree with me.

[RUTH stands next to JULIA in agreement. Both the girls look at TAMERA.]

JOSH

Tamera?

TAMERA

[Pause.] I was actually going to talk to her–

JOSH

Why weren't you talking to her earlier?

TAMERA

Because I don't like her, but that doesn't matter-

JOSH

Mark, any words?

MARK

You are not pulling me into this, brother.

PAUL

I just wanted a drama-free Christmas dinner. Was that really too much to ask?

MARK

We're getting older and adding more people to the family. Did you really think the peace would last this long?

JOSH

Julia, I love Amy, and she's going to be a part of this family, whether you like it or not.

JULIA

You don't think you're rushing into this?

JOSH

You're asking me if I'm rushing into this when you have Tamera and Jacob?

JACOB

Whoa, she said she was going to go talk to her.

JULIA

Don't drag them into this. It took her nearly a year to finally bring him here.

RUTH

Yeah, we were starting to wonder what was wrong with you.

JACOB

Thank you...I think.

JULIA

This is not about them. It's about you rushing into another one of your stupid doomed relationships.

JOSH

They're married, Julia! *[Silence.]*

JULIA

What? No, they're not. *[Looks at TAMERA.]* No, you're not. Right? *[Silence. Everybody looks at TAMERA and JACOB.]*

RUTH

Oh my god, they are.

MARK
No way.

JULIA
Tamera? Sweet cousin. You're not married, are you? You wouldn't get married without telling me, right? *[Silence.]* Jacob, you wouldn't marry my cousin without talking to one of us, right? *[Silence.]* Right?

JACOB
[Pause.] It was her idea.

TAMERA
Oh my god.

JULIA
What?!

CHARLES
You're right, this is a great Christmas.

JULIA
Why does Josh know and I don't?

TAMERA
[Looks at JACOB.] I don't know. *[To JULIA.]* It's been like a month, and it wasn't a big deal.

JULIA
Why does Josh know and I don't, Tamera?! Are you pregnant? *[To JACOB.]* Did you get my cousin pregnant?

MARK
Did you?

JACOB
What? No! It was just a spur of the moment. We were in Vegas.

RUTH
A Vegas marriage? Girl. Really?

TAMERA
I know, I know.

JULIA
So why is it that Josh knew before any of us, particularly me?

PAUL
Calm down, Julia.

JULIA
No! Why?! Tamera, we share everything together! You couldn't call me?

JACOB
I think it was me. I talked to Amy–

[NIKKI ENTERS.]

NIKKI
Hi. Um, is this a bad time?

PAUL
You know what, fuck it. No, Nikki, it's fine. *[Drinks.]*

MARK
Is everything okay?

NIKKI
Yeah, everything is great. Amy left.

JOSH
What?

NIKKI
Amy left. She kind of heard...well, all of the things.

JOSH
[Gathering his stuff.] Do you know where she went?

NIKKI
She headed down that way. She, um, she took the car.

JOSH
Of course, she did. *[Looks at CHARLES.]* Can you help a future brother-in-law out?

CHARLES
[Looks at RUTH.] I kind of feel like I should help him.

RUTH
Fine.

PAUL
We really need to work on your backbone, Charlie.

CHARLES
Hey, I'm in this for the long hall, and that means picking my battles.

[CHARLES, and JOSH begin to EXIT.]

NIKKI
I'll go with you. I saw where she headed. Mark, are you good?

MARK
Oh, I'm great.

NIKKI
Okay. *[She starts to EXIT with them.]*

JOSH

Let's go.

JULIA

We're not done.

JOSH

Oh, I think we are.

[The three of them EXIT. Silence. MARK, JULIA, and RUTH all turn their attention to TAMERA and JACOB.]

JACOB

[Pause.] Merry Christmas?

PAUL

[Lifts a glass.] Welcome to the family.
[Blackout. End Scene.]

Act II

[Scene opens on the kitchen. AMY is in the kitchen cleaning dishes. This goes on for awhile. JULIA ENTERS. AMY looks up at her. They both just look at each other. AMY continues cleaning dishes.]

JULIA
You don't need to do that.

AMY
It's okay. I want to. *[Silence. She continues cleaning.]*

JULIA
I'll dry.

AMY
Sure.

[They both clean dishes in silence.]

JULIA
Your potato salad was good.

AMY
No, it wasn't.

JULIA
[Pause.] Well...at least you were here.

AMY
Would you have honestly cared if something bad had happened to me?

JULIA
For your information, yes. Yes, I would have, goodness. I'm not heartless. My twin loves you. I have to care. *[Silence.]* You didn't go far.

AMY
Yeah, I know.

JULIA
Good idea. Telling everybody that my cousin was married. *[Silence.]*

AMY
I didn't tell anybody-

JULIA
Yes, you did. *[Silence.]*

AMY
Jake told me.

JULIA
Yeah, I know he told me. You guys really have a spouse group chat going?

AMY
Yeah, being with you guys is stressful. Especially when you're not liked. *[Silence.]* Are you mad at him?

JULIA
A little, but we talked. He makes my cousin happy, so it's fine.

AMY
Are you serious?

[RUTH ENTERS to get a bottle of wine.]

JULIA
Why does my approval matter so much to you?

AMY
It's not just me—it's all of us.

JULIA
Yeah, I noticed, why is that? I'm not mom.

RUTH
Yes, you are. Where's the wine opener?

AMY
[Hands it to her.] Here.

RUTH
Thank you.

JULIA
When did I become mom?

RUTH
Like five years ago. You didn't notice?

JULIA
But the point of these holiday dinners is to avoid all this-

RUTH
We're African, Julia. We were going to get older, and it was going to happen. Family approval is important, and you're the matriarch. Deal with it.

JULIA
When did I become the matriarch?

RUTH
You've been the matriarch.

JULIA
I don't know if I like this.

RUTH
[Pours her wine.] It's the way things are.

[TAMERA and NIKKI ENTER.]

TAMERA

Paul sent us in to make sure you're not being mean.

JULIA

Oh my god. Paul!

PAUL

[From outside.] Be nice!

NIKKI

Why aren't we making the guys clean the dishes?

TAMERA

Charlie and Jacob think they aren't allowed in here. It's sacred or something.

RUTH

[Laughs.] It is.

JULIA

No, it's not.

[NIKKI and AMY just look at her and nod.]
Really?

TAMERA

Oh yeah.

RUTH

Told you.

JULIA

[Pause.] Well. It's sacred, apparently, and you're in here cleaning dishes.

AMY

Yep.

[Silence. RUTH moves over to where JULIA is. TAMERA, seeing she's on the same side as them tries to move over to NIKKI and AMY'S side. RUTH pulls her back.]

RUTH

Nope, they need to experience this.

[Silence. They all look at each other]

NIKKI

Ask her.

AMY

I can't. I'm scared.

NIKKI

She'll respect you more, ask her.

AMY

Okay. So. Since you're obviously the one in charge...why don't you like me?

JULIA

I never said that-

TAMERA/RUTH
Yes, you did.

JULIA
[Pause.] Fine. Maybe I alluded to-

AMY
The only reason I'm in the kitchen right now is because I'm cleaning dishes.

NIKKI
It's true.

JULIA
But that shouldn't matter.

AMY
But it-

JULIA
No, Amy, that should not matter. That's why I don't like you. You care too much about what we think. You're weak. [Silence.]

AMY
I'm weak?

JULIA
Yes, you're weak.

AMY
I'm weak.

JULIA
Yes, you are, and I don't mean to be offensive, but that is not what my brother needs.

RUTH
It's true.

[Everybody looks at TAMERA.]

TAMERA
What?

AMY
Am I weak, Tamera?

TAMERA
[Pause.] Yeah... and, I mean, you don't exactly acknowledge my existence.

AMY
[Puts dishes down.] Excuse me?

TAMERA
You don't.

RUTH
You really don't.

JULIA
It's true.

AMY
I didn't know I had to.

RUTH
Really?!

NIKKI
Hang on, give her a minute. *[Silence.]*

TAMERA
You didn't know?

AMY
No. There's like sixty of you.

JULIA
There's only five of us.

TAMERA
She's talking about cousins.

AMY
It's hard to keep up with all of you.

TAMERA
[Pause. Quietly.] There's eighty of us.

AMY
What?

TAMERA
There's eighty. There are eighty first cousins.

AMY
Eighty?!

JULIA
Josh didn't tell you?

AMY
I mean, I knew, but I didn't take it seriously.

RUTH
Oh yes, honey.

NIKKI
I think it's a third world thing.

AMY
Well, then why is she so special?!

JULIA
Excuse me?

AMY
There's eighty cousins, why is Tam so special?!

RUTH
See, this is why I said I didn't like her.

NIKKI
You barely like Jacob, calm down.

RUTH
I am not going to calm down-

TAMERA
It's because my dad died. *[Pause.]* In our family, when a father figure passes, the closest uncle takes up the mantle. I know it's old school patriarchal, but it's what we do. It's been in our bones for...generations honestly. You just, take care of your family. That's what it is. So yeah, I'm their cousin...but I kind of became their sister. The funny part is I don't live near them honestly, I'm far away, but...I still feel like their sister. Because in our family, that's what's expected.

[Silence.]

JULIA
We don't have cousins once removed. That's not a thing. If you're a first cousin, you are an aunt or uncle. That's the way it is. *[Pause.]* I thought it was an original African thing, but I guess it's in our DNA too.

RUTH
We're first gen. We're not that far removed.

NIKKI
My family's the same way. I mean, a little different, but the same. I think America just does things differently. *[Pause.]* But I can also see why it's hard to keep up...especially if you're a white woman.

RUTH
Oh, hell no!

JULIA
Absolutely not!

NIKKI
It's the truth!

TAMERA
She's right! *[Silence.]* I mean, she is. This is different. *[Pause.]* So. Go on, Amy. Ask us questions.

AMY
You don't like me.

JULIA
That's pretty far-

[They all look at her.]

Okay fine.

AMY
Why? And I don't want to just hear from Julia. I want to hear from each of you.

TAMERA
I don't have a problem-

AMY
Yes, you do. Just tell me the truth. *[Pause.]*

NIKKI
Julia?

JULIA
[Pause.] I don't trust you. I know it's silly and simple, but I don't. And it's not personal, you're just the first woman Josh has dated since he got sober. I legit thought his "one" was going to be somebody like Nicole, but here you are. I just...I love you, and I love how Josh adores you, but I don't trust you.

[AMY looks at NIKKI. AMY nods..]

NIKKI
Okay. Ruth?

RUTH
She said it earlier: she's weak.

NIKKI
Hey, be ni-

TAMERA
[Stops her.]

RUTH
My brother needs a woman who is strong, and that is not you. That's why I don't like you, period. Josh is going to do his own thing, that's who he is. What happens if he falls off the wagon? Since you got here, you've been crying about getting us to love you. That's weakness in my book. I need to know you can handle him, and right now there is no evidence that you can. *[Silence.]*

NIKKI
Okay. Tam.

TAMERA
It's really not that-

NIKKI
Tamera?

TAMERA
[Pause.] You don't acknowledge me as a member of this family, and as much as I want to support you, it's hard. You just don't acknowledge me.

AMY
It's because I don't know how this family works! I have fallen in love with a man

whose sisters and mothers are in power. Now as much as a feminist I love that, this is really fucking different.

RUTH
It's different because we're women of color.

NIKKI
Ruth!

RUTH
It's true.

AMY
Yes, well, I am a big woman! *[Pause.]* So yes, our insecurities are different, but they are also the same. *[Tears.]* Look at you. You are all beautiful, confident. Me? I'm just here, trying to survive. *[More tears. NIKKI holds her. TAMER goes over.]*

TAMERA
Literally the only reason why we're confident is because we're with our tribe. That's it. Nicole is a part of our tribe, so we accept her. *[Pause]* We're just still trying to figure you out. It's weird.

AMY
But you married Jacob, and they all seem to be fine-

TAMERA
Because he's white, and Africans like white men better.

JULIA
That is not why we-

RUTH
It's kind of close.

JULIA
[Looks at her.]

RUTH
It's true.

TAMERA
You need to show us why you're good enough, besides just "earning our respect." Why should we relax at the idea of you being with Josh?

AMY
So you marrying Jacob without telling anybody is just going to get looked over?

TAMERA
I did it because I knew we could be together. I didn't need approval.

NIKKI
Oh that's sweet.

JULIA
Also, we're going to have a serious talk about you eloping.

TAMERA
You said you didn't care.

JULIA
Yes, and I don't. You're an adult, you do what you want.

[JACOB ENTERS on his phone.]

JACOB
Hey, I hate to interrupt, but who told *US Weekly* that I was married?

[TAMERA looks at JULIA. JULIA looks at AMY. AMY looks at NIKKI. All look at RUTH.]

RUTH
What, you thought I was going to keep this secret to myself?

JACOB
Cool. Uh, Tam, your mom's called me six times, so yeah.

[EXITS.]

TAMERA
[To RUTH.] Really?

RUTH
Again. Did you expect me to keep this to myself?

JULIA
[Looks at her phone.] Oh, yeah, there's our mom calling.

TAMERA
[Looking at her phone.] Yep, ten missed phone calls. [Looks at RUTH.] Really?

RUTH
Yep.

NIKKI
See, this is why we eloped.

JULIA
Don't encourage her.

NIKKI
It's true! Your family is very stressful! Why do you think I'm here? I'm supporting her!

JULIA
Okay fine! Tam, you eloped without telling me.

TAMERA

And I'm sorry, it just seemed easier-

JULIA

You still didn't tell me! I have known you our whole life, and you didn't tell me you were getting married?

TAMERA

What was I supposed to do? Text you the week of and say, "Hey girl, I'm getting married in Vegas, come on down."

JULIA

Yes! Yes, you were supposed to text me that! I would've said wait and texted the others. We would've put our money together and figured out a way to get all four of us and your mother down there! At most the wedding would've been delayed a day or two, as long as we were there. *[Pause]* Tam, we would've been there. *[Silence.]*

TAMERA

[Looks at RUTH.] You feel this way?

RUTH

[Pause.] I mean, you know me and Charlie are going to elope, so…

JULIA

I'm sorry, excuse me?

AMY

Not the time, Julia.

NIKKI

Good work.

RUTH

But yeah, finding out you got married without us kind of hurts. I mean, I understand why, weddings are awful…but yeah. It hurts. *[Silence.]*

TAMERA

I'm sorry. I just…I didn't want to deal with all the drama.

JULIA

And I get it. Believe me, I do. *[Pause.]* But we're called The Five for a reason. I mean, Josh and Mark are bummed. They really wanted to walk you down the aisle.

TAMERA

They can walk Ruth down the aisle.

RUTH

And they will, but they still want to walk you down the aisle, god dammit. Shit.

NIKKI

[Pause.] I mean…I kind of wanted to see it.

TAMERA
No, you didn't.

NIKKI
Yes, I did. Mark talks about you all the time. Plus, I've witnessed one Kenyan wedding. You guys know how to throw down.

TAMERA
Okay. So, I'm married, and I screwed up getting married without telling you. What should I do?

AMY
[Long pause.] Um...I'm an event planner.

TAMERA
But we're already married.

[JACOB ENTERS.]

JACOB
Hey, Ruth, why is the *HuffPost* calling me?

RUTH
Don't worry about it, we'll deal with it later.

JACOB
But you work for them…

RUTH
Don't worry about it.

[Annoyed, JACOB EXITS.]

AMY
I can plan your ceremony.

TAMERA
But we're already married.

AMY
People elope and have wedding ceremonies later all the time. Let's be honest, wedding ceremonies are for the family anyway. I mean, yeah, they're for the bride and groom ...but they're for the family. They want to see the person they love most be sent off into a new season. It's kind of beautiful. *[Silence. AMY sits on a chair. She motions for TAMERA to sit next to her.]* Why did you elope?

TAMERA
I was overwhelmed and having a panic attack, so we just did it.

RUTH
What?

JULIA
How long have you been having panic?

AMY
Just look at me. Why else?

TAMERA
[Pause.] I was scared.

[RUTH and JULIA start to interfere. NIKKI stops them.]

AMY
Why were you scared?

TAMERA
Because….it's a lot. Planning, calling, texting, emailing, setting a budget, finding a space. It's a lot.

AMY
But you have friends and family who will do that for you.

TAMERA
[Overwhelmed.] Yes, and then they'll ask for their debt repaid a year later, and you can't do it before you have no idea what you're talking about! *[She cries.]* Weddings suck. I love them, but they suck. *[To RUTH and JULIA.]* So yes, that's why I got married before anybody knew. *[Silence.]*

RUTH
But in Vegas though? That's so basic.

JULIA
That's not important, Ruth. *[She moves closer to TAMERA. She takes her hands.]* You love him?

TAMERA
Yeah.

JULIA
Can he take care of you?

TAMERA
[Pulls her closer.] We can take care of each other.

JULIA
Ndio? *[Swahili for "yeah"]*

TAMERA
[Pause.] Ndio.

[JULIA and TAMERA hug. RUTH Steps in. Pulls TAMERA to her.]

RUTH
[In Swahili] Do you love him? *[Google translation: unampenda?]*

TAMERA
Ndio.

RUTH
[In Swahili] Does he love you? [Google translation: anakupenda?]

TAMERA
[Long pause. Looks at both her "sisters".] Ndio. Ndio. [They all hug. This goes for awhile.]

JULIA
Okay. Amy. You need to show us that you can take care of our little sister.

RUTH
She needs to have a dope ass wedding, not whatever happened in Vegas.

NIKKI
You're really hung up on this Vegas thing, aren't you?

RUTH
It wasn't a drive through wedding, was it?

TAMERA
[Long pause.] It was.

RUTH
Oh, hell no! No woman in our family does a drive through wedding! Amy, this ceremony needs to be fire.

AMY
[Writing things down.] Yes ma'am.

JULIA
Also please plan two ceremonies. We're going to need a big one at home.

TAMERA
Wait, what? No!

RUTH
Bitch, did you think you had a choice? Not everybody can fly here from Kenya.

JULIA
If I had to do it, so do you.

NIKKI
I had to do it too.

AMY
Two ceremonies, got it.

TAMERA
I honestly don't think I can handle-

AMY
[Looks at her. Reassuring.] I was diagnosed with OCD when I was nine. I'm on the spectrum, and honestly, I have some level of undiagnosed paranoia. Let's not even talk about the body dysphoria and bulimia. You

are the favorite in my book. I have you. Please trust me. *[Silence.]*

TAMERA
Okay.

AMY
Okay. You're going to love it. I promise. *[Continues writing.]* Anything else I need to know?

TAMERA
I like being the center of attention, so if you and Josh get married around the same time as me, I might hate you.

JULIA
Tamera, that is ru-

AMY
[Continues writing.] Got it. Don't get married within six months of wedding. Ruth, when do you want to get married?

JULIA
That does not matter-

RUTH
I'm good to wait a year.

AMY
Perfect, we can make that work.

JULIA
Really?

RUTH
They're married already. They need to have a ceremony.

AMY
Let's make it happen.

TAMERA
But what about your wedding?

AMY
My wedding will happen no matter who or what is in it. You're the next bride. You're what's important. I'm good.

TAMERA
Thank you, Amy. You're great. Like, really. *[Hugs AMY.]* I'm sorry.

AMY
It's okay. I get it.

TAMERA
[To RUTH and JULIA.] We're doing a shot.

JULIA

We don't need a shot-

NIKKI

[Pouring shots.] Yes, you do.

TAMERA

You're dry.

NIKKI

Doesn't matter, you all need shots…

RUTH

I'm here for it. Nikki, pour yourself an ounce of that punch.

NIKKI

[Pouring] Already ahead of you. *[After pouring herself a shot, she makes a toast.]* To our new family, new friendship, *[looks at AMY]* and new confidence. Amy...welcome.

JULIA

[Pause.] Yeah. Welcome. *[They all cheers. AMY is tearful.]*

AMY

Thank you. Like really, thank you.

RUTH

[Pause.] So we just gonna act like the guys haven't been listening this whole time?

[JOSH and MARK ENTER.]

JOSH

Is it safe to come in?

NIKKI

You tell us.

MARK

We weren't listening to everything.

[JACOB, CHARLES, and a drunk PAUL ENTER.]

JOSH

Jake, guess what, you're getting a pain in the ass wedding ceremony after all.

PAUL

Haha, you thought you could avoid that. Merry Christmas, everybody!

JULIA

Oh, Paul…

CHARLES

He'll be fine, he's just having a good time.

RUTH

You're drunk too, aren't you?

CHARLES
Oh extremely.

MARK
[Puts JACOB in the middle.] Jacob. *[Looks around to see nobody except JOSH is standing with him.]* Boys!

[The men gather.]

You married my cousin without my permission.

TAMERA
Uh, this is 2019-

MARK
You married my cousin without my permission. What do you have to say?

[Silence.]

JACOB
Um, I don't need permission because she wanted to marry me? *[Pause.]*

MARK
Yeah, you're right, you passed.

JOSH
Welcome to the family.

MARK
But I would like the opportunity to give her away. You kind of robbed me of that.

JOSH
How do you know it's going to be you? She might want me to walk her down the aisle.

TAMERA
Mark's going to do it. He's older and reliable.

JOSH
Hey, I'm reliable.

AMY
Meh.

JOSH
Hey!

TAMERA
[Her phone goes off.] Shit, it's Kensie. And I Have six missed phone calls from mom.

PAUL
You're in trouble.

JACOB
Yeah, I just went ahead and turned my phone off altogether.

TAMERA

This is becoming a thing. I didn't want it to be a thing.

JACOB

[Goes to her.] Hey. It'll be fine.

TAMERA

We didn't want this to be a thing though.

RUTH

Y'all really thought you could sneak off and elope without involving the family?

CHARLES

Yeah, weddings aren't about you.

PAUL

Selfish.

JULIA

It'll be great. You have all of us. Plus, Amy's helping with planning. It'll be great.

TAMERA

Okay. *[Smiles.]* You know you're going to be my maid of honor, right?

JULIA

Oh, I've already decided that.

RUTH

I'm in the wedding party too. So is Nikki.

NIKKI

She might not want me in it.

TAMERA

I didn't even want a ceremony. I have no say in this.

JULIA

She's right. Aw you guys, this is so great. We need to take a picture.

MARK

Let's do it on the porch out back. The parents are going to go nuts.

TAMERA

They're already going nuts. *[Looks at RUTH.]*

RUTH

You're welcome.

[They all start to EXIT.]

PAUL

Hang on! All spouses hang back!

[JULIA looks at PAUL. He winks at her. She smiles.]

JULIA
You heard him. Let's go, we'll be outside.

[A baby starts to cry. JULIA stops.]

AMY
You guys go, I'll get him. *[AMY EXITS.]*

JULIA
[Looks at JOSH.] Um.

JOSH
[Just looks at her.]

JULIA
Okay then. Don't forget to bring him out when you're done, okay guys?

PAUL
You got it.

JULIA
Come on, fam.

[She, JOSH, MARK, TAMERA, and RUTH start to EXIT.]

RUTH
You really going to let her hold him?

JOSH
Ruth!

RUTH
What?

[The siblings EXIT laughing. Before TAMERA can EXIT, JACOB goes to her, pulls her close, and kisses her. They smile.]

PAUL
Gross.

CHARLES
Get a room.

TAMERA
[Rolls her eyes.] I'll see you out there. *[She EXITS.]*

[PAUL brings gets some glasses and pulls out a bottle of really good bourbon.]

PAUL
Gather around, my friends. We're toasting.

CHARLES
Thank God.

NIKKI
You've been drinking all night.

CHARLES
I can still show gratitude!

[AMY ENTERS holding KING.]

AMY
Look who I found.

[She joins the group. Everybody "Oohs" and "ahs" over the baby.]

PAUL
You gave us the least amount of trouble, little man.

CHARLES
Don't grow up.

PAUL
[He begins pouring bourbon.] Jacob, you want to grab Nikki a glass of punch?

NIKKI
Oh, I got it. *[She gets herself a glass.]*

CHARLES
Hey, Jake. You think you gonna have one of those?

JACOB
Eventually. Not for awhile.

CHARLES
Oh. But not like now?

JACOB
Are you asking me if the wedding was a shotgun?

CHARLES
Yeah. *[JACOB just laughs. Pause.]* I mean, was it?

JACOB
No!

NIKKI
She's been drinking all night, Charles!

CHARLES
You can still drink while you're pregnant.

PAUL
No, you can't, everybody knows that.

CHARLES
You can have wine. Ruth's been drinking wine.

NIKKI
Yeah, so?

AMY
Oh my god, Ruth's pregnant, isn't she?

[Everybody stops. Silence. CHARLES is guilty.]

JACOB
And you let them get mad at me?

NIKKI
The family is going to kill you.

PAUL
You know what? Nope, no. I'm officially creating a spouse pact. *[Hands out glasses.]* We keep that between all of us for now. Lord knows the family is going to jump down your throat. Let's all agree not to do the same with each other. We need to have each other's backs. Agree?

NIKKI
[Pause.] Okay.

AMY
Yeah.

JACOB
Agreed.

CHARLES
Thanks, guys.

PAUL
We survived Christmas.

AMY
Barely.

JACOB
No shit.

PAUL
But we did. Congrats to the newest brother-in-law. Welcome to the family. Get used to all of this.

NIKKI
You haven't met your new aunt yet.

CHARLES
Good luck with that. You're gonna need it.

JACOB
Sounds like you're going to need it.

CHARLES
Oh god, you're right.

PAUL
You'll be fine. We got you. *[Raises glass.]* Merry Christmas, guys.

EVERYBODY ELSE
Merry Christmas. *[They all toast. Music begins to play lightly.]*

PAUL
Let's get out there before Julia-

JULIA
Paul!

PAUL
Yep, let's go.

AMY
[To KING.] Let's go see mommy.

[They all start to EXIT.]

CHARLES
You know as far as holiday dinners go, this wasn't awful.

JACOB
Yeah, I actually enjoyed myself a little.

NIKKI
We're doing it again next year right?

PAUL
Every year. It's a tradition.

JACOB
Tam says she wants to host one next year.

AMY
Oh, that'll be fun. I love New York.

CHARLES
You think you're gonna be here next year?

PAUL
Hey.

AMY
I don't plan on leaving anytime soon.

NIKKI
Good. We actually kind of like you.

AMY
Aw thanks.

[They all EXIT. PAUL is the last one left. He looks at the group of new and old friends he just made. It's nice to finally have some allies he can relate to. He looks at the audience.]

PAUL
I love this family.

JULIA
Paul!

PAUL
Coming dear. *[To the audience.]* Merry Christmas.
[He downs his drink and EXITS. Christmas music swells. Lights fade. End scene.]

THE END.

www.ingramcontent.com/pod-product-compliance
Lightning Source LLC
Chambersburg PA
CBHW081438070526
44586CB00019B/2168